SMASH HIT

SMASH HIT

RACE, CRIME, AND CULTURE IN BOXING FILMS

DAVID CURCIO

ARMINLEAR

LOC Library of Congress Number: 2023942534

ISBN (hardback): 978-1-956450-81-1
ISBN (paperback): 978-1-956450-80-4
ISBN (eBook): 978-1-956450-82-8

Armin Lear Press Inc
215 W Riverside Drive, #4362
Estes Park, CO 80517

Primo Carnera, Myrna Loy, and Max Baer
in The Prizefighter and the Lady, 1933

ACKNOWLEDGMENTS

Big thanks to Bob Bachelor, Michael Carbert, Nigel Collins, Katie Kopple, Don Mcrea, John McKaskill, Andrew Rihn, Glen Sharp, and Mike Silver for their time, encouragement, and feedback throughout various stages of the manuscript. A shout out to J.G., whose two-word text suggested a title that left me wondering why I hadn't thought of it myself. Jenn Smith's edits not only made for better reading but made me a better writer. I am eternally grateful for her boundless support. Resounding gratitude to my agent, Maryann Karinch, who believed in my vision from the get-go. Finally, the deepest love to my mother Ginnie for her read-throughs and nixing those meandering digressions and lurid Hollywood hearsay nobody should have to read.

The abundance of films *not* discussed, paired with personal taste and historical interest would, in the hands of a thousand different writers, produce a thousand different narratives. My gratitude soars toward those who believed in this one.

CONTENTS

AUTHOR'S NOTE

The films in the present volume are structured under shifting and evolving twentieth-century mores rather than release dates. Their range in quality is vast. While efforts are made to cover as much history as possible, a completist's survey would mean a lot of ink wasted on sub-par films. Conversely, a handful of worthy films are omitted as their inclusion would stilt the overarching narrative.

All films discussed in this book are available through streaming services

INTRODUCTION

"Every fight is in front of an audience."
-W.C. Heinz, *The Professional*

While the pairing of fistic combat and drama has over three thousand years of tradition to back it up, it is almost impossible to convey the allure that boxing exerted upon the American zeitgeist throughout most of the twentieth century. Its recent drop in popularity is elucidated by its current ranking among America's most-watched sports. Though still a multi-million-dollar industry, the game has nevertheless been eclipsed by unified, corporate behemoths including football, baseball, basketball, hockey, motorsports, golf, and the more extreme brutality of mixed martial arts (MMA). The age of fight results and rivalries splashed across the front page is gone. Except for significant pay-per-view fights, coverage is relegated to a small square of real estate in the Sunday sports section.

Amid this drop in viewership, boxing's perpetual subsistence in the cinematic realm is cast into ever-deeper relief. As boxing (without all that boxing) packs theaters, the lion's share of public appeal no longer lies in the sport itself but in its depiction, via fiction and loose biopics, on the big screen.

During the turn of the century, cinematic recordings of fights ranked among the medium's most popular subjects. With short films that initially manifested as naive entertainments and slapstick routines, the sport was a shoo-in during Hollywood's rise in the teens and twenties. Amid organized crime's increasing squeeze on the game, mid-century anxieties brought spiraling darkness to a genre reflective of the day's shifting sociological landscape.

While this made sense throughout most of the twentieth century, boxing films continue to outnumber all other sport-themed films—more than doubling the number of baseball films, the second most popular cinematic sport. Considering boxing's dwindling viewership, the genre's durability is notable.

Few boxing films in recent years have garnered critical acclaim or cleaned up at the box office, and as the past twenty years demonstrate, the genre has yet to generate a so-called classic in the new millennium. Not that it matters: the sheer quantity of newer boxing films is legion, if a bit muddled considering hybrids featuring bare-knuckle brawlers or MMA. But if the goal of studios is to fill seats and make money, boxing remains as viable a subject today as it was during the sport's heyday.

Whether enacted in the ring or the Colosseum, a lizard-brain, atavistic attraction to violence has always existed among humans. In recent years, the phenomenon has extended beyond film to video games, YouTube scraps captured on iPhones, and endless cruelties streamed on the internet. While recent pushback over the causal effects of various media on society's more "suggestible" demographics is nothing new, no amount of handwringing has curbed ticket sales, purchases, or mouse-clicks.

"For some," writes film critic Hal Hinson, "the process of distinguishing mindless violence in film and meaningful, expressive violence is an intrusion on their idea of what art should be." But if 1980's *Raging Bull* spills considerably more blood than 1974's *The Texas Chain Saw Massacre* (it does), does this even matter? If innate aggressions—conscious or not—are expunged within the safe space of a theater or a boxing ring rather than on the street or in the home, surely its overall effect is more ameliorating than harmful to society.

With an air of macho swagger, Jack London asserted that "Men want to see fights because of the old red blood of Adam in them that will not die down." In an era when boxing was still derided within dignified circles, the artist George Bellows willingly conceded to the id. "I don't know

anything about boxing," he wrote in 1921. "I am just painting two men trying to kill each other."

Across the Atlantic, Sigmund Freud was investigating
how the appeal of violence was at once advantageous and
damaging to the collective human psyche. His final work,
Civilization and Its Discontents (1930), reads like an obituary
to nineteenth-century Victorian repression wherein the
moribund psychoanalyst asserts that no one is blameless
as regards the violent impulse. Humanity's ongoing rec-
onciliation with its savagery, manifested in the so-called
death drive, dubbed *Thanatos* by Freud from the Greek
"to disappear," lies not in eliminating these urges but in
their acceptance. His conclusion—that no one is exempt
from such appetites—was unpopular at best in disrupting
Victorian ideals of individual agency.

Critic and essayist Robert Warshow examines the
paradox from an angle considerably less reductive than
Freud's. "One of the well-known peculiarities of modern
civilized opinion," he writes in his essay, *The Westerner,*
"is its refusal to acknowledge the value of violence. This
refusal is a virtue, but like many virtues, it involves certain
willful blindness and encourages hypocrisy." However, the
catharsis derived by the decidedly non-hypocritical boxing
spectator, to say nothing of the shared emotional valence
with an audience, is modified by the knowledge that the
violence in the ring is accurate and, in theory, safe.

Of course, the two guys in the ring aren't there to

mollify the spectators' fluctuating neurotic impulses. They're in there to get paid.

In his essay *What Boxing is For*, Sam Sheridan contends, "If you're not poor, you shouldn't box." Joyce Carol Oates extends this logic to metaphor, writing that "impoverished people prostitute themselves in ways available to them, and boxing on its lowest levels offers an opportunity for men to make a living of a kind." Ex-World Heavyweight Champion Larry Holmes applies the same analogy: "All fighters are prostitutes, and all promoters are pimps."

Neither was the first to make the comparison. In 1897, the Reverend Levi Gilbert of Cleveland thumped fire-and-brimstone sermons decrying the world's first wide-distribution film, known today as *The Corbett-Fitzsimmons Fight*. The film's popularity prompted the Reverend to boom that, "such men sell their bodies for merchandise, as indeed as the harlots of the streets." Societal components of prizefighting also came under attack. Fifty-five years before Gilbert made his appeals from the pulpit, New York magistrate Jasper J. Golden lamented the "gamblers, bullies, pickpockets and thieves; the idle, disorderly and dissolute" that descended on his state for a much-touted bare-knuckle match.

According to a 1962 Gallup poll, nearly forty percent of Americans thought boxing should be outlawed, a sentiment echoed the same year on the big screen when *Requiem for a Heavyweight*'s incredulous manager barked, "Sport? If there were headroom, they'd hold these things in sewers!" Nevertheless, there's little doubt that the father of modern psychoanalysis would condone the endeavor if only to safeguard the greater good while hampering violence of a more extreme nature.

Salty analogies of sex workers and sewers notwith- standing, few endeavors stand as infallible a bellwether for race relations throughout the twentieth century than boxing. In their 2019 article "Life Expectancy of White and Non-White Elite Heavyweight Boxers," Thang S. Han et al. conclude, "those who are attracted to boxing often come from inner cities and single-parent households and have limited formal education." This dearth of "social opportunities makes boxing attractive to young men from minority groups."

Amid pre-existing animosities and fistic score-settling, the close of the nineteenth century saw an unprecedented influx of second-generation Irish and English immigrants dominate the ring, a trend that shifted to Jewish and Italian fighters during the following three decades. A 1955 study concluded that second-generation Americans were more likely to turn to boxing.

Most early twentieth-century fighters began training on the streets: stealing, mugging, and defending themselves and their neighborhoods from rival ethnic gangs with fists, baseball bats, and the occasional heavier artillery. Protection of ethnic integrity and the support of one's family were often inextricably linked, rendering the profession's life-saving purses worth getting hit for.

Considering financial and racial disparities, it's no surprise that Black fighters were common long before opposition to mixed-race bouts dissipated during the 1920s-30s. Boxing was one of the few pursuits that leveled the playing field and, temporarily at least, curtailed the so-called color line. Not only was it a means of escape from the menial labor to which Black Americans were confined, it also put their earning potential on par with Whites.

With the promise of security for war veterans via job training courses and colleges, the economy's midcentury boom saw the number of professional prizefighters drop by fifty percent. At this point, Black and Latino boxers began to dominate the ring in earnest, and from 1949 to 1999, only five of the forty-three Heavyweight Champions have been White. In the twenty-first century, a full twenty-one of the thirty reigning heavyweights have been foreign, the preponderance hailing from Eastern Europe. The remaining nine Americans have, without exception, been Black. Meanwhile, championship titles grow ever-more muddled amid the sport's numerous sanctioning bodies. What is certain is that Black and Latino fighters, still the most disenfranchised groups within the U.S., remain perennially enmeshed in the game.

The ties uniting boxing and cinema bring the narrative back to the turn of the century when, by dint of extraordinary coincidence, the country's most crucial new contraption turned its lens on the newly modernized fight game. If necessity is the mother of invention, the introduction of the moving picture served as midwife to the dissemination of prizefights, already in high demand.

In the last decade of the nineteenth century, Thomas Edison opened a laboratory for the study of the emerging medium of film and photography. His collaborator, Eadweard Muybridge, had already made a name for himself in 1878 with his *Horse in Motion*, wherein twelve photographic frames provided visual evidence that all four equine legs simultaneously lift from the ground at a gallop. But Edison's real interest lay in the coordination of image with sound, a technology that would not come to fruition for another thirty-five years, and he soon passed the project to his assistant, William K.L. Dickson.

Dickson's development of celluloid film, in collaboration with the Eastman Kodak Company, allowed him to build the earliest device through which the public could view moving pictures. Dubbed the Kinetoscope (from the Greek *kineto* as in "movement," *scopos*, "to view"), the machine resembled a standing vista-viewer upon which two eye-holes allowed for private viewing. Unveiled to the public in 1891, it employed the durable 35-millimeter film originally contrived by Dickson and Edison in 1887, setting an industry standard for the next century.

In 1894, chemist-turned-cinema technician Woodville Latham joined forces with Enoch Rector (an early promoter of boxing films) to open the first Kinetoscope parlor. With Manhattan as their flagship venue, subject matter was initially limited to vaudevillian "dumb acts," so named because they required no sound. But the public was only willing to drop so many pennies to see the same contortionists, wrestlers, and cock fights. The twenty-second running-time imposed by film reel-length was no easy sell, and rote circus-staples got tiresome quickly. The question arose: what could keep customers feeding the machines throughout a single visit? Latham's son Gray contrived the filming and display of prizefights to ensure viewers would keep the pennies coming through to their finales.

Boxing was still outlawed in most states, but no laws prevented its display in reproductive form. As parlors began cropping up in every major U.S. city, even women—banned from live fights until 1916—could get a gander.

In June 1894, *The Leonard-Cushing Fight* made its Kinetoscopic debut using an eight-foot ring, roughly a third of the standard size, to accommodate the camera's narrow frame. Within five months, Dickson's improvements on the Kinetograph (a similar, less wieldy device also developed with Edison) brought running time to a full minute. The same year, the Edison Manufacturing Company produced *The Boxing Cats,* portending the legions of felines that saturate the internet. On the human front, *Corbett and Courtney Before the Kinetograph* featured six one-minute exhibition rounds of Gentleman Jim Corbett outclassing the hopeless underdog Peter Courtney. Only a fraction of a single reel remains intact.

Meanwhile, Gray Latham was already looking to the next advancement and, with characteristic ingenuity, set about devising a means of projection. This was only partly to cut down on the queues that wended through parlors. A larger viewing surface would mean a shared, collective experience and higher admission prices. The great distance required to shoot a full-size ring had thus far reduced the action to a small, thin viewing strip. Latham's horizontal, elongated frame could film from much closer, so setting another industry standard: the widescreen aspect ratio format. Developed in tandem with Rector's hand-cranked camera dubbed the Veriscope, Latham's projector contained thousands of feet of film that allowed for eight minutes of uninterrupted shooting. In less than a decade, the Kinetoscope's capacity had multiplied fortyfold.

In 1897, the actor and manager William A. Brady produced the first filmed bout. Directed by Rector, *The Corbett-Fitzsimmons Fight* was also the first motion picture displayed to a mass audience. It was the world's first feature-length film. The use of three Veriscopes not only ensured for no pause in the action but allowed for an estimated one-hundred-minute running time, consuming over four miles of film.

America's first cinemas opened in 1902 and provided audiences with a new, affordable means of communal entertainment. From the comfort of actual seats (or disarrayed chairs, as the case often was), customers no longer had to stand bent over stanchions peering into eyeholes or get arrested attending illegal bouts. Within three years, more than three thousand theaters had opened in the United States. Those lucky enough to live within a reasonable distance of a movie house no longer had to rely on blow-by-blow newspaper accounts when a ringside seat could be secured in the confines of nascent movie theaters for a fraction of the gate price.

The earliest evidence of formalized fisticuffs is seen in Egyptian bruisers etched in limestone and quartzite dating around 3,500 B.C.E. along with depictions of the carnal Freudian love drive *Eros* that comprise some of civilization's original smut. Roughly three thousand years later, pugs painted in clay slip on Greek amphorae again shared equal time with boinking couples and group romps. In 688 B.C.E., the sport was added to the official Olympic Games. 650 years later, Virgil described a fallen boxer "spitting out clots of blood from his mouth, teeth amongst them."

The gladiatorial clashes that peaked from the first century B.C.E. to the second century A.D. saw stadium events like running and discus-throwing take a backseat to pummel and mutilation in amphitheaters. With the allowance of weaponry including swords and spiked gloves, the spectacles enjoyed the same regard as the twentieth century's most anticipated prizefights.

"Roman drama," writes Robert Brustein, artistic director of the American Repertory Theater, "was extremely bloody and violent. The Elizabethan drama was bloody and violent, the Jacobean drama was bloody and violent, and 19th-century Romantic drama was also bloody and violent." As modern physical combat moves ever closer toward the intentional theater of World Wrestling Entertainment (WWE) or the extremities of MMA, boxing's strict set of rules continues to manifest as a spontaneous spectacle played out in twelve acts.

A famous stage actor once told the 1930s heavyweight Max Schmeling, "If I kill dozens of people playing *Richard III*, the curtain falls, we all stand up and take our bows... With you, it's really a matter of life and death... Your blood isn't make-up." A valid point: while every production of *Romeo and Juliet* ends with the same double suicide, boxing—unscripted, unrehearsed, and wholly unpredictable—is performance at its most raw. Promoter Lou DiBella concurs. "If it's not theater you're fucking up in presenting."

The esteem in which boxers were held as defenders of ethnicity and race was further bolstered when, by dint of fortuitous timing, they were established as the world's first movie stars with the release of *The Corbett-Fitzsimmons Fight*. Since then, the boxer has stood as a singular cinematic figure, his artless *mano y mano* trade ensuring a durable, anguished hero alone in his struggles for acceptance, accountability, and maybe even glory. A cousin to such existential heroes and sinners as the solo shamus and the lone cowboy on the plain, the boxer's iron-clad moral code is frequently warped, bullied, or seduced into ambiguity through the discovery that he might be the only honest guy left in a corrupt universe where, unlike those private dicks and gunslingers, he has no connections at the precinct house or fellow gunmen to rouse to action. Despite sympathetic managers and doting love interests, the boxer is alone from the moment he steps under the ropes, where physical pain is a matter of course.

The topical themes that run through the genre follow a precise, steady chronology that concretely reflects contemporary sociological mores. With the exception of the horror film (a genre that carries its own brand of cathartic savagery), this phenomenon is most evident in the dark corners of humiliation and bright lights of victory inherent to the genre under discussion.

During the middle of the nineteenth century, an emphasis on fitness developed among the same American middle class that, not so long before, decried the sanctioning of boxing. No longer the sole dominion of the callous rabble, the end of the century saw droves of top-hatted dandies with pince-nez attend bouts both legal and clandestine. Although most remained spectators, some turned Sunday practitioners to shed the flab and "damnable feminization" that came to be associated with Victorian languor. Suddenly, sitting around parlors, reciting verse, and playing the piano didn't seem so tough.

As attraction grew, local tavern owners held non-publicized bouts with admission charges and small purses for the fighters. Still, most middle-class Americans objected to the practice, partly due to puritanical Victorian ideology, the culture of the Enlightenment, and a wish to distance themselves from British culture. The accompanying rise in gambling that brought all manner of lowlifes and sharps into town didn't help matters. On a state-by-state basis, boxing's legality waxed and waned.

Casual practitioners lauded for their commitment to fitness were nevertheless useless in the professional bare-knuckle brawls held in dirt patches like those back in the combatants' native England and Ireland. There were no set time limits on bouts, the longest on record having gone 276 rounds over the course of four and a half hours when Jack Jones beat Patsy Tunney in Cheshire in 1825. While brief rest periods were allowed in the case of knockdowns, a fight wasn't over until one man was unable to rise or continue. Supervision was lax. Fighters didn't always play fair. Some still don't.

In 1867, the Scottish nobleman John Sholto Douglas, better known by his formal title of the ninth Marquis de Queensberry, devised a set of guidelines that fast became the new standard for pugilistic combat. Under the Marquis's refinements, the so-called Queensberry rules instituted three-minute round times with one-minute rests. Square rings of roughly twenty-four feet replaced rounded dirt tracts. A felled opponent who could not rise within ten seconds was declared loser by knockout, and eight different weight classes were recognized to make for fair competition. The implementation of padded gloves helped protect the face and, more importantly, the seventy-two bones of each hand.

These adjustments, far more palatable to the average spectator than the lawless eye-gouging and head-butting of the bare-knucklers, earned the sport the moniker "the gentlemanly art of self-defense." Today, the nickname "the sweet science," coined by British sportswriter Pierce Egan decades before the introduction of the Queensberry rules, has replaced the dandified moniker to invoke the unification of cunning, artistry, and intellect.

The Queensberry rules might have made boxing safer, but boxing has never been safe. A boxer undergoes an initial M.R.I. to obtain a professional license long before he has the chance to suffer any professional damage. No medical follow-ups are required. The accumulation of concussions that disrupt the brain's stability within the skull can lead to brain damage known as chronic traumatic encephalopathy (CTE), or *dementia pugilistica,* which often does not manifest until after a fighter's career is ended. In a sport where the average retirement age is thirty-five, a lack of unions, health-care benefits, and pensions have left many retirees bereft of more than just money. "The brain damage detected in so many ex-fighters," writes Ivan G. Goldman in the *Columbia Journalism Review,* "makes the sport basically indefensible."

Where the sheer quantity of fights once proved a valuable means of cutting one's teeth even in the case of losses, a record of one win and three losses today would be career-ending. Given the meager quantity of fights in which today's boxers partake, the question arises: is the sport doomed to extinction? Mike Tyson is skeptical but remains agnostic. "Most boxers today," he writes, "... are not inspired enough to go to the past ... not only to find out about the fighters but to research their associations. Which one hung out with Dickens? Do they know [the eighth Heavyweight Champion] Gene Tunney and [teens and twenties Lightweight Champion] Benny Leonard were friends with George Bernard Shaw?"

While Tyson's assessment rests on a cultural level, boxing scribe Mike Silver is considerably less assured when considering the twenty-first-century crop of sluggers with over-muscled physiques that run counter to the litheness essential to effective movement: "Let's be perfectly clear, there are no great fighters today... [and] I'm not overly optimistic that any positive changes will actually take place." Boxing writer Gary Lee Moser blames a shortage of publicized rivalries over the past twenty-five years for the sport's drop in popularity, without which it "will remain doomed to the shadows." In his essay *Post-Primes and Career Arcs: Navigating Boxing's All-Time Rankings*, Michael Ezra encapsulates the contemporary scene as "mired in an eternal post-prime."

Promoter J. Russell Peltz laments the current state of boxing less for its quality of fighters than for its copious and scattered divisions. Unlike the consolidated leagues organizing baseball, football, and practically every other professional sport, boxing has not one but four sanctioning bodies, each of which contains seventeen weight classes (up from the Marquis's original eight) to make for no less than sixty-eight so-called "world titles." Nor is it uncommon for champions to vary within these bodies. Contemporary fighters who attract widespread attention outside the sport's adherents are noted not for skill or personality but for their astronomical purses. "Lots of people in boxing today are not boxing lifers," Peltz continues. "They're lawyers, accountants, doctors, and they invest. They don't get it. These people don't love boxing. They love the money." Quotes Michael Benson when discussing 2017's aptly nicknamed "Money Fight" between Floyd "Money" Mayweather Jr. and Conor McGregor (the second most lucrative bout in the sport's history), "the reason for a potential rematch is in truth very simple – money, more money."

In his *New York Times* review of 2010's *The Fighter*, film critic A.O. Scott writes, "no film genre is more strictly governed by conventions—or enslaved by clichés." With Thanatos at one pole and Eros at the other, Scott's only allowable exception is the romantic comedy. Although recent decades have brought a ring of validity to Scott's blanket statement, the critic neglects to mention the genre's evolution over the past century. In other words, different times necessarily call for different trends and formulas, neither of which are confined to the boxing film or, for that matter, the romantic comedy.

The following chapters are meant to elucidate themes and variation through which social trends have morphed the boxing film through white-washed melodrama, morally ambiguous crime stories, endless biopics, and cartoonish franchises. As motifs continue to fold, overlap, and evolve, filmmakers will continue to mine the sport in all its manifestations of triumph, tragedy, and crushing mediocrity.

1
THE SET-UP

Directed by Robert Wise
RKO Studios, 1949

The clock outside the Cozy Hotel juts from its black post, a sentry to the seedy end of a town that doesn't have a quaint side. Its apathetic face reads 8:05. Cars shoot by in every direction. Nightclubs and penny arcades loom like oracles. A kid hawking newspapers cuts in front of a middle-aged guy trying to do the same. When the older guy says he has to make a buck too, the kid won't give him a glance. "Aw, go take a walk!" The city's no place for the old.

A tracking shot wends through rows of men caught mid-conversation and navigates cement pathways through arched doors to reveal the buzzing activity tucked under awnings and inside the alleys of Paradise City. Customers negotiate and scheme in the gray night, betting, losing, and if they're lucky... but they're never lucky. Everyone's tie is a bit too short. Their cuffs are frayed and their cigars are stumpy. The women appear worried and indecisive. The men look like their last buck is folded in their sock. A guy steering the claw game at the arcade snatches a brand-new camera only to watch it drop back into the pile at the last second. In a city devoid of sentimentality, fate is forever propelled by forces as impartial as the camera-dropping claw.

Based on Joseph Moncure March's 1928 verse narrative of the same name, RKO Studios purchased *The Set-up* from its author for a piddling $1,000. Whitewashing its source material, the Black fighter of the poem is switched out for the blond Robert Ryan. Director Robert Wise later explained that he had initially cast the Black boxer-turned-actor Canada Lee for the role when the notoriously racist Howard Hughes, who helmed RKO from 1948 to 1955, summarily nixed the proposed lead. Pansy, the boxer of the poem, *"had the stuff/but his skin was brown."* Moncure March, the former Managing Editor at the *New Yorker*, justifiably griped that in removing the racial subtext, the studio had "evaded the whole basic issue of discrimination against the Negro."

Screenwriter Art Cohn's locker room is a dank melting pot of colorblind, mutually supportive young men, among whom the only college student is notably Black. It's a sweaty concentration of lower-class America, where everyone's sure that *they'll* be the one to ascend from the filth of a thousand cities like this onto something approaching immortality—if only temporarily.

Cohn's variant of Pansy is the over-the-hill Bill "Stoker" Thompson (Ryan), the archetypal tragic hero. Against all advice and reason, Stoker refuses to accept what is sure to be his imminent failure, and with child-like credulity, epitomizes something more akin to nervous desperation. Lacking the gentler ring name "Pansy," "Stoker" suggests the Sisyphean effort of keeping one's inner spark alight. Meanwhile, the viewer looks on while it gutters and dims as surely as the hands on the clock outside creep forward.

Ryan was an ideal choice to portray the waning pugilist. His four-year stretch at Dartmouth as Heavyweight Champion, from which he sported some scars of his own, freed him from the lack of veracity that thwarts actors who pretend at a physical skill that takes years to hone. Liberal and outspokenly anti-racist, the actor ironically found his greatest success in war films, westerns, and wherever else his mitts came in handy. A pacifist to the end, Ryan even read poetry with Pete Seeger and Bob Dylan at a Woody Guthrie Tribute Concert in 1968. But in front of the camera, weighing in at an even 190 and a lean six-foot-four, he was a tough guy by any standard.

Aging by the hour ("Get 'im a wheelchair!" a woman hoots from the crowd), Stoker brings in small purses as cannon fodder for up-and-comers looking to pad their records with wins. Traveling from town to town in cheap hotel rooms with his wife Julie (Audrey Totter), he clings to his hopeless aspiration like a rosary. But tonight will be different. Tonight he'll bring home that five hundred bucks and poise himself for a title fight—the ultimate shot at glory. Then he and Julie can retire in style. "Just one punch away," he tells her, but Julie's not so sure. Her husband's been saying that for a long time. But so quickly is the viewer invested in Stoker's imminent destiny that there's no one they'd rather accompany on his death march.

The opening moments at The Cozy fast reveal that pride is the tragic flaw to which Stoker is bound and damned. Indeed, it is forged on his face like the head on a coin whose inverse displays another deadly sin embodied by the racketeers' greed. Most people would put the chances of the coin toss at around fifty-fifty, but self-assuredness doesn't stand a chance against avarice around here. Stoker leaves his house in a suit and tie, his gym bag like a briefcase. Dragging his way to the stadium, he looks like just another working stiff, which is precisely what he is.

At thirty-five, Stoker's ankles are starting to buckle. The reflexes of youth have slowed down, and the hands on the clock outside move in one just direction. As the film unfolds in real-time, the city's anonymity envelopes the viewer like a fog over a terse seventy-two minutes. With no artificial soundtrack, the brassy strains of sidewalk bands, the din of the penny arcade, and the blare of jukeboxes that pour out of the clubs bring a welcome respite from the silence of The Cozy or the din of the ring.

The Set-up exemplifies and clarifies the tropes inherent to what has come to be defined under the umbrella classification "film noir." Considering the sheer number of boxing films that fall under noir's protean motifs, the designations that define the genre, as such, are worth discussing in some detail.

A confluence of intellectual and stylistic themes, the classification "film noir" became common parlance just as its stylistic leanings began to abate during the mid-sixties. Often lurid in its focus on reprobates and moral conflict, contemporary screenwriter and director Paul Schrader notes that until its introduction in the thirties, studios had never "dared to take such a harsh, uncomplimentary view of American life."

In 1869, the American psychiatrist George M. Beard coined the term *Neurasthenia* to denote the social disconnect that emerged amid the proximity of overpopulation. In the wake of the Industrial Revolution, a pandemic of nervous exhaustion, depression, and chronic fatigue plagued cities. As dispassionate as the whims of nature or the indifferent claw-machine, film noir directly opposed the idealism foisted upon the public through all media, from musicals and radio shows to the *Saturday Evening Post*.

In the mid-forties, thousands of disillusioned veterans returned from the war to a newly urbanized America awash in alienation. "Simply reflecting on what a monstrous thing this city is," Wade Miller wrote in his 1950 pulp novel *Devil on Two Sticks*, "I can't believe it does anyone good to feel small." By the fifties, three-fifths of the country's population lived in cities. Film noir directly addressed the loneliness and constant threat of violence incited by city life through an almost-singular emphasis on crime.

In his book *Dark City: The Lost World of Film Noir*, film historian Eddie Muller describes an age when "the city arose as a special environment ...that diminished the forces of nature's random onslaughts, and reduced the menace of wild animals [to] the more predatory tribes of men." Two years into the Great Depression's span from 1929 to 1939, messages alerting audiences to the criminal element taking hold of their cities *at this very moment* preceded films including William A. Wellman's *The Public Enemy* and Mervyn LeRoy's *Little Caesar* (both from 1931). While intended as earnest pleas, this sensationalism only served to bolster interest among the public—especially with the promise that the following material was "based on fact." The final overture, *"What will YOU do about it?"* urged viewers to write their local lawmakers. As to the films themselves, *New York Times* reporter Fred Stanley was emphatic in his condemnation of what he dubbed "red meat" productions. The Depression had changed public appetite from escapism to the urgent realism of the purgatorial metropolis.

Veiled or conspicuous, the city's perils are exemplified in noir's intrinsic visual severity, and Paradise City is the Main Street of the American Dream reflected in a broken mirror. Corners and streets emerge from the inky mist and recede beyond invisible vanishing points that lead to the cloudy void outside the city lines. Such muscular imagery ran concomitantly with the influx of immigrants fleeing Germany and Eastern Europe where, a quarter century prior, the hatched contrasts inherent to German Expressionism were exerted to hallucinatory extremes in Robert Wiene's *The Cabinet of Dr. Caligari* (1921), F.W. Murnau's *Nosferatu* (1922), and Fritz Lang's *Metropolis* (1927) and *M* (1931). Amid this urban boom, it was a logical leap to reinterpret these tropes through the city's jagged angularity.

Wise offers similarly disorienting perspectives where bodies contrast under febrile overhead floods and blazing streetlights stretch their neighbors' shadows across sidewalks to creep up brick walls. A houseplant's serrated leaves on the windowsill of The Cozy manifest in a black explosion. Behind it, the intersection through the window evokes the vertiginous anxiety of a chattering woodcut. In the source poem, Moncure March describes the lights that make:

...great shadows sprawl
Over the crumbling brown wall,
...bringing out the rigid shapes
Of long, slanting fire escapes...

The ebb in crime following the Great Depression nevertheless saw the mob continue its aggressive operations as the bootlegging racket quite literally dried up with the end of Prohibition in 1933. One channel through which they sought new means of income was the control of fighters. With their promise of financial advancement, quick purses, and easy paydays, gangsters were not without their appeal to countless uneducated, struggling pugs whose frequently poor grasp of the English language and lack of financial savvy made them easy targets to be used and discarded at will.

As for the managers, they could always be bought. If they couldn't, there were other means of persuasion, and rare is the mid-twentieth-century fighter who got anywhere without mob backing. Getting in with the wise guys almost always involved a trial of loyalty, often carried out through a fixed bout that served as a testament to a fighter's fidelity to his "owners." It was a guaranteed score for the hoods, though such pressures have eroded the moral core of many an onscreen boxer and countless real ones. With his imperious office and manicured hands, the boxing noir villain is more akin to the starched-collar capitalist than the Tommy-gun-toting public enemy. As the men pulling the strings, the gangsters' play for control of the fighter is the impasse wherein the hero's principles and morals are put to the test.

Exuding down-at-heels desperation bolstered by a nasty streak fatter than his cigar, Stoker's manager Tiny (George Tobias) approaches a thinly mustachioed gangster with the foreboding moniker of Little Boy. Played with steely, sterile menace by Alan Baxter, Little Boy's the best-dressed guy in Paradise City and only too happy to take a piece of the Stoker action. Figuring the washed-up bum is a sure loss, the gangster initiates a series of bets wherein Stoker will go down any time after the second round of the evening's fight. There's just one problem with this fix: Tiny never bothers to let Stoker in on it, figuring he'll make it two rounds alright, but not much more. Why bother? Like he said, "There's no percentage in smart'nin' up a chump." Tony, the racketeer's original incarnation in the poem, agrees:

"The best man wins' —like hell!"
Said Tony.
"That stuff is all so much baloney!"

Moncure March paints his B-level hoods in the broadest of strokes to reveal a concentration of unwavering callousness. Despite the 1,500 years that separates the crowd from the slavering attendees at the Circus Maximus, thumbs down and crying for blood, some things never change. Just look at the bookmakers, or betters like Fingers MacPhail, who *"looked like something/Lost in the mail."* Should the reader puzzle as to how this slick, would-be thief sunk to such degradation, Moncure March explains that MacPhail *"Drifted into the fight racket"* after he *"tried one safe, but couldn't crack it."* Wise assembles a similar micro-society, and if the viewer gazes hard enough into the film's mulling congregations, they may get a gander at old Fingers himself.

In *Lonely Places: Film Noir Beyond the City*, Imogen Sara Smith identifies a critical facet of noir as an intense but fleeting investment in its characters on the viewer's part. Noble or sordid, they are casualties of their environment whose trials fade quickly from memory shortly after the final reel. A character as misguided as Stoker may elicit sympathy, but can this sympathy last? Like the intrepid cowpoke or valiant swashbuckler, the boxing noir hero is destined for physical confrontation. But unlike his contemporaries, his victory is far from certain in an urban jungle teeming with "predatory tribes of men." The fight sequence, which occupies a full quarter of the film complete with three-minute rounds and one-minute rests, indicates that Stoker may have reached the end of the line. But the viewer remains undeterred in their commitment to stay with him throughout the fight—if only to sponge the blood from his face.

To capture the thrashing flesh, hissing mobs, and slanted perspectives of the arena, cinematographer Milton Krasner employed three cameras: one set to cover the ring in full, a second placed beside the ring to track the fighters, and a hand-held used for close-ups. With the indifference of a newsreel, no lens shies from the brutal head blows and rib-splintering hooks Stoker absorbs. In a tongue-in-cheek nod to the mundanity of violence amid perpetual urban hysteria, Arthur "Weegee" Fellig, known for his iconic photographs of some of the era's most gruesome crime scenes, was cast as timekeeper.

No boxing match exists without an audience. Anything else is just a brawl, and as the bout unfolds during the film's third act, the viewer is privy to more barbarism outside the ring than in. The displaced masochism of the crowd is on full display: spectators respond with glee to every blow. Every clinch provokes hoots of displeasure. The death instinct resonates in the stands like a balm for confinement—the eruption of the urban herd mentality in one unified frenzy. Psychoanalytic readings are without end, but in this auditorium, the one sure tie that binds is a taste for blood. That's entertainment.

In Moncure March's arena, *"Even whores of the cheapest sort/Avoided this dismal palace of sport." The Set-up*'s venue may seem more palatable, but no one's immune to the contagious and collective forces of a good rampage. Even the demure woman who fretted and squirmed outside the venue just minutes ago is up on her feet screaming, *"KILL 'IM.!"* as ropey sinews protrude from her neck. The air drained from her lungs, it is she, not the announcer, who serves as the fight's vocal emissary.

The most notable spectator among these philistines is a blind man facing the ring while his companion gives him a verbal blow-by-blow. Based on a fixture at the prize-fights Wise attended as a boy, it is significant that the most measured and focused attendee cannot see the butchery that unfolds before him. Just knowing that it's there is enough.

When Stoker puts his man down for good in the fifth, he's strayed from a script he never knew existed. But as far as Little Boy's concerned, whatever Stoker knew or didn't know about the set-up is irrelevant. There has to be some payback. Luckily for Stoker, the pre-Motion Picture Association of America (MPAA) Hays Code would not allow for the hero's demise unless the perps were killed too (see Chapter 3). Fried in the chair, swinging from the gallows, or gunned-down in the street, the Codes didn't care much as to the whys or hows, but they were firm: "If screen characters engaged in crime," writes Sheri Chinen Biesen in her essay *Censoring and Selling Film Noir*, "they had to be punished, die or go to prison." Pansy, who unwittingly provoked the vengeance of the gangsters, wasn't as fortunate as Stoker. And Stoker's isn't fortunate at all.

It's a good night in Paradise City if no one gets killed. Little Boy and Tiny vanish into the underbrush of the lamp-lit jungle where the laws of humanity will continue to get battered, mangled, and generally ignored. As to Stoker, his path is no more apparent to him than it is to the viewer, his pyrrhic victory having forever barred him from the only path he's known. Returning to The Cozy, Stoker stands before Julie and looks down at his fist, worked over by Little Boy's goons with a brick. After an eternity of drifting from town to town from one humiliation to the next, one can't help but wonder if they did him a favor.

The camera moves to the window one last time to linger on a city that doesn't care if Stoker stays or goes. Traffic stops and starts. The lights in the arcades flash bright and go dim again. 9:17 p.m.

2
KID GALAHAD

Directed by Michael Curtiz
Warner Bros., 1937

The fighters pound away while Nick Donati (Edward G. Robinson) keens from ringside, waving puppet arms and yelling to his boy to watch the McGraw kid's right. Beside him is his best girl, Fluff (Bette Davis), and it's pretty clear that it's not the fight she's worried about. A couple of rows back, the vicious gangster Turkey Morgan (Humphrey Bogart, in a suit with shoulder padding stacked like a Simmons mattress) leans in with eyes that flit furtively at Donati of their own accord. But Donati's too absorbed in his fighter's flagrant disregard for instruction. He knows bad acting when he sees it, especially when his own fighter flashes a knowing smirk at Morgan before dropping to the canvas to play-nap through the count. Donati can also tell when a boxer's being strong-armed, and he's pretty sure who owns his.

Released in a decade when film noir had firmly planted its flag into American culture, *Kid Galahad* was the first popular boxing film to provide the public an unabashed glimpse into the illicit transactions that were part and parcel of the fight game by the 1920s. It was an easy sell. Boxing had already established itself as a viable subject in silent films. Buster Keaton's comedy *The Battling Butler* (1926) depicts a wimpy rich boy who impersonates a fighter to woo his beloved, while Alfred Hitchcock's *The Ring* (1927) features two suitors duke it out over a mutual love interest. Five years later, Roy Del Ruth's talkie *Winner Take All* (1932) featured James Cagney in another cautionary tale that fightin' and broads don't mix.

But *Kid Galahad* was new: while it wasn't the first boxing film to feature a gangster, it was the first full-blown cinematic glamorization of the criminal activity that had muscled in on boxing during the 1920s and turned into a lucrative industry long after prohibition. Amid the perils of a growing urban landscape, the film set new expectations and standards that spurred a thematic template few boxing films of significance would neglect as the subject gained momentum in the following decades.

Adapted from Francis Wallace's 1936 serialized *Saturday Evening Post* story of the same name, screenwriter Seton I. Miller preserves the drama of its source while elevating the script to a morality play on how boxing makes money for other people. Bogart and Robinson's felonious creeps serve as incessant reminders that fighters are little more than cash machines for lowlifes. But bad guys have problems too, and this was *Kid Galahad*'s primary attraction. If audiences wanted to watch a fighter, they'd have gone to the fights. They're here for the bad guys.

Warner Bros. fast garnered its reputation for films that rejected the notion of cinema as escapism, earning them the moniker "the gangster studio." Actors including Cagney, Alan Ladd, and the present Bogart-Davis-Robinson trifecta played to public appetite through thinly veiled incarnations of the hoods that consumed as much newspaper real estate as a top-ranked heavyweight.

The rise in criminal activity during the Great Depression sparked the enactment of the Lindbergh Law, which allowed for the increased jurisdiction of the Federal Bureau of Investigation under its proactive, vigilant director J. Edgar Hoover. But as public faith in government dropped and its appetite for the lurid increased, each new sensational massacre or bust saw a rise in gangsters' near-mythical status. Although the economy's recovery in 1934 marked a drop in the national homicide rate by twenty percent over the following three years, the die was cast, and the public was hooked. Fight-fixing figured largely into the mix, and New York District Attorney Frank Hogan's 1946 crusade to clean up racketeering in the game only increased demand for ever-more exploitative narratives in life and art.

Under director Michael Curtiz's severe lens, by turns bleached in light and shrouded in shadow, the powerhouse trio turns a ten-cent crime yarn into a drama of pointed, if sometimes ambiguous, morality. As archetypes in a modest parable, *Kid Galahad*'s characters embody blunt, psychological paradigms wherein fate and motivation are as varied as the individuals that wheel from altruistic to venal to a confused, inchoate blend of the two.

The managers of several boxing films to follow would be chewed alive by Robinson's Nick Donati. Course, truculent, and *almost* heartless, he maintains a sloppy, self-serving moral compass. And while self-serving morality isn't altogether moral, Robinson brings tenderness to a role for whom, per the pulpy novelization, "the price was the important thing." In this business, a guy can't afford to be forgiving.

Donati's vindictive streak stems from navigating an amicable but uneasy relationship with the mob while keeping his good eye on Fluff. A diamond in a mine of vice and foil to the manager's natural proclivity toward corruption, the novel's cast list reductively sums her up as having "dubbed the kid with a kiss and sent him out to get his lumps." The shrewdest of the lot, her independence lies in polar opposition to the cheap molls and kept women that populated the nascent film noir, probably because she's not kept at all.

Author and podcaster Karina Longworth characterizes Bette Davis's relegation to an "eight" by Hollywood beauty standards as having garnered her appeal among female filmgoers insecure with the endless string of tens to which audiences of both sexes had grown accustomed. With distinguished poise, professionally applied make-up, tailored wardrobes, and flattering light and angles devised by cinematographers to hide her flaws, Davis made it all seem attainable—despite her early self-assessment as "Beautiful, never, striking, sometimes, if I'm lucky."

Like Fluff, the young Davis embodied both the virgin and the vamp: a dangerous cupcake and catalyst for the neurosis specific to males dubbed the "Madonna-whore complex" (aka "psychic impotence") by Freud. Longworth identifies the source of this contradiction in an industry where nearly all financial backing came from men who "fantasize about having sex with young, unspoiled women who lack the age and maturity and life experiences of their own wives." Perpetually insecure with her looks and sex appeal, Davis wrote in her private journal that "sex was god's joke on mankind." Initially uncomfortable among the cattiness of film divas, she ultimately out-catted them all while transcending the Madonna-whore dichotomy altogether. Even a bemused Bogart had to admit it: "She scared the bejesus out of me." (Davis, who appeared with Bogart in her first film, Hobart Henley's 1931 *Bad Sister*, found the actor crass, arrogant, and churlish. As for Bogart, his intimidation was short-lived: "What she needs is a good screw from a man who knows how to give it.")

Davis's transition didn't happen overnight. In 1936,

she accepted two roles in England, breaking her contract with Warner Bros. for what she hoped were greener pastures. The studio took legal action, and the barrister representing Jack Warner told Davis she was "a naughty young lady" before promptly sending her back to the States. When Davis asked if she was legally bound to accept any role the studio assigned her under contract "whether it is distasteful or cheap," a retaliative Warner summarily cast her as a prostitute in Lloyd Bacon's *Marked Woman* the same year *Galahad* was released. At twenty-eight, Davis was about to enjoy her second run as an ingénue. Returning to Hollywood in full-on diva mode, she studiously avoided appearing soft or forgiving on screen, and it is only by dint of Bogart and Robinson's asperity that she doesn't chew the scenery in characteristic fashion.

A hotel suite fills with guests for a party that Fluff and Donati throw with the shrimpy two grand brought in from the thrown bout, prompting Fluff to remark, "We can swim after that splash." When a bellhop named Ward Guisenberry (Wayne Morris) is sent up to help with the drinks, his entrance assumes a tidal tug to the loins of every woman in the room. They caress his lapels in a frenzied blitzkrieg and smear his face with lipstick. But Donati's amusement turns to rage upon hearing that his fighter just took that dive for a whopping $25,000 at the behest of Turkey Morgan. Just as he suspected.

With the country still reeling from the Great Depression, Warner Bros. was the first studio to aggressively hire actors from the massive influx of immigrants and working-class ethnicities. George Raft was German, Paul Muni was Austro-Hungarian, Cagney was Irish, and Robinson was Jewish. Bogart was a New York Brahmin whose ancestral chart traced back to the Mayflower. Curtiz, a cantankerous Eastern-European immigrant who came to America partly to escape Hungary's communist government, would make an astonishing forty-six films between 1930 and 1939—six with Bogart, of which *Galahad* was the first.

The thirties saw Bogart typically cast as petty gangsters and hoods. Within a few years, he was entrusted with more complex roles in films that included *Dark Victory* (1939), *High Sierra* (1941), *The Maltese Falcon*, and *Casablanca* (both from 1942, the latter directed by Curtiz). But in 1937, he was still playing routine punks, and it fell to the actor to imbue the two-dimensional gangster with concentrated menace in an amalgamation of three of the source story's hoods: the racket king Terry Winkler (*"He and his gorillas made champs and broke them, just as easy as that"*); the nimble-named Buzz Beaver (*"A little fellow who... lined six men up against a wall during Prohibition and let them have it"*); and the muscle named for that ungainly bird.

Donati's first thought is to hire a cheap gunman and nix the gangster, but if you go after Turkey Morgan, the grave you dig may well be your own. Tension descends on the party like a change in the weather when Morgan enters with his top fighter, heavyweight contender Chuck McGraw, the hopeful's brother (the same McGraw that just took a dive on Donati's dime), and other assorted riffraff pulled from central casting.

Even Morgan's girl can't resist the bellhop's allure. Her push-up bra hoists her nipples to rub against his chest and her lips press against his. Morgan opens his blade to fastidiously cut off Guisenberry's pant legs. Following a brief melee during which the contender gets rough with Fluff, the bellhop puts the boxer on the rug with a neat hook. It makes a hell of an impression on Donati, but not enough to let the kid hang around with no pant legs.

Although Guisenberry's dream is to have his own farm, Donati recognizes a good right when he sees one. If he hitches his wagon to Donati's, the kid can buy ten farms.

After some trouble from Morgan, Donati brings his fighter to his mother's house to lay low. With so much time spent together under the same roof, Guisenberry and Donati's sister Marie become well acquainted. But they squabble quite a bit. Perhaps a little too much. Can this be love?

A fighter's climb from a non-professional to a top-card contender is a well-worn trope of countless boxing films that culminated forty years later in 1976's *Rocky*. The square-off between an inexperienced fighter with no record or ranking and a champion is pure fantasy, a plot device that capitulates to the notion that any big guy who can fight will rise to the top ranks in about a month. But who cares? The onscreen fights here are little more than a backdrop to the warring thugs and a facile device to forward the real drama between the handlers. For Guisenberry, the choice is clear.

Despite Donati's brutish nature, the farm boy knows which side his bread is buttered on, and who buttered it for him.

Fluff dubs Guisenberry "Kid Galahad," after the son of Sir Lancelot, renowned for his unbidden readiness to lay his cape or detached pant legs over puddles in the service of gentrified ladies and scullery maids alike. Yet from the get-go, it's clear that the six-foot-two dreamboat is little more than a MacGuffin around which the real drama between Donati, Morgan, and Fluff can play out.

As Galahad, the *New York Times* dubbed Wayne Morris "the Warners' latest astronomical discovery." But upon his return from four years in the Naval Reserve, the actor found that the studio known to build up their players via constant exposure had moved on in pushing other pretty boys to A-list status. Relegated to the limbo of low-budget westerns, Morris's untimely death from a heart attack at age forty-five is especially tragic considering his healthy living. A forward-thinking environmentalist, his agriculture and pastoral ecology studies are mirrored in the bellhop-fighter's bucolic aspirations that run wholly antithetical to film noir's urban dread.

Notwithstanding the experience Robert Ryan brought to *The Set-up*, credible fight scenes often try on actors with brief or lackluster preparation for a role. A plausible fight scene is necessarily the product of inventive camerawork and inspired editing. Curtiz, who made realistic ring action his top priority, was less than thrilled with Morris' performance, repeatedly blaring through a megaphone in his thick Hungarian accent, "Retake! Fake fight! Awful!" Meanwhile, the actor was busy knocking his training opponents, some of them professionals, out cold.

But if the stage is set, why bother with training in deference to forwarding the crime drama the audience paid for? When McGraw starts baiting Galahad in the ring with lewd digs at Fluff, he's put down for the count. Living up to his name, the white knight's two most significant blows have been thrown in defense of Fluff's honor. But there's a problem: Donati, who doesn't think his kid's ready for a championship bout, explicitly told him to carry the fight to a decision. Now he feels betrayed, and as evinced in the film's opening dive, he's not a forgiving man.

The championship bout between Galahad and Chuck McGraw is set to take place within the month. Donati's temper, already well-established in his stubborn refusal to absolve fighters who stray from the script, hits the roof when a headline featuring Galahad and Marie locked in a smooch makes the front page. With vindictiveness notable even for a guy who built his fortune holding grudges, Donati instructs Galahad to come into the McGraw fight swinging like a saddle bronc in an early expenditure of energy guaranteed to be a losing strategy.

There are several ways to fix a fight that don't involve a fighter taking a dive, and despite what the overwhelming spate of boxing films would have the viewer believe, boxers were rarely murdered over fixed fights. Nevertheless, anyone who financially benefits from a pre-ordained outcome operates in illicit territory. Their methods are manifold: cherry-picked opponents, forged medical records, bribes, morally flexible managers, judges, referees, promotors, scorekeepers, and yes, the occasional, straight-up dive. "Anybody who spends his own money advancing a fighter... engages in some form of fight-fixing," writes Charles Farrell in his essay *Why I Fixed Fights*, and Donati has to look after number one. That means he's pretty comfortable jerking around one of his own when he's crossed. The money doesn't hurt, either. Rather than dump the kid, he throws him to the wolves and bets a hefty sum on McGraw to recoup his loss.

The fight occupies about ten minutes of screen time. "Keep away from him!" Donati yells to his fighter, knowing that McGraw can put some momentum behind his blows and do some real damage with a little distance. Fluff and Marie implore Donati to throw in the sponge, and while that 150 grand he stands to win is tempting, he assures them that the kid will be alright. Donati's principles, which lie far outside the realm of moral calculation, remain unfathomable and intentionally ambiguous.

The final round brings a surprise knockout the viewer saw coming from the start, and this time it's Donati who's strayed from his own unwritten script in which he and Morgan stood to make a pile. Instead, they've taken a financial blow to the jewels, and as the new champ blushingly raises his arms, the showdown is nigh. Once again, it's time to give the viewers what they've been waiting for.

Two shots ring out through the haze of cinematographer Tony Gaudio's mezzotint blacks and grays. When the smoke clears, it's obvious that these two corpses won't be collecting from anyone. Donati's parting words to Fluff ("We did what we set out to do... We got a champ") are considerably less consoling in the source story, where his last words of consequence are, "I won't have to be lookin' at that bum no more." If Donati's jealous vulnerability toward Fluff redeems him with the viewer, so does his dying, which also exonerated him under the Hays Code.

Amid the chaos, Fluff emerges as the de facto hero in plain sight, albeit the feminized hero for 1937, where the size of your heart matters more than the length of your barrel. Navigating the era's patriarchal landscape not as a scheming fatale or hoodwinked boob, her independence remains a source of strength that assures her place as the last "man" standing. Even her name is a demure provocation to the hard guys surrounding her, and she's made no secret that she is not long for the gangster life.

For Donati, love is a one-way street, and in the end, he emerges as a man who has everything money can buy but also knows that money can't buy everything. As for Fluff, an aura of mystery surrounds her from the start. There was never a question about Davis's outsized personality, but Fluff's effortless displacement of the masculine world to which she refuses to be bound was a notably feminist statement on Warner's part for 1937.

A casualty of the final shoot-out is dutifully mourned,

but when you lie down with gangsters, you should plan on dying like one. Fluff accepts Donati's passing like the dawning of a new day, though her thoughts that comprise the source material's last sentence belie any bildungsroman design: "Nicky had done a lot of good—by dying."

The heroine's capacity to survive without a man resonates as the film's most powerful message with modern viewers. One can only imagine the confidence it bolstered among contemporary female audiences who, until recently, had regarded themselves as plain "eights." In the oppressive stadium still hung with cordite, Fluff moves through the bloodless carnage and out the stadium's back door. Gazing at a poster of the kid they used to call Galahad, she glides with unhurried stealth through slashing shadows to emerge into the bright city night, turning the page to a chapter the audience will never get to read.

3

CHAMPION

Directed by Mark Robson
United Artists, 1949

The stadium's full. The ring is empty. The crowd and the canvas are thirsty for blood. A disembodied voice mourns a fallen fighter in perfunctory, colorless praise. "He was a champion... a credit to the fight game. Until the very end."

Not so fast.

The eulogy gives way to the subterranean corridors beneath the stadium, where three dim cylinders of light wilt from the overhead spots and recede into the darkness like stepping stones to hell. Two wise guys emerge from the shadows, moving like missiles toward the camera, up the stairs, and into the arena.

If *The Set-up* is a portrait of an honest fighter navigating an indifferent world devoid of morality, *Champion*, released the same year, is its evil black shadow; the leering, bullying relative at the boxing-noir Thanksgiving table who had to be invited. Both films are hammering parables of doomed predestination, and neither ends well. But unlike Robert Ryan's noble, albeit delusional, Stoker, *Champion* offers up an odious lout steeped in emotional violence so implacable as to drift into exploitation. Call it cruelty porn. This will be a rough ninety-seven minutes.

Ring Lardner's mercilessly grim, seemingly unfilmable short story of the same name appeared in the October 1916 issue of *Metropolitan* magazine and was adapted for the screen three decades later by screenwriter Carl Foreman. Franz Planer's cinematography imbues even the most placid passages with a dread equal to his frenzied fight scenes while Dimitri Tiompkin's pugnacious score flips on a dime from meandering trots to bombastic discord.

Foreman, Planer, and Tiompkin all garnered Oscar nominations, while Harry W. Gerstad took home the statuette for Best Editor for his seamless shifts from quiet anxiety to explosive violence. Also nominated was Kirk Douglas, a thirty-three-year-old up-and-comer whose eighth role as the boxer Midge Kelly garnered him Hollywood A-list status. Writing in the *New York Times*, Bosley Crowther called attention to the actor's "slight inclination to over-eagerness," ostensibly for histrionics so extreme as to forever ground the character in the two-dimensional. But it's with more than a "slight inclination" that Douglas delivers his malicious cackles and malignant glowers.

Twenty-two years after *Kid Galahad* advanced the boxing noir by attracting top-tier actors and satiating public fascination with the game's criminal ties, *Champion* channeled Douglas's smug aggression into a conflation of boxer and villain. Never mind those hoods in cocked fedoras heading into the stadium. Midge is the bad guy here.

A textbook narcissist, Midge Kelley's avarice borders on the pathological, condemning him to forever swipe at a brass ring that isn't there. In a genre where conflict often spurs self-awareness and moral epiphanies, the illusory goals plaguing Midge only make him double down on his barbarity. With no hope for redemption, *Champion* demonstrates that rules are more recognizable—and necessary—when broken.

Ring Lardner, an early twentieth-century sports and theater columnist, was also a renowned satirist who counted F. Scott Fitzgerald and Virginia Woolf among his friends. His son, screenwriter Ring Lardner Jr., was a primary target of the communist witch hunts that seized Hollywood at the height of the Cold War. Called to testify before the House Un-American Activities Committee (HUAC) in 1947 and asked the standard, "Are you or have you ever been a member of the Communist Party?" Lardner Jr. responded, "I could answer the question... but if I did, I would hate myself in the morning." His flippancy earned him a top place among the infamously blacklisted "Hollywood Ten" (ten producers, directors, and screenwriters who refused to answer questions regarding communist affiliations October 1947) and a year in Danbury Prison.

The anecdote is pertinent because Douglas played his own curious role in the Hollywood Red Scare. Eleven years after *Champion*'s release, the actor had garnered considerable sway as a leading man and hired screenwriter Dalton Trumbo (another member of the Ten) to collaborate on Stanley Kubrick's 1960 film *Spartacus*. Despite the actor's clout, it was still a bold move for which Douglas publicly credited himself with single-handedly breaking the blacklist. To call this an exaggeration would be generous at best. Among others, *Spartacus* author Howard Fast, a blacklisted, full-fledged Red on whose 1951 historical novel the film was based, rejected the actor's claims entirely.

Upon publication of Douglas's second autobiography-cum-memoir, 2012's *I Am Spartacus!: Making a Film, Breaking the Blacklist*, John Meroney and Sean Coons of the *Atlantic* cite an interview with *Spartacus* producer Edward Lewis in which he recounts Douglas's initial resistance to bring Trumbo on board. (The year after *Champion* was released, its screenwriter Carl Foreman became another casualty of the witch hunts.) Douglas's top priority laid in maintaining his A-list status, and although he hired Trumbo to re-write his next film, Gottfried Reinhardt's *Town Without Pity* (1961), he did not allow the writer's name to appear on the screen. Trumbo's daughter Mitzi sheds further light on this working relationship: "Kirk Douglas was paying my father only a small fraction of what his salary would have been had he not been blacklisted." Communist writers were notoriously underpaid, and in 1959, Douglas's production company had four on its payroll.

Midge Kelley rides the boxcars with his disabled brother Connie (Arthur Kennedy, with a bum leg and a cane). Thumbing it on the highway, a handsome car with the top-down pulls over. Sitting at the wheel is Dunne (John Daheim), a top heavyweight contender on his way to Kansas City for tonight's fight. In the passenger seat, his girlfriend, Grace Diamond (Marilyn Maxwell) wears a fox stole around her long white neck and eyes the scraggy brothers with icy disdain.

A wrestler during his four years at college, Douglas boasted an impressive build that Dunne studies with care. With that body, Midge could make a quick $35.00 as an undercard at tonight's fight, and it isn't long before Midge (sans professional boxing license) comes charging from his corner in a ring in Kansas City and floors his opponent with erratic, malicious blows.

It's the first of many beatings Midge metes out during the film, and Douglas's rancor is etched into his face as though he were already practicing for his upcoming turns playing cocky, egocentric brutes. Even as a newcomer, the actor was fearless in exposing humanity's uglier sides. With systematic methodology, "playing antiheroic heroes soon became the Douglas specialty," wrote film critic Nigel

Andrews in the actor's 2020 *Financial Times* obituary. The so-called "ultimate Hollywood shark," Douglas was quick to win the public's hearts—and wallets.

Midge's slappy performance and first-round kayo pique the attention of Tommy Haley (Paul Stewart), a professional manager who sees potential behind all that discordant flailing. Handing Midge his card, he tells him to stop by the gym when he arrives in L.A. Haley will be there. He's always there.

There's no conspicuous fraternal bond between Midge and Connie, a backstory that's mercifully absent considering the opening line of Lardner's story: "Midge Kelley scored his first knockout when he was seventeen. The knockee was his brother, Connie, three years his junior and a cripple."

The brothers arrive at a restaurant, of which they were made to believe they own a share, only to discover they've been scammed. The owner takes pity; he could use another dishwasher and line cook. He even has rooms available. There's just one caveat: "Stay away from my daughter."

To no one's surprise, Midge is caught red-handed with the girl in question. Unassuming and diffident, Emma (Ruth Roman) stands stoically as vows are exchanged in a literal shotgun wedding where Midge pockets his ring before the pastor can finish presiding. Lardner's account is again more callous, the post-connubial "gift of the groom" arriving as "a crushing blow on the bride's pale cheek."

Wise to the pesky loopholes to which he was subjected back in Kansas City when he got handed a tenner in lieu of the promised thirty-five, Midge knows how expenses add up and that the so-called purse doesn't always correspond with the net. It's a formula in no way confined to film, especially at a time when the mob was constantly con- triving new means of fleecing fighters through arbitrary, bogus expenses.

An indifferent Haley leans against a ring where two men spar and tells Midge that he's retired since last they met. "Take a deep breath," he says, sucking in a lungful of stank air steeped in cigar smoke. "It stinks in here. And it's not sweat. It's *no good*." Then this should be easy: "No good" is Midge's most vital asset, and against his better instincts, Haley returns to the game he's come to despise.

Midge's singular focus is to clinch the title. As his unbroken string of wins—all by kayo—continues to grow, he becomes meaner, and Lardner conveys Midge's sports- manship in the first person: *"I'll kill 'em all."*

The film offers its sympathetic leads in Connie, Haley, and Emma, who allow for the conveyance of Midge's ques- tionable ethics in and out of the ring. Following an early bout, Connie speaks to his brother with concern. "You looked like you wanted to kill that guy." Midge is silent. Of course he did.

Midge must wait his turn like any other good boy if he wants his shot. Nobody pulls off a title fight in this town without the go-ahead from the mild-mannered gangster Harris (Luis Van Rooten). Sober, austere, and without the faintest glint of hostility behind his poker-face façade,

Harris has been watching Midge, and he'll get his shot. But there's a process, and for now, the title should rest with Dunne—the heavyweight who gave Midge a lift to his first fight. The guy's earned it, and he's not getting any younger. But with a little patience, Midge is a lock for next year. So long as he loses tonight, because that's also part of the process.

"They don't own me!" rages Midge, whose compulsion to define and delineate ownership is most pronounced concerning people, especially Emma, whom he's abandoned for over a year during his travels. But it's too late now. The fix is in, and the fighter has no time for grousing about ownership. It's still a payday, and Midge won't lose his status as a contender. But he doesn't like it. No fighter would, but most of them would understand. Midge doesn't.

Pretty soon, Grace Diamond of the Mannerist neck and fox stole wonders if she judged Midge a little harshly. Dunne may be her main squeeze, but Midge is raking it in. Grace loves money—especially what it buys. The arrangement works well since Midge loves to spend it.

The fight's underway, and Tiompkin's score meanders along with the preliminaries like Muzak before it slowly transitions into strident, fearsome swells. The air's thick with violence, and Gerstad abuses Dunne and the viewer with skittering edits that underscore Midge's singular maxim: *Kill 'em all*. Turning ringside to Grace with the primitive glare of an ape mauling a troop member in front of his mate, Midge drops his man fast.

For Midge, the spoils of victory are twofold, and purse notwithstanding, neither one is very nice. Haley's lost some serious credibility, and Harris isn't happy either. But Midge won't let his own social politics—more akin to those of the animal kingdom than the prize ring—be swayed by civility. It's time he learned Newton's third law of motion, where one action invokes an equal, opposite reaction. It's also time he realized that sometimes that opposite reaction is a bit less equal and a lot bloodier.

In a post-fight ambush, Midge is pursued down the same gloomy hallway beneath the stadium that opened the film. Maybe this *is* what hell looks like as Robson plays the impartial Virgil to Midge's hot-footing Dante bounding over those three circles of muddy light. Shadows crawl blackly down the stands where Midge slips under the ropes and into the ring. An overhead shot reveals a dozen shades of gray that overlap and dance under the dim floodlights. The first enforcer steps out of the darkness like a well-dressed ghost. Then the others emerge: from doorways, black corners, and thin air. The film's only moment wherein Midge is made vulnerable, he endures the ungloved blows of a dozen fists. Luckily for him, he still has earning potential, and as this business is run on a case-by-case basis, he's let off with a cursory beating. Consider it a wake-up call. Still, no championship belt has ever felt more meaningless.

In Larder's telling, Midge abandons his family for good, saddling Emma with a baby shortly after scoring his first victory. He's averaging $1,000 a fight when a letter from Emma arrives informing him that "the baby... cant live much longer unless I give her better food and thats impossible the way things are." Midge balks at her request for $36.00. A second letter, this time from his mother, informs him that Connie "hasnt got out of bed in over 3 yrs." Midge rips her appeal for "medisin" money into "a hundred pieces." The infant dies.

A third letter is destroyed, this one from Grace Diamond, who, as painted by Lardner, is just another casualty of Midge's bile. But faithful to her name, combining as it does docile refinement with the price tag on her stole, Grace almost attains the embodiment of the prototypical noir femme fatale. She's been feeling available since Midge gave her man that beat-down, and when the new champ leans in and makes his move, she warns him, "I'm expensive."

This notion of the femme fatale has been steeped in misogyny since a conniving snake induced Eve to pluck that apple from the Tree of the Knowledge. Literally the "deadly" or "poison woman," the term entered common parlance in late nineteenth-century Europe amid failed bohemian aspirations to free love and a rampant outbreak of syphilis (of which sex workers comprised the largest demographic of the infected). Jealousy, triangulation, and illness fostered the debasement of the sexual woman, vilified as parasitic and dangerous in any medium.

Champion's inversion of the femme fatale's allure vindicates scores of chumps wrung dry and thrown to the curb by scores of greedy sirens. Of course, love's a two-way street, and many a doe-eyed *femme docile* has been chewed up and discarded by numberless, caddish *hommes fatale*. If the male protagonist's handling of the poisonous woman is a way to gauge his moral strengths and failings, Grace doesn't stand a chance. Greed recognizes greed, and Midge sniffs it out as Robson turns the noir mainstay of the fatale on its ear.

With laughable hypocrisy, Grace scolds Midge for his proclivity to spend like a sailor but walks away smelling fresh as a daisy when Midge beats her to the punch: "You'd better register yourself another meal ticket." Of course, she will; Midge isn't the only cash machine in town. Exit the treacherous fatale.

Midge begins to wonder why he's giving Haley a cut when he can just as easily go it alone. No percentages, no kickbacks, no waiting on promoters and racketeers. But once again, there's a process, and Midge's refusal to play ball won't do him any favors. But the way he sees it, business is just another bloodsport. Like boxing, like love, it all comes down to the same thing: more money.

Haley rues the "golem" he saw in Midge in Kansas City, an appropriate word denoting an incomplete, unfinished monster evinced in Midge's social pathology. But the words "truth" and "death" that activated the fabled golem of Prague's Jewish ghetto don't carry the same weight as "money," the magic word that stirs Midge from his own slumber. "And for what?" Haley barks before he leaves, "to fill a hole? To win bets for someone you didn't even know?" It would appear so, and Midge's next stop is Harris, who, not so long ago, had him worked over for beating Dunne. But that was just business. Maybe now they can make some money.

Luis van Rooten plays Harris as forever mitigating his austerity with nervous, eagle-eyed disquietude. No matter how many goons he keeps around, he still comes across more like a CPA or a banker, which, in an unofficial capacity, he is. Still, nobody sits behind that desk without having erased a few pugs who didn't listen so well. But he knows Midge isn't ready for the scrap heap yet. The kid's a sadist, but filmgoers still wanted their champion. While the obsession with bad guys continued to grow concurrent with the mob's chokehold on the sport, the public willingly tolerated a scum fighter to sate its appetite. It was no coincidence that both *The Set-up* and *Champion* arrived at the cusp of the most egregiously corrupt decade the sport has seen.

Midge signs on with Harris and, the ink still wet on the contract, makes his play for the gangster's girl, Palmer (Lola Albright). With morals clouded from years in the moll racket, her integrity lies comfortably between Emma's wary, honest resignation and Grace's calculating avarice. She knows how Harris makes his living, and she doesn't care. It's a good one, and that's what matters.

Harris inadvertently hands Midge a new bargaining chip. If Midge drops Palmer, Harris will wipe out all debt incurred when Midge fought under Haley. He'll also give Midge a $65,000 purse for a rematch with Dunne. It's a generous offer, especially considering that most hoods would shoot Midge full of holes no matter how good an earner he is. Nevertheless, Harris's parting words are ominous: "You better train for this one."

When Palmer shockingly, inexplicably, outlandishly falls in love with Midge, he leans his sweaty head back, laughs his peculiar brand of perverse exuberance, and tells her he's already married. It's the most thought he's given to his wife in months. The latest casualty of Midge's demented bile, Palmer is the only character who might have known better, considering the company she keeps.

After a four-year abandonment, Midge returns to the diner to learn that Emma wants a divorce. She and Connie are in love, which is alright with Midge, but he's used to making the decisions. Packing her bags, Emma tells Midge that she never hated him. "But you're afraid of me." His voice is calm as he moves upon her and the screen fills with the camera's glaring white of his bare back. "You're my wife."

Unsurprisingly, the implied rape was subject to the scrutiny of the newly formed Motion Picture Production Code. Indirectly spurred by silent film star Fatty Arbuckle's 1921 sexual assault on Virginia Rappe and helmed by Republican Postmaster General and Indiana Presbyterian Will H. Hays, the so-called Hays Code issued a formal list of thirty-six "Don'ts" and "Be Carefuls" in 1927. Twelve of the thirty-six off-limits themes were sexual in nature, including the inscrutably worded "inference of sex perversion," among which rape figured prominently. While the Codes were self-imposed by the industry to avoid more stringent government oversight, producers and distributors could still be fined up to $25,000 for breaking even one such stricture. But as discussed, there were ways around this, which invariably meant killing off the offender, and Midge crossed a line that could not be uncrossed. (A discussion of Douglas's alleged 1955 rape of the sixteen-year-old Natalie Wood, revealed in 2018 by Wood's younger sister Lana, will be passed over here as it cannot contribute to the narrative at hand.)

This time, the sorely unprepared champion is on the receiving end of Dunne's hammering mitts. There's no sadistic nihilism or scornful misanthropy here; it's just how the game works. Although Dunne draws on his ire toward Midge for stealing Grace, the viewer is too busy reveling in their own schadenfreude to consider such minutiae.

Douglas unleashes a sketchbook of facial acrobatics by turns agonized, wounded, and feral. The actor draws on every face and neck muscle to twist and tighten in a savage parody of snarls. The public and the press ate up every leer and grimace. Although several ringside cameras were employed, Robson's POV focus on Midge's face through Dunne's eyes is the best indicator of the action—and the outcome. There's only so much punishment the viewer (never mind Midge) can tolerate as Douglas's chiseled, rectilinear features and beloved cleft are tenderized to spongey curves.

Back in his dressing room, Midge rants deliriously

about the "fat bellies with big cigars" who would try to own him, fleece him, and steal from him. (Most boxers wait until *before* a fight to launch such tirades.) When a fast-acting brain hemorrhage kills him, Connie, Emma, and Haley—all of whom have followed Midge through the dark catacomb of cement—breathe a sigh of relief.

Shortly before the film's release, drama ensued when RKO honcho Howard Hughes slapped *Champion* producer Stanley Kramer with a lawsuit contending that the film was too close in tone to *The Set-up*. (*Champion* was released in January of 1949, *The Set-up* in April.) While both are boxing films, the similarities end there. Following a back-to-back viewing, the judge agreed and ruled that Kramer alter two sentences and cut one minute before dismissing the case. *Champion* was a smash, dwarfing *The Set-up*'s box office intake with its rags-to-riches appeal, though Hughes must have fumed when Gerstad, a one-time assistant to *The Set-up* director Robert Wise, clinched that Oscar for Best Editor. Five years later, screenwriter Carl Foreman was blacklisted. As for Douglas, so confident was the young actor that the film would be a success that he deferred his salary and agreed to be paid only if the film saw a profit. He made his money.

As the eulogy from the flashback opening recommences, the viewer is surprised to see Haley behind the microphone. His cadence is guarded, his words devoid of grief or grudge. His golem has returned to clay, dried, crumbled, and doomed to swirl in a fetid breeze.

Emma and Connie move through the evil hallway and over the same three rings with their backs to the viewer, mirroring the approaching hoods from the film's opening to disappear into the shadows and vanish into an unknown future. As for Haley, it's a safe bet that he's out of the fight game for good this time.

Lardner's story closes at a newspaper office where sportswriters try to compose a flattering obituary for an unrepentant dirtbag. The champ was a sleaze, but his vilification "would never have passed the sporting editor." Instead, feats of generosity are invented for a laudatory puff piece that his wife and mother never get to read, "for the news on Sunday is a nickel a copy."

Seven years after *Champion*, Robson directed what is perhaps the most scathing indictment of corruption in all of boxing cinema. With a singular focus on the fight game's partnership with the mob, *The Harder They Fall* (Chapter 8) is a sweeping critique-cum-exposé of the sport on a social level. But *Champion* gets personal, an uneasy reminder that the worst of human nature isn't always brought to bear by outside forces. Sometimes it's just bred in the bone.

4
GENTLEMAN JIM

Directed by Raoul Walsh
Warner Bros., 1942

"I think the boxing game is supposed to be a gentleman's sport," said the fighter Joseph Parker in 2015. To build upon his proclamation is a quotation attributed to Lana Turner: "A gentleman is simply a patient wolf." Though the two are not mutually exclusive, the nickname "Gentleman" Jim was a still stretch for the world's second Heavyweight Champion, James J. Corbett.

"Gentleman" Jim held the heavyweight title from 1882 to 1887, the most crucial years of boxing's move from its gloveless, eye-gouging roots to the modern "sweet science." Corbett was no street tough, nor did he engage in brawls as a child. Excepting his expulsion from elementary school for breaking a bully's nose, he preferred to hone his skills in professional sparring clubs.

The best-dressed dude in the game in an era when clothes made the man, Corbett was the first champion to fight exclusively under the Queensberry rules. He was also a weaselly, albeit charming, manipulator, philanderer, and stubborn grudge-holder whose charisma, along with his wardrobe, earned him his ring moniker. The sobriquet might seem applicable to any number of boxers who came to the game on the heels of the bare-knuckle roughnecks, though "Gentleman" is most apt when applied to the calculated, scientific methodology that Corbett introduced to the sport. "Before [Corbett] came on the scene," said his manager William A. Brady, "boxing was not quite respectable. He brought education, brain power, and talent to the ring... The sport became legitimate." Boxing was banned in most states, and the public derided its practice. With showy pizzazz, Corbett's slick persona brought an air of dignity wholly at odds to the beer-soaked bluster of John L. Sullivan, the world's first Heavyweight Champion and a student of the far more brutal bare-knuckle London Prize Ring Rules.

Raoul Walsh's enormously popular *Gentleman Jim* was notable for its departure from crime-centric plots. (Robert F. Hill's *Flying Fists*, released the same year as *Kid Galahad*, and Zachary Mamoulian's 1939 *Golden Boy* were also among the few mid-century boxing films that were not structured around crime.) The film's primary appeal was Warner Bros.'

casting of Errol Flynn, whose swashbuckling, eponymous *Captain Blood* (released in 1935 and directed by Michael Curtiz two years prior to making *Kid Galahad*) turned the unknown Australian into Hollywood's most alluring male lead practically overnight.

Flynn's relationship with Jack Warner was less than amicable from the get-go. Warner considered Flynn a drunk and an antisemite and is reported to have referred to him as "a lousy Irish beachcomber" whose career he could "unmake" at will. Luckily, for Flynn and Walsh, Warner was out of town during filming, where he would not interfere with their process and dialogue tweaks. Yet for all their animosity, Flynn conceded in his infamous 1959 autobiography *My Wicked, Wicked Ways* that "Jack Warner's faith set me on my career."

Flynn's dreamboat veneer was nearly shattered in 1943 when he was charged with two counts of statutory rape. The charges were dropped not because the actor reminded the court that he "need[ed] a baseball bat to keep the girls away" but because the women redacted. Although he was acquitted, widespread coverage of the trial wreaked severe damage to the status Flynn had cultivated over his eight years as a romantic lead. Grandstanding blather, including "I like my whiskey old and my women young," didn't help his cause. Nor did his frank answer to a reporter's query as to why he surrounded himself with underage women: "'cause they fuck so good."

At thirty-three, Flynn's ongoing bouts of malaria,

tuberculosis, and a litany of venereal diseases had virtually sapped the actor's stamina. His rampant alcoholism and numberless liaisons that gave birth to the idiom "in like Flynn" didn't help matters, though his autobiography tells a different story in which he claims to have been in excellent physical condition when training for and filming *Gentleman Jim*. After getting punched in the face by a professional sparring partner three times in one day, he wrote, "For once, I loved making a picture."

In *Errol Flynn: The Untold Story*, Charles Higham quotes the Hollywood boxing advisor and one-time Welterweight World Champion Mushy Callahan, who was to train Kirk Douglas seven years later for *Champion*: "I had to teach [Flynn]... to move very fast on his feet...Luckily, he had excellent footwork, he was dodgy, and he could duck faster than anybody I saw. And by the time I was through with him, he'd jab, jab, jab with his left like a veteran." But training came at a cost: Flynn's overexertion caused him to collapse from a minor heart attack during filming.

While the press portrayed him as the picture of health, Flynn chewed oranges soaked in vodka to steady himself during filming. He also consumed "vitamins" laced with morphine that lead to a full-blown heroin addiction by his forties. The Warner Bros. publicity department went into damage-control mode, concocting a story that the actor had won an Olympic gold medal for boxing in 1932. No one thought to question the bogus claim.

As Flynn was in decline, director Raul Walsh's career

blossomed following his move to Warner Bros. In 1939, he directed Humphrey Bogart and James Cagney in *The Roaring Twenties*, commencing a fifteen-year run during which he made his most memorable films—much of them hard-nosed noir featuring Warner's top leads.

The standard Hollywood biopic unfolds in a predictably linear narrative that invariably clouds the subject in a barrage of connected bullet points. In this way, even the most critical milestones are rendered blips in a timeline. Although Corbett had been dead nine years before the release of *Gentleman Jim*, the film is cautious in safeguarding his reputation while taking enormous liberties with his life outside the ring, especially the deus ex machina of a wholly fictionalized love interest. Based on Corbett's own autobiography, *The Roar of the Crowd* (1925), Vincent Lawrence and novelist Horace McCoy's screenplay superfluously colors the facts in every hue. But to varying degrees, so did Corbett.

An heirloom scrapbook opens to reveal Flynn's name in whorling cursive, undoubtedly the most handsome penmanship in the history of the boxing film. *Auld Lang Syne* interpolates the old Irish ditty *The Fountain in the Park* in a page-flipping credit sequence. As the photograph on the final page blends seamlessly into downtown San Francisco, a beat cop with a face like braised meat tries to block access to an illegal bare-knuckle bout between two punchy, wobbly gladiators. When the ring of a whistle announces the arrival of the fuzz, the fighters turn on the cops. The year is 1887.

Back at the police station, the "scandalized" judge

rants about the "crazy state laws" that outlaw boxing and do more harm than good to the sport's reputation, to which one of the apprehended pugs asks, "Why haven't you changed the laws?" The judge blames Black fighters—"big muscle-bound tramps from the Barbary Coast [that] have killed the fight game." (The disparagement of Black fighters was prompted by the lower gate costs they garnered and the so-called color line wherein —due to a blend of fear and old-fashioned racism—White fighters fastidiously avoided Blacks.) To add some class to the game, the judge imports the dapper Englishman Harry Watson (Rhys Williams), a real-life figure who trained the Prince of Wales in the art of the sweet science. "Since we can't make you fighters into gentlemen," the judge announces, "we'll make gentlemen into fighters."

Corbett is introduced working as a teller at the Nevada Bank of San Francisco, a job he held prior to becoming a fighter. It's relatively menial labor, but his love for money runs deep. He likes being around the stuff, and his obsequious treatment of higher-ups is wincing. Before Corbett even made money as a boxer, he confessed to a penchant for "the good life—the high silk hats, the gold watch chains, the refinement that comes with money." In a well-executed bid for popularity, he sneaks himself and several high-ranking bankers into an illegal bout, making him only slightly more likable with the top brass.

When Victoria Ware (Alexis Smith) withdraws a haul of silver for her father, a top player in the local *haut monde* and the owner of the real-life Olympic Club, the pugilist-cashier spots an opening. That silver's heavy, so the sycophantic Gent carries it to the club himself.

There never was a Victoria Ware, though when Corbett was nineteen, he eloped with a woman named Olive Lake. (The year was 1886, and Corbett would have been fresh off an 1885 divorce from Lake at this point in the film.) Ostensibly, the marriage was annulled for having taken place when the couple was underage. More likely is that Corbett, who'd already begun planning his wedding to the actress Vera Stanwood, wanted out. Stanwood, who moonlit as a sex worker, tolerated Corbett's infidelities as he did her line of work. Despite the acrimony that plagued the marriage (Stanwood sued him for divorce more than once), they remained together for thirty-eight bitter, unfaithful years. As a love interest befitting a gentleman, Miss Ware serves as a barely recognizable composite of Corbett's two wives.

Inside the foyer of the Olympic Club is a reproduction of Douglas Tildon's 1892 bronze statue, *The Tired Boxer.* An homage to millennia-old sculpture like the piteous Hellenistic *Boxer of the Quirinal* and the heartrending *Dying Gaul,* Tildon's seated boxer reaches warily for a single glove in resolution to rise, if only for one final round. The piece establishes the club as a gateway to boxing. Smelling money, Corbett unabashedly insinuates himself into the club's milieu.

When Corbett encounters Harry Watson (the fellow brought in to make "fighters out of gentlemen") teaching boxing to club members, he removes his jacket, laces up the gloves, and effortlessly slips Watson's swipes with bodily torques and circling footwork. It's unlike anything Watson—who can't manage to so much as tap the young banker—has seen before. But facts belie the retelling: the Welshman put Corbett down repeatedly during their first spar, though he later declared that "a scientific fighter always has the edge over a slugger."

No novelty pint of green beer can equal the Irish stereotypes that play out among the rowdy brood back at the Corbett house. Pat and Ma Corbett, Jim's two uncouth stevedore brothers (Corbett was in fact one of ten sons), and the grinning Father Burke (probably based on Corbett's uncle, a Catholic priest and no stranger to dustups) whoop and yell across the dinner table. The brothers needle each other incessantly before they take it outside, much to the delight the man-of-the-cloth. Corbett's father Pat's brogue is most conspicuous when he shows up at inopportune moments singing Irish shanties. A far darker character than the fiction suggests, Pat was a violently loose cannon who murdered his wife and killed himself when Jim was thirty-two.

Despite the fledgling fighter's chutzpah, the old guard cuts him some slack when they realize his natural pugilistic sophistication can prove an asset to the club. Setting a date for a bout with the heavyweight Jack Burke is a win-win: either Corbett beats the Chicagoan and the club makes some money, or Burke knocks the annoying upstart on his ass and they revoke his membership.

Corbett shows up to the bout in a rented top hat and tails as the announcer blares that this will be the first fight under the Queensberry rules. (It wasn't. The first record of such a fight is from Virginia City, Nevada, in 1876—the rules did not become standard practice for another thirteen years.) For the viewer's benefit, the display in the ring emphasizes the emerging civilizing climate of the sport in a forgery of Corbett's movements. The short bout is as enjoyable to the viewer as it was unpleasant for the dissipated Flynn, who could only perform for about a minute at a time.

As a crowd gathers at the Olympic Club to celebrate Corbett's knockout victory (the fight was in fact a draw), Victoria Ware seems disappointed: she was looking forward to her pursuer getting some of that arrogance beaten out of him.

Jim's second fight is injected here into what looks to be the day after his first victory as he kayos the boxer and wrestler "Professor" William Miller in Salt Lake City. (It was in fact Corbett's fourteenth fight, not his second, and it occurred in San Francisco, not Salt Lake City.) A less surprising liberty is the historical fiction of Corbett's victory over Miller as a kayo rather than his win by decision, as was the case. It would be sorely naive to consider the movie anything more than a half-fiction, and the viewer must settle for a yarn in which these blunders take a back seat to a smooth but ambiguous chronology.

Corbett's first and most frequent opponent was the Jewish boxer Joe Choynski (not Jack Burke as portrayed in the film). Considered defenders of their respective ethnicities, the two met for the first time in 1884 and fought three more times in the space of six weeks in 1889 when Corbett was twenty-two years old.

Their third battle holds a singular place in modern boxing history. Duly recreated here with pointed efforts to mimic Corbett's science, the fight occurred on a floating grain barge in Benicia Harbor in California's North Bay region, far from police jurisdiction. Of Corbett's many bouts, the highly unconventional "Battle on the Barge" demands recreation.

On a canvas placed over wooden slats, Flynn's languid movements reveal the decline of an actor who held his own against fencing champion Basil Rathbone in *Captain Blood* just seven years prior. But that was a long time ago.

By 1942, Flynn began to welcome the occasional stand-ins. The shuffling forgeries of Corbett's footwork are enacted with fluid grace by Callahan, who continued step in as needed for the rapidly dissipating actor. As Callahan's feet shimmy in place, a club member remarks that Corbett "should have been a dancer."

Scandal struck that June evening when Choynski's gloves mysteriously disappeared. Long suspected of "forgetting" them to turn the meeting into a bare-knuckle bout, his cornerman is shown surreptitiously nudging them overboard. Ever the gent, Corbett conceded to Choynski's use of thin riding gloves while he opted for five-ounce padded gloves as ordained by the Queensberry rules.

A fantastic spectacle follows as the two actors (and a few overworked stunt doubles) stage a thwacking slugfest in which every blow resounds like a thunderclap courtesy of an overeager sound effects department. Knocked overboard, Corbett pulls himself back on deck seconds before the ten-count. In the original battle, Corbett broke his left hand on Choynski's skull which, along with a dislocated thumb from their last meeting less than a week prior, meant fighting under excruciating pain. It took twenty-seven rounds for Corbett to make a mess of Choynski's face and, with both men ready to collapse, score a knockout with the first hook on record. (A blow formalized, if not invented, by Corbett, a hook involves stiffening the arm at roughly ninety degrees and using the legs, hips, torso, and shoulders for propulsion.) Five weeks later, the two met again where, despite the pain in Corbett's hands, Choynski lost by decision.

The final championship bout under the bare-knuckled London Prize Ring rules took place on July 8, 1889, when John L. Sullivan, aka "The Boston Strong Boy," made good on his boast that he could "lick any son of a bitch in the world" by pounding Jake Kilrain to the dust over the course of an astonishing seventy-five rounds. Seven months later, Corbett's victory over Kilrain (this time under the

Queensberry rules) elevated him to one of the Olympic Club's most esteemed members, a standing he accepts with the faux humility befitting an arrogant pest. Still aching to see him put down, Victoria attends his fights like a vulture wheeling patiently overhead.

John L. Sullivan (a hammy Ward Bond) was among the most revered figures in late nineteenth-century America. With no pretenses to valor or science, he was nevertheless quick to embrace the Queensberry rules, making him both the last champion of the bare-knuckle era and, de facto, the first champion in the illustrious litany of modern heavyweights. With his larger-than-life presence and hard-drinking Boston-Irish bravado, Sullivan delighted in buying rounds for the house while repeating his boast about licking sons of bitches with the compulsion of a facial tic.

Sullivan's booming salutation at the local watering hole is tweaked here: "I can lick any man in the world!" (This was 1942, after all.) Although Bond employs his absurd Irish lilt to comedic effect, the accent was closer to that of the real-life Corbett, though Flynn insisted on maintaining the smooth elocution befitting Hollywood royalty. Considering his condition, it's also likely that he was too lazy to ape the Hibernian intonation.

The public still believed that Sullivan could lick any son of a bitch, including the Gent, who had to raise $25,000 in purse funds to get his shot at the champ. An increasingly spiteful Victoria digs into her coffers for the required funds, so strong is her wish to see the wind knocked out of her "tin horn shanty Irishman." Her only stipulation is that Corbett never finds out where the money came from. (In truth, Corbett and his manager hastily raised the money themselves.)

Despite his eight-year age advantage, Corbett was the underdog with the bookmakers. Reluctant to let go of their aging hero, the public concocted the rallying cry, *though Corbett placed his blows quite well, we won't go back on our John L.* When it came time for the fighters to step into the ring, Sullivan insisted that as champion, he should enter first. (The practice of the champion entering second has long since become customary.) Following the ego-driven standoff, the two enter together, though the Strong Boy's indignation assured that Corbett had already won the preliminary psych-out.

Flynn managed a modicum of fluidity as filmed in one-minute intervals while Bond plays the lurching spaz, spinning like a whirling dervish who can barely locate his opponent within the twenty-four square-feet. With telegraph updates from around the world superimposed over the action, Sullivan deftly slips a punch only to wind up wrapped in the ropes like a fly caught in a web.

Breaking the Bostonian's nose in the third round, Corbett continued his assault while a steady stream of blood poured from Sullivan's face. The cascade continued throughout the fight's remaining seventy minutes, during which Corbett took over entirely and dropped his man in the twenty-first. Say hello to the world's second Heavyweight Champion.

The following day, the *Police Gazette* (a defunct men's lifestyle magazine featuring pin-ups and boxing coverage among other pre-Hefner material) praised Corbett for having "lifted boxing out of the barroom slough, the evil influences of its habitués and start[ing] it towards its moral revolution."

Even Sullivan congratulates Corbett on his creative, technique-driven methodology. It was reported that John L. consented—through a maw far more bloody than the Codes would allow—that Corbett "beat me fair and square. I'm thankful that when my time came to lose, I lost to an American." Here, his praise is laced with a potshot at Jim's affectations. "I don't know what all the gentleman talk is about," Bond's Sullivan tells Corbett back at the pub. "But," he concedes, "maybe you're bringing somethin' to the fight game." The Strong Boy was not to fight again and soon became a formidable voice in, of all things, the temperance movement. Although the public accepted Jim as both champion and a new breed of sex symbol, they continued to mourn the fallen John L.

Victoria's profession of her love for Jim is an about-face that mines the depths of misogyny. For all the Gentleman's foot-in-the-door tactics, the mid-century notion that aggressive pursuit wins the girl has not aged well. The long-predicted climax culminates in a kiss that lasts exactly as long as the Codes would accept. But while coming on strong might have been acceptable in 1942, statutory rape was not, and Warner Bros. had difficulty gauging the effect of Flynn's charges on the film's reception, where tag lines like *"THE SHAMROCK SLUGGER! He could love as well as fight!"* carried an uncomfortable aftertaste.

Corbett lost the title on May 11, 1897, to the British fighter Bob Fitzsimmons, nine years his junior and seventeen pounds lighter. As discussed in the Introduction, the bout corresponded with Enoch Rector's perfection of the Kinetograph machine to become the first film available for large screen viewing. Released eleven days after the bout, *The Corbett-Fitzsimmons Fight* held the longest continuous running time of any movie for the next thirteen years and consumed over 48,000 feet of stock. The fighters spent more time quibbling over the film proceeds than the purses or gate receipts from the fight.

Corbett failed to regain the title six years later when he fought Jim Jeffries, famously dubbed the "Great White Hope" (see the following chapter). The Gent had put on thirty pounds and, at thirty-seven, was nine years Jeffries's senior.

Vera filed for divorce shortly after Corbett's retirement and publicly testified that his penultimate fight against Kid McCoy (whose name circuitously gave rise to the expression "the real McCoy") was fixed. Nevertheless, the two remained together until Corbett's death from liver cancer in 1933, which had wasted him down to a meager 140 pounds. He was sixty-six.

Widely credited with elevating boxing from the brutish spectacle of hard-drinking gasbags to calculating, civil sportsmanship, Corbett's outsized ego and innovations under boxing's newly sanctioned rules are best summarized by Lord Byron when he wrote that, "If necessity obliges a man to be a blackguard, he may as well be scientific." Jim Corbett was both, rolled into one nasty, graceful package.

5
THE GREAT WHITE HOPE

Directed by Martin Ritt
20th Century Fox, 1970

Chicago District Attorney Al Cameron (Hal Holbrook) sits at his desk ruminating about the Black Heavyweight Champion Jack Jefferson's taboo-smashing lifestyle. The boxer (a strapping James Earl Jones with a shaved head) is setting a dangerous precedent for Black America, so Cameron holds a meeting where he gingerly puts the screws to the fighter's White common-law wife, Eleanor (Jane Alexander). How did they meet? Did Mr. Jefferson get her drunk? What about pills? Did he buy her things? Cameron's at a loss. Then he hits on their ace in the hole: what about busting Jefferson on the Mann Act? "But she's not a pro," he's reminded. Well, maybe they can work around that.

Based on Howard Sackler's 1967 play of the same name, *The Great White Hope* is a speculative account of the reign of Jack Johnson, boxing's fifth Heavyweight Champion and the first Black heavyweight to hold the title (1908-1915). A towering and provocative figure in the opening decades of the twentieth century, Johnson cheerfully humiliated White opponents in the ring, flaunted his exorbitant wealth, and, most distressingly for the time, openly indulged his penchant for White women. He was also, by dint of luck, the world's first major film star.

After *The Corbett-Fitzsimmons Fight* premiered in 1897, public demand for widespread film distribution led to more sophisticated cameras, durable celluloid film, and a proliferation of movie houses. To the White public, the fate of boxing (and for many, the dignity of the White race) lay with the 1910 title bout in which Gentleman Jim Corbett's dethroner Jim Jeffries was to come out of retirement and return the belt to the White race.

Jeffries didn't stand a chance, and original footage affords indisputable visual evidence of his brutalization at the hands of the grinning Johnson. Throughout the country and across the Atlantic, moviegoers came in droves to see for themselves. If boxing was the first subject on which Rector and his contemporaries unveiled their cinematic invention, the original masscult of filmgoers was sparked by racism, emasculation, and the emerging fascination with and fear of the Black body.

Through the barely fictional Jack Jefferson, *The Great*

White Hope interprets Johnson's avatar by turns gloating in defiance of White norms and seething in self-imposed exile. The standard trope in which a fighter rises from a poor scrapper and on to glory tends to ignore what is often that same fighter's slow, ignominious downfall. *The Great White Hope* shrewdly opens with Jefferson at the top, where *nobody* stays forever. As boxing scribe Budd Schulberg observed, "Fighters don't grow old, they just die slowly in front of your eyes." *The Great White Hope* is that rare biopic illustrating how even a juggernaut like Johnson had a shelf-life. With charm and venom in equal parts, Jones portrays the titan's inevitable decline with gusto, dignity, and not a shred of regret.

Contemporaneous reportage and credible but unsubstantiated anecdotes provide endless instances of Johnson's brash defiance cloaked in jovial showmanship and nonchalance. Among the most famous recounts his being pulled over for speeding and issued a fifty-dollar ticket, roughly $1,300 in modern currency. Peeling a hundred from a roll of bills, the cop said there was no way he could change that kind of cash. Jack told him to keep it. "I'll be coming back the same way."

Covering the years 1910 through 1915, *The Great White Hope* focuses on the second half of Johnson's prime fighting years as the witch hunts against him reached a fever pitch. Although the men trying to take Jefferson down have less presence regarding speaking roles than in the play, their pursuit of the fighter hangs over the film with claustrophobic

oppression underscored by Jefferson's low-ceilinged training quarters. So sprawling is Sackler's play in its casting and
locales that the film, whittling seventeen acts down to nine,
is intimate by comparison.

Jones, who played Jefferson in the original stage
production, bares a fair resemblance—albeit considerably
lighter skinned—to the lithe, muscled champion. With eyes
that burn white heat inside a deep brow, the actor interprets
Ritt's Jefferson as a man whose countenance can swing on
a dime from buoyant to indignant. Johnson may have worn
a happy face for the public, but he was dead serious in his
pursuit of White opponents.

Born in 1878 in Galveston, Texas, John Arthur "Jack"
Johnson was raised in a racially integrated neighborhood
where it was not unusual for Black children to play alongside Whites. When he was sixteen, he moved north to work
in a Manhattan gym where he learned to box. His fistic
skills were further honed through participation in spectacles known as "battles royale," impromptu street fights or
organized affairs in which four or five kids (usually, but not
always Black) could earn upwards of $1.50 swinging, usually
blindfolded, until only one was left standing. In his novel
The Invisible Man, Ralph Ellison's protagonist describes the
terror and humiliation inherent to these contests: "I had no
dignity... It was complete anarchy." But dignity didn't worry
Johnson and anarchy didn't faze him. Always the last one
on his feet, what he really liked was the money.

Johnson's ability to absorb blows with superhuman

resilience was rendered almost entirely moot by his capacity to catch just about any punch his opponent could throw. A plodding, defensive fighter, he let his aggression build as the rounds accumulated and his opponents tired. He'd happily have floored them in the first, but the fighter walked a fine line: Blacks who beat Whites too early in the bout were often ducked by other Whites—a prime motivator behind the color line. They also risked disfavor and even violence at the hands of White spectators who wanted a full show. Johnson was always happy to take his time.

A group of fight organizers and pressmen kick around the Burbank dirt waiting for a glimpse of the man who's sure to put the Black champion down for good. Still, they have to give Jefferson credit for following the previous champ all the way to Australia to take the title. Their prattle serves as a backdrop as to how, forty years after Lincoln signed the Emancipation Proclamation Act, this son of former slaves held what was then considered the world's most illustrious distinction.

In 1908, the heavyweight title was held by a Canadian named Tommy Burns, the same fighter (unnamed in play or film) the men grudgingly praise Jefferson for chasing halfway around the world. Burns talked a good game about taking all comers regardless of race, but he dodged Johnson like the plague, demanding astronomical purses to weasel out of a title bout. When Burns split the country for Sydney, Johnson was in hot pursuit.

To prove the fight was not financially driven so much

as a means of silencing, taunting, and further humiliating his White detractors, Johnson agreed to accept a paltry £1,000 purse to Burns's £6,000. Tommy had run out of excuses, and on the day after Christmas, 15,000 spectators paid witness to nothing short of a slaughter at Sydney Stadium. As the sun glinted on Johnson's gold tooth, he battered Burns with fists and words: "Poor little Tommy, who told you you were a fighter?" The bout was stopped in the fourteenth.

John L. Sullivan, whom the reader met in the previous chapter, was among the first to congratulate Johnson on his victory. It was especially sporting coming from the man who once told Colored Heavyweight Champion George Godfrey that he'd give him a shot when he was "ready to fight rats, dogs, pigs, and niggers."

The White populace immediately turned to petition the ex-champion Jim Jeffries (renamed Frank Brady in play and film) to come out of his four-year retirement and take back the title. Among Jeffries's supplicants was author Jack London, who coined the term "great white hope" to denote the man who would return the belt to the White race. Although the writer readily praised Johnson's skill in his reportage, London's rallying cry resounded throughout saloons, church sermons, the halls of Congress, and across the pond from English pubs to the House of Parliament: "*Jeff, it's up to you!*"

After two years of supplications, the ex-champ finally caved. His return to the ring proved considerably more challenging to the retiree than the film suggests. After settling on his alfalfa farm, Jeffries had gained a hundred pounds before drawing the color line in order to duck Johnson. Of course, the fat farmer was scared out of his mind, and needed at least another year to get back into fighting shape. In the film, Frank Brady emerges from his Burbank farmhouse fit as a butcher's dog. The venue was set for the burgeoning city of Reno, Nevada. Newly accessible by rail, The Biggest Little City in the World was ripe for action.

Jack Jefferson pounds at a sand-filled heavy bag in his small, makeshift gym. The year is 1910, although as the film moves forward, leeway is given to minor chronological lapses and time compressions. Neither play nor film pretends to factual biography, best displayed in Eleanor, Jefferson's common-law wife who the DA grilled and a loose amalgamation of Johnson's first and second wives, Etta Duryea (who shot herself in 1912) and Lucille Cameron.

Eleanor sits silently in a corner as Jack's manager enters the gym to announce the fight date, the irony of which sets Jefferson ringing with laughter. The Fourth of July. The day of independence... something with which his dark-skinned brothers and sisters are not wholly familiar. With the press due to arrive, Jefferson's manager suggests his "girlfriend" disappear for a while. Such coupling—in front of reporters, no less—is bound to push public sentiment over the edge. But Jefferson knows that ship sailed the moment he took the title. Miscegenation's just salt in the wound, which is exactly what he wants.

The influx of nonwhites into cities at the close of the nineteenth century gave rise to a distinct strain of negrophobia among a flabby, indolent Victorian elite. Bogus socio-Darwinian theories ran rampant, one stating that Blacks possessed thicker skulls and so were less susceptible to pain. Nevertheless, the frequent sight of Black bodies, considerably fitter due to the work to which they were confined, sparked what might be called the first fitness craze among the newly emasculated gentry. Scholar Ronald L. Jackson frames this Victorian exercise fad in a wholly racial context: "bodies [were] assigned social meanings."

Johnson was regarded as an exotic fetish among a significant swath of the female upper class in his fomenting of verboten thrills and forbidden fantasies. Morley Callaghan's 1951 novel *The Loved and The Lost* illustrates this allure as "gentle innocence ... attracted perversely to violence, like a temperament seeking its opposite." In a contemporaneous reading of Freud's *Totem and Taboo* (written five years into Johnson's reign), the fighter would be perceived as breaking humanity's oldest codes, including "the protection of important persons" (*i.e.*, White women, per the DA's commission), "the safeguarding of the weak" (ditto), and "the guarding of the chief acts of life" including "marriage and sexual functions." Not only were Johnson's interracial couplings taboo but so was Johnson himself.

"If black men beat white men in the ring," writes Theresa Runstedtler in her book *Jack Johnson: Rebel Sojourner*, "It was not a stretch that they would feel entitled to ravish white women in the bedroom."

Eleanor stands in the corner as the press pours in. Jefferson's brooding scowl turns to delight when a reporter asks him about his so-called "yellow streak," a famous taunt the patently terrified Jeffries threw at Johnson as a feeble palliative for the anxious White public. Jefferson moons the group a flash of his yellow underwear. Another reporter expresses the collective prediction for the fight's outcome, and all clear-headed bets are on Jefferson: "Your only problem is picking the round."

On July 3, the Reno Special chugs to a halt in a dusty boomtown thronged with crowds both Black and White. Stuffed pickaninny dolls with banana-sized lips are paraded in effigy. Protesters hold signs calling for the eradication of boxing, and the din of flimflammers, pickpockets, sharpies, and two-dollar girls is drowned out by the brassy blast of marching bands. In the background, the freshly constructed wooden stadium looms like an oracle.

Jefferson encounters a Black reverend and his informal, ticketless flock where a teenage member tells him that, by tomorrow, he'll be proud of his Black skin. Jefferson fixes his gaze on the kid like a dagger and hisses. "Country boy, if you ain't there already, all the boxing and all the nigger-praying ain't gonna get you there." The message was clear: Black folks don't need to pray for *him*. They have to look out for themselves.

The mercury hit 110 degrees that Fourth. Always obliging, Johnson volunteered to take the less desirable sun-facing corner customarily determined by a coin toss. From the opening bell, he teased and toyed with the lurching farmer. When Jeffries fell against him in a clinch, Johnson consoled him: "I'll love you if you want me to." As an ungentlemanly Jim Corbett spewed vile racial epitaphs from Jeffries's corner, Johnson turned to him and smiled. "Where do you want me to put him, Mr. Corbett?" before lovingly bullying Jeffries to the canvas. Just like the Sydney newspapers described him, grumbles one of the reporters back in Burbank, "grinning all the time... making smarts remarks to the crowds."

Since no stage production can convincingly recreate a boxing match, Sackler ingeniously set the action outside the venue, where ticketless spectators watch over the stadium wall to relay the action to the crowd on the ground. Although the cinematic format allowed Ritt to bring the viewer over that wall and into the fight, the grinning Jefferson instead faces the camera and throws punches as though the viewer were Brady himself. "The Fight of the Century," as it was billed, consumes less than ten seconds of Jones's terrifying, intimidating exuberance cloaked in a shiny smile.

Johnson's cakewalk victory precipitated riots in more than fifty cities nationwide. A contemporary AP announcement read that the "cost of Johnson's victory in human lives cannot be estimated because of varying reports." More than twenty Blacks were were murdered, several by lynching. Hundreds of others were severely injured. Although most of the violence was inflicted by Whites, the press spotlit the scant instances in which Blacks were implicated as instigators. A Washington newspaper bewailed the "hundreds of drunken negroes [who] paraded the streets making the night hideous with their cries." A Memphis paper issued the warning, "Let No Fool Negro get Biggidy."

The fight was one of the first wide-distribution bioscopic films following Recter's ninety-minute *Corbett-Fitzsimmons Fight* thirteen years prior. But while the popularity of *Corbett-Fitzsimmons* was in part due to the unveiling of the new medium, the politicization of *Johnson vs. Jeffries* cannot be overstated. The consternation incited by the film's ubiquity, in tandem with cinematic advancements including longer takes, was the one-two stroke of timing that poised Johnson as the world's first movie star. American journalists called an end to the film's dissemination with the claim that it posed a threat to Caucasian morale. Here was concrete, visual evidence of the perceived physical predomination of the Black race. "Johnson's triumph and its film recording," writes Runstedtler, "had put white people on notice."

In 1912, the film was banned by Congress. It was the most widely viewed motion picture until the 1915 release of D.W. Griffith's three-hour epic *The Birth of a Nation*. A shameless glorification of the Ku Klux Klan and a big hit at the White House, *Birth*'s all-White cast featured actors in blackface committing a litany of atrocities, including assaults on White women. It was a blockbuster.

Johnson's interracial couplings also cost him popularity with the Black community, who were beginning to wonder if the Champion's comportment was a legitimate step toward racial equality or yet another impediment to the Black cause. His habitual refusal to fight other Blacks with the claim that the purses were too small prompted the Colored Heavyweight Champion Joe Jeanette to lament that "Jack forgot about his old friends after he became champion and drew the color line against his people."

Among Johnson's harshest critics was author and educator Booker T. Washington, who wrote, "In misrepresenting the colored people of this country, this man is harming himself the least." But this wasn't a popularity contest: "I ain't runnin' for congress!" Like he told the congregation back in Reno: there's no time to wait around for collaborative group action that might never happen. Racial advancement begins with the individual. Black or White, it's every man for himself.

Despite constant hassle at the hands of the police, Johnson was gainfully employed, his record was clean, and even his relationships with White women were thus far technically legal. But as he wrote in his 1927 autobiography *In the Ring and Out*, "certain unfair persons, piqued because I was champion, decided if they could not get me one way they would another."

Cameron's decisive recourse comes with his envisioning the Mann Act following his grilling of Eleanor. Instituted in 1912, the so-called White Slave Traffic Act forbade the transportation of interracial couples across state lines for purposes of prostitution, "debauchery," and other vaguely worded "crimes against nature." And from streetwalkers to the pricier upstairs girls, Johnson was a regular customer. Even his wives Lucille, and possibly Etta, were sex workers. In 1909, Johnson was twice caught driving from Chicago to Milwaukee, each time with a different White woman. Although the "violations" were committed over three years before the institution of the Mann Act, Cameron finds his opening in a newly minted law even the government couldn't clearly define.

In 1912, Johnson was convicted for transporting a White prostitute and former girlfriend across state lines four years prior. Federal marshals arrest Jefferson, slapping him with the same 366-day prison sentence and $1,000 fine handed down to Johnson. Life as a fugitive looked pretty appealing, and in a scene derived from a possibly spurious anecdote, Jefferson dons a National Colored Baseball League uniform and escapes to Canada with the rest of the team. From there, it's off to London with Eleanor.

It was almost impossible for Johnson to secure a fight in Europe, yet he remained intransigent in his refusal to take on Black challengers. Instead, he performed in several humiliating, highly popular European stage adaptations of Harriet Beecher Stowe's 1852 anti-slavery novel *Uncle*

Tom's Cabin. In vaudevillian slave garb, Jefferson's cheerless incantations to a half-full cabaret in Budapest indicate that it's time to leave Europe. With anxieties of impending war sweeping the Continent, Jefferson and Eleanor decide things will be much quieter in Mexico.

The border isn't much of a stretch for the long arm back home, and when Eleanor calls their exile "slow poison," Jefferson turns on her with a dangerous sneer. Maybe it's time for her to go back to her *own* kind. She protests and rages as Jack whips her with his towel in a harrowing, pungent allusion to slavery. As Eleanor flees, he wraps his taped hand around his crotch. She can return to the States if she wants, but he's not going with her. "I'd rather cut it off."

The quarreling couple is interrupted by two U.S. Marshals. Some legal matters require attention back home. There's even added incentive were Jefferson to cooperate: if he returns for a fight with the new white hope, it's likely that 366-day sentence will be reduced. Before he can answer, Eleanor's drowned and broken body is carried in. In a gut-wrenching method of self-slaughter, she's thrown herself down a well in a bleak and sobering reference to Johnson's first wife's suicide. It's July of 1915 (Etta shot herself in 1913), and the fighter had been lamming it for seven years. Jefferson isn't ready to go home yet, but he'll fight the big guy, just as Johnson did, in Havana.

At six-foot-six and 242 pounds, Johnson's challenger Jess Willard (renamed "The Kid" in the film and play) prompted the Champion to quip, "If they make white hopes any bigger, I'll have to get stilts." Following Ritt's ambiguous, vaguely terrifying enactment of the Brady fight, Jefferson's cumulative fury is unleashed in a climactic brawl soaked in blood and no shortage of tears from Black spectators.

Jefferson comes out in full force, and the viewer fast loses track of how many times he drops The Kid. But their blood stains the canvas together. When The Kid takes over, Jefferson's manager begs Jack to stay down. "They'll kill you," and it's not The Kid he's talking about. Like Johnson, Jefferson's been wearing the belt like a death writ for almost seven years. The racist White public had had enough.

The reenactment is singular in its fixation on Jefferson's degradation. At forty-three, Johnson was finished. As boxing writer Randy Roberts succinctly words it, "He was old, overweight, and that was it. It was time to go." It would be seven years before interracial bouts were reinstated and another twenty-two before Joe "The Brown Bomber" Louis would take the heavyweight title.

Johnson did less than a year at Leavenworth in Kansas. He even insisted on driving himself to prison and payed his fine with a thousand-dollar bill. The guards complained that the "pugilist chauffeur," as Johnson wrote under "profession" upon incarceration, believed "the rules did not apply to him." A favorite with the warden, the fighter's transition back to the States couldn't have been smoother.

In the *New York Times*, Vincent Canby described *The*

Great White Hope as "one of those liberal... uncontroversial works that pretend to tackle contemporary problems by finding analogies at a safe remove in history." Sackler was abashed. "It's a metaphor of struggle between man and the outside world," he responded. "People spoke of the play as if it were a cliché of white liberalism, but ... it wasn't a case of blacks being good and whites being bad." Released when Muhammad Ali was regarded as both hero and villain for his refusal of military induction and his allegiance to the Nation of Islam, both play and film translate as a harsh critique of contemporary domestic race relations. In what sounds like a plea for a mid-career Ali biopic, Canby expressed the more pressing need for a film "that dared touch on some really controversial issues, including the [Vietnam] war, the draft, the black Muslims, [and] black separatism." As Ali filled TV screens with his antics and espousal of the Nation of Islam's racial segregation, Canby's initial criticism of *The Great White Hope*'s so-called "safe remove from history" isn't altogether invalid. Even Ail was said to have proclaimed, "You just change the time, date, and the details, and it's about me!" Alas, such elements are problematic in that they cannot be changed.

After a late retirement with diminishing returns, Johnson continued his peripatetic excursions and mingled in the café society of neutral Spain. In 1920, he returned to the States through Mexico by way of Havana. On a June evening in 1946, he confronted the racist proprietor at a

North Carolina diner when he was refused service. After storming out, he smashed his car while speeding along a dark road outside Raleigh. He was sixty-eight.

Requests for a posthumous pardon for Johnson's Mann Act violation under President George W. Bush failed to pass the Senate in 2008. Following an appeal launched by Senators John McCain, Harry Reid, documentarian Ken Burns, and Mike Tyson, the pardon was finally signed by President Donald Trump on May 24, 2018. By dark happenstance, the signature came the day after the NFL announced that it would fine teams whose players "do not stand and show respect for the flag and the anthem."

As Jefferson prepares to flee the country with the Bluejays, his mother sits in a rocker recounting her son's early years. "I tried to learn him like you got to learn a colored child.... I hit him with my hand, and he say, 'So what.' I hit him with my shoe. He look up at me and smile. I took a razor strap to him... but then he'd do a funny dance and ask me for a nickel."

Nearly thirty-five years after the film's release, James Earl Jones expressed the staunch fortitude and autonomy with which Johnson by turns scorned and ignored White public sentiment. "He walked out into a world that was not ready to accept a Black man as a total person, and he didn't know how to function otherwise." As to Johnson's disinterest in the forwarding of race relations, it's like the reverend said back in Reno when Jefferson scorned his prayers: "Give him the light to understand why." *The Great White Hope* suggests, correctly, that he never really did.

6
CINDERELLA MAN

Directed by Ron Howard
Universal Pictures, 2005

A diverse succession of three Heavyweight Champions dominated the mid-1930s—overlapping and inextricably bound within the annals of boxing, crime, the exalted and abused. There was the strong-armed Italian giant Primo Carnera, remembered primarily as a fourth-rate pawn to the mob; the clowning playboy Max Baer; and James J. Braddock, the gentle-natured New Jersey bruiser dubbed the "Cinderella Man" by journalist Damon Runyan. At the cusp of the eleven-year reign of the great Joe Louis—the first fighter to revivify the million-dollar gates commanded by the previous decade's sensational Jack Dempsey—the trio's collective four-year reign from 1933 to 1937 held a country's attention against the swinging backdrop of the Roaring Twenties through bleakest years of the Great Depression.

"In all the history of the boxing game," wrote Runyan, you'll find no human interest story to compare with the life narrative of James J. Braddock." The same quote opens Ron Howard's easy, self-ennobled *Cinderella Man*. Anyone familiar with the fighter's stocky frame and gentle smile will find as perfect an A-lister as they could hope for in Russell Crowe, an actor whose reputation has cast him as considerably more pugnacious than the man he portrays.

The scourge of the Depression punctuates the crucial years of a fighter who emerged as the consummate Everyman to millions of poverty-stricken Americans bereft of work, home, and shelter. With a pendulous career that brought hope and heartbreak to their collective plight, Braddock's life wended from rags to riches, swiftly and ignominiously back into poverty and, finally, through patience soaked in humiliation and blood, to financial stability and universal validation.

James Braddock was born in the tough-as-nails Irish neighborhood of Hell's Kitchen on Manhattan's West Side. Known for its marauding gangs and rat-infested tenements, railroad apartments and cold-water flats, the Kitchen boasts gangsters "Lucky" Luciano, Dutch Schultz, actor and wannabe wise guy George Raft, and Owney "The Killer" Madden, one of the most prominent fight-fixers of the day, among its native sons. The story, probably spurious, is that when a rookie cop referred to the putrid, blazing stretch of midtown as "Hell," his veteran partner told him that this was worse. This was Hell's *Kitchen*.

Braddock began fighting as an amateur when he was twenty-one to support his parents and six siblings. The year was 1923, and America was in the throes of booming economic growth. Work was plentiful, and the industry expansion created thousands of new jobs in steel production, automobile manufacturing, and construction. Ownership of cars, electric household appliances, and radios was commonplace. The Prohibition law was revoked in New York as the first Yankee Stadium opened in the Bronx. On the West Coast, the iconic Hollywood sign was constructed, Warner Bros. was formally incorporated, and Roy and Walt Disney commenced building their empire. In Washington, Vice President Calvin Coolidge had stepped in for Warren Harding when the latter died of a heart attack amid a myriad of damning scandals. Through it all, the charismatic heavyweight Jack Dempsey dominated the fight game.

Braddock clinched the New Jersey Middleweight and Light Heavyweight amateur titles two years in a row, at one point going thirty-eight bouts without a loss. In 1926, he turned professional and finished the year with a record of 14-0 over eight months. It was a promising start. Moving to the heavyweight division the following year, where the money was better, Braddock garnered attention as the decade ended. He was no wunderkind, and his fluctuation between near-contender status and the low cards was cause for constant financial anxiety. He shrugged at the newspaper wags who derided his skill. "I was always more or less the underdog. But it didn't make no difference to me."

With a bullish, brawling style, Braddock compensated for his lack of nuance with an iron chin and a punishing right cross. Grace took a back seat to punching power, and the blows he meted out early in his career floored most takers. With the newspaper and bookies' odds stacked against him in all his significant fights, Braddock's rise from the dustbin of pugs to the extolled brass ring of Heavyweight Champion was the stuff of fairy tales minus the pumpkin, though a few turtles got involved.

Despite his precarious record in a decade that boasted an overabundance of great heavyweights, Braddock was a perennial favorite with the fans. When the Depression hit six years into his professional career, the combination of his pecuniary hardships with his tenacity in the ring made him an underdog worth rooting for. When he finally clinched the title, Braddock had just entered his thirties, an age when many fighters begin to show some wear. He did not fight again until his loss to Joe Louis two years later in 1937, retiring with the worst record of any Heavyweight Champion before or since: fifty-one wins, twenty-six losses, and seven draws.

Despite the attention Braddock garnered as an up-and-comer, it didn't pay the bills, and he spent his days working the Hoboken docks as a stevedore. When there was no work at the docks, he walked the three miles to see if anything was happening at the Weehawken railroad yards. A faithful husband to his wife Mae, played here by Renée Zellweger, Braddock eschewed (nor could he afford) the pricey threads sported by other fighters or the nightclubs where they palmed maître-d's with C-notes and stuck twenties in the cleavage of cigarette girls. Among the most cautious of champions, Braddock invested in stocks where his money would ostensibly remain secure. When the film begins at the tail end of November 1928, few could have predicted the catastrophe that would descend upon the country that Tuesday afternoon eleven months later.

In 1926, a young entrepreneur named Joe Gould spotted Braddock working the docks. Their meeting became a full-on partnership that lasted the duration of Braddock's twelve-year career. Who cared that Gould had virtually no experience in the game outside of organizing a few bouts in the Navy or that he was friendly with a few wise guys? He had one of the keenest eyes in the biz when spotting weaknesses in other fighters.

Braddock and Gould (Paul Giamatti, who manages to make smarmy sarcasm and mild exasperation endearing) sit in the back of the limo minutes after Braddock bullies the formidable Tuffy Griffith to the canvas in the film's opening minutes. Gould peels Braddock's $8,000 cut from a wad of bills. Pretty good for one night's work, but there's no post-fight party for Braddock, who goes home to Mae and his two kids. The couple weren't married until 1930 and so would not yet have children, though the time compression bares no effect on the film's trajectory. (Still, the viewer should note that Mae Braddock spoke with a refined elocution wholly antithetical to Zellweger's grating bridge-and-tunnel whine.)

The film takes an abrupt leap to 1933 via a twist on the well-worn device of the spinning headline. As the luckless Braddock returns from the docks under a raw, steady downpour, his boot squelches a newspaper into the mud. The top fold announces that domestic unemployment is up by twenty-five percent. Meanwhile, the Braddocks have added a third mouth to their brood and downsized to a one-room flat. Past-due notices start to replace the milk bottles that used to appear on the step. The heat is turned off for non-payment. Like countless Americans whose savings were tied up in stocks, Braddock's wealth vanished overnight.

In 1928, Braddock broke his right hand—something he was to do at least three more times throughout his career—in his fight with Paul Swiderski. This would sound the death knell to a career for most fighters, especially less desperate ones. "Hands," wrote W.C. Heinz in his novel *The Professional*, "are a fighter's tools... A fighter busts his hands, and he's nothin'." But Braddock couldn't afford to stop. Besides, he was still a favorite with the public for that rough-and-tumble style. He may have lacked the polish of other heavyweights, but he sure was fun to watch. Unfortunately, his bum right (and several broken ribs into the bargain) meant fighting under chronic pain throughout his career. While *Cinderella Man* acknowledges this affliction as an integral facet of Braddock's inglorious fall and astonishing rise, Howard skips over crucial years that leave the viewer puzzling as to why the man who was just handed a stack of eighty hundred-dollar-bills is still skulking around the docks to get the heat back on.

The most plausible explanation for this lapse is that a depressing string of losses in the six years between Braddock's professional debut and Black Tuesday would not make for rousing viewing. By 1932, his record stood at thirty-eight wins and fifteen losses, reducing the fighter to cannon fodder for up-and-comers looking for name recognition with which to pad their records.

The game itself was also suffering. Boxing and cinema were still America's most popular forms of escapism during the Depression, but people weren't spending like they used to. This meant smaller gate intakes which, in turn, meant smaller purses. Braddock's income had shrunk exponentially. He could no longer afford gym fees or sparring partners. Medical bills weren't cheap either and, in 1933, he broke his hand again. An anecdote from Jeremy Schaap's 2010 biography of the fighter recounts a doctor approving Braddock's suggestion that rather than pay to have the hand re-broken professionally in order to heal correctly, he'd save the money by re-breaking it in the ring.

Minutes before Braddock's fight with Abe Feldman in February of that year, Giamatti's Gould catches his fighter wincing as he clenches his taped fist. Braddock supplicates. He *needs* this fight to feed his family and to get the utilities back and running. The pain brought on by the few right crosses he does land reverberates through his nervous system as accentuated by the slo-mo camerawork, a meteoric flash of light, and warbling sound effects that almost every post-1980 boxing film uses to convey disorienting blows to the head. The crowd grows restive and boos Braddock's underwhelming performance. When Braddock again broke his hand—this time in three different places—the fight was declared a no-contest (i.e., stoppage for reasons out of the fighters' control). At twenty-eight, Braddock was already looking washed-up.

Ten months later, mayhem abounds as 1933 draws to a close. Fences are busted up for firewood. Husbands walk out on their wives and babies. Hoovervilles spread like pestilence under bridges and along riverbanks. As the Braddock children sleep, thin wisps of steam rise from their mouths while their father separates bills and coins at a desk under a crucifix nailed to the wall. Counting six dollars and twenty-four cents, Braddock is forced to swallow the bitter pill of government relief aid. His brawn made him a frequent pick from the masses clamoring for work at the docks, where he masked his red and swollen right with shoe polish. Using his left to heft 150-pound bales for eight-hour stretches strengthened the arm and earned him the nickname "Jabbin' Jim" as he employed his left jab to spare his throbbing right.

In 1934, Gould arranged for Braddock to fight John "Corn" Griffin, a vicious puncher on his way to contender status. Braddock was already being talked about in the past tense with columnists and bookmakers. Still, the fight would provide worldwide exposure to both men as the top undercard in the title bout between the above-mentioned Primo Carnera and Max Baer. It was Braddock's first fight since re-breaking his hand on Feldman's head ten months prior, which, despite the go-ahead from the doctor, hadn't gone as planned. Griffin may have regarded him as just another chump, but a payday's a payday.

There was a catch. The fight had been arranged in such haste that Braddock had just two days to prepare, yet those forty-eight hours proved enough. Defying the diminutive odds and confounding the bookies and bettors, Braddock beat Griffin on a technical knockout in the third round. ("Imagine what I could do on a steak," he tells Gould after scoffing down a bowl of hash with his hands before the fight.) The purse was a scant $250, but it got the heat back on.

Next up was the Black fighter John Henry Lewis. The majority of White America still frowned on the mixing of the races within boxing, as in practically every other facet of society, and mixed-race bouts, while not infrequent, continued to mean smaller gate intakes. But to Braddock, a fight was a fight, a man was a man, and a purse was a purse. Not all boxers agreed, and the color line of the recent past reared its head with renewed ferocity throughout the decade as the shadow of Joe Louis hung over the game. The first Black Heavyweight Champion since Jack Johnson twenty-two years prior, Louis was quiet, humble, and in every respect Johnson's opposite. When Braddock defeated John Henry Lewis, he again shocked the bettors as his growing fan base vicariously played out their own comebacks.

Most of the action is shot from inside the ring, an approach that became de rigueur after its use in *Raging Bull* (1980). Cinematographer Salvatore Totino ingeniously hung a foam-covered camera from the arena's ceiling for the actors to hit, so bringing the POV shot to a new level in which the lens itself takes a punch.

Braddock had just conquered the two top contenders for the title in a stunning ascent that prompted promoters to create a series of elimination tournaments. The victor would fight the new champion, Max Baer, who took the title from Primo Carnera with playful alacrity. It was March of 1935, and Braddock, with ribs that refused to heal, was paired against the formidable Russian-Jewish fighter Art Lasky.

Despite Crowe's limber hooks, the actor's face registers agony with every right cross. A blow to the jaw by Lansky sends his mouthpiece soaring across the ring like a spinning white moth. Braddock walks with deliberation to pick it up with his glove and puts it back in his mouth. It's not over yet, and his victory by unanimous decision—again, to the dismay of anyone with a vested financial interest—gets him his title shot at Baer.

Braddock's last few purses may have amounted to so much chump change. Still, the $4,100 brought in by the Lasky fight allowed him to return to the New Jersey Relief

Department to wait in line and repay the government relief money he'd received—in full and with interest. It's an action scene in itself as a winding roomful of friends, neighbors, and fellow workers, fans all, recognize the fighter. They know what he's doing and that he won't be back at the docks anytime soon. His diet had so improved that he gained eleven pounds and, according to legend, grew a full inch in height.

The mendicant of barely six months ago was now the top contender for the heavyweight belt. Asked by the press about his rare and charitable gesture of returning the relief money, Braddock explains that since it got his own family through some hard times, maybe it can do the same for another. "I believe we live in a great country, a country that's great enough to help a man when he's financially in trouble. I've had some good fortune ...and thought I should return it." And what about his upcoming bout with Max Baer? A poker-faced Braddock tells the hounds with their pads and flashbulbs that it's sure to be a great fight for all.

Max Baer (played with smarmy, cocksure swagger by Craig Bierko) is presented early in the film as he ducks under the ropes for his title fight with Primo Carnera. Flashing a wink ringside to his adoring *belle du jour*, he moves in on the Italian. (This being Braddock's show, the fight is not reenacted here.) Almost a year later, Baer's manager visits a hotel room where his boy stands shirtless under the doorjamb as two wiggling young women coo and crawl over the bed in their teddies. The fighter's affable timbre is swapped for a peevish, nasal whine. "I'm not gonna fight Jimmy Braddock. He's a chump." But whatever power the champ wields, he can't afford to break his contract. Baer knows this as well as anyone.

Tragedy cast Baer in an ominous light after a 1930 bout in which his opponent, Frankie Campbell, was so concussed that his doctors described his brain as having been "knocked completely loose from his skull." A distraught Baer accompanied Campbell in the ambulance and wept bitterly when he died. With tearful attempts to console Campbell's widow, Baer provided ongoing financial support for her family. Three years later, the boxer Ernie Schaaf died of a relatively benign blow by Primo Carnera. Although the fighter's death cannot entirely be attributed to boxing (Schaaf was suffering from meningitis and recovering from influenza), it was believed the Italian's punch was the straw that broke him on the heels of a devastating beating at the hands of Baer five months prior.

So fraudulent is Baer's portrayal in *Cinderella Man* (to wit, his braggadocio over his "kills") that his family filed a lawsuit against Howard for the debasement of their father's legacy. Baer's son James explained that his father "would often pull punches late in his career because he didn't want to inflict permanent damage on his opponents." Several boxing historians concur, noting the cautious approach Baer later adopted for fear of having a third victim's blood on his hands. Long after retirement, Baer regularly suffered nightmares and panic attacks.

The papers anticipated the real possibility that Braddock would meet the same fate as Campell and Schaaf, the United Press calling the fight "the most one-sided... in history" before it even took place. It was a sentiment few would have disputed. With the odds stacked against him at 10-1, Braddock was unfazed. "How many guys," he asks the cold-eyed, opportunistic promoter Jimmy Johnston, "died the other night ...cause guys like you have not quite figured out a way to make money off watching guys like [Schaaf] die?" Johnston puts business to bed for the night and invites Braddock, Gould, and their wives to dine at his restaurant. When a coiffed, tuxedoed Max Baer saddles up to the bar, Braddock carefully sets down his napkin and walks over to greet the champ. They shake hands. The underdog is confident that the bout will be mutually beneficial. But he also asks Baer to lay up on telling the press of the likelihood of another kill. Braddock's got a family. It's upsetting them. Although Baer made no such prophecies, his veiled threats further vilify his character as he leans in to remind Braddock that "people die in fairy tales all the time."

The majority of early mid-century fighters maintained what were at the very least amicable relationships with their opponents outside the ring. Few embodied this respect and affection for their fellow boxers more than the man the press dubbed "The Larruping Lothario of Pugilism." A former butcher and a ranch hand from the Bay Area, Baer didn't enjoy fighting, but the money was good, and so was he.

Baer did enjoy the lifestyle fame brought, especially in the unending string of women from coat-check girls and cocktail waitresses to ingénues and A-listers. His legendary womanizing made many bed-hopping Hollywood idols look limp by comparison. With movie star good looks, a goofy personality, and a self-deprecating sense of humor ("I got a million-dollar body and a ten-cent brain"), Baer was the life of any party. Unlike his attitude going into the Braddock bout as shown in the film, his philosophy is best conveyed by way of original documentation: "Jimmy Braddock has a terrific right hand, and if he hits me on the chin with that right hand... the band's bound to play *Moving Day for Little Maxie*." Baer set up a trust to ensure his savings weren't sapped by a largess that ranged from exorbitant tips to financial compensation for the fighters he hospitalized. Nevertheless, he was so caught up in society fêtes and nighttime romps that he's gone down in the books as one of boxing's laziest champions. He couldn't have cared less.

The atmospheres at Braddock and Baer's respective training camps in the Catskills could not have been more different. Braddock worked under the tutelage of a young New Yorker named Ray Arcel, a national boxing treasure who was to become one of the sport's greatest trainers. From roadwork to sparring to diet, Braddock was under strict guidance at what the press dubbed "Homicide Hall" for its grueling training regimen. By contrast, Baer's camp was a circus of female celebrities, women, ladies, and dames. Training was the least of his priorities, and he expressed no concern over the upcoming bout. As for Braddock, when asked by reporters if he was worried, he shrugged again. "Let Max worry; he's got the title."

Mae's attempts to dissuade her husband from going up against this "murderer" is another fiction that lends some Hollywood drama to the bout. Mae Braddock had complete confidence in the skills her husband had honed under Arcel, as did Gould. But Braddock kept his physical handicaps to himself. His hand had suffered another break after the Lasky fight. His fractured ribs had gotten worse. But he wasn't the only one in the ring with a damaged paw on fight night: Baer went in with no less than two of them, and his doctors advised a postponement which the fighter characteristically ignored.

Fight day arrives, and Braddock kisses his family like he's going off to war, and to the millions of fans preparing for a comeback to prefigure their own, he is. Like a knight heading into battle, it was the stuff of fairy tales, but while his namesake's foot size saved her from a life spent sweeping ashes, there was no lucky slipper for Braddock.

Dead silence hangs over Madison Square Garden, then a single cheer from the stands and a roar of applause explodes as Braddock enters the ring. A bored-looking Baer tells his handlers, "I'll kick this Mick's balls up to the roof of his mouth," though with the first bell, Braddock charges in using his jab and improved legwork he'd honed under Arcel. Switching to short, inside blows (considerably easier on the hands), he falls into clinches to stave off the momentum of

Baer's fearsome right. Unlike Howard's reenactment, Baer issued no taunts during the fight, though Braddock later admitted to a few playful cracks of his own. "I think that took a little out of him."

With one low blow, one illegal clinch, two backhands, and one punch after the bell, Baer fouled no less than five times during the fight, though the film suggests the number resides somewhere in the double digits. In either case, Braddock could have easily had Baer disqualified, but he wanted a definitive win.

Victory looks like a lock for the hero, but this wouldn't be a boxing film if there wasn't that small chance that he might yet lose. Despite swallowing those numerous fouls, Braddock dominates almost every round as Baer tries for the knockout that never comes.

Speculation as to whether Baer took it easy on Braddock proves baseless when studying footage of the fight, and Max became a furious puncher upon the realization that the bout wasn't the cakewalk he'd anticipated.

Theories persist that the gangster and fight-fixer Owney Madden, who controlled Primo Carnera, had gotten his hooks into Baer by way of his friendship with Gould. (As mentioned, Braddock's manager moved in some unsavory crowds.) But as was the case with Braddock, it's unlikely that Madden ever made much money off Baer, who had, in so many words, told the gangster to go fuck himself when Madden approached him in his dressing room. Still, Gould's palling around with wise guys has led more than one expert to conclude that there was indeed *something* fishy about the fight. Such is the course in which memory, fact, and evidence grow muddier as events recede into the haze of history.

The film delivers the victory the viewer paid for but jazzes it up for entertainment. The actual bout was quite dull, the *New York Times* calling it "one of the worst heavyweight championship contests in the long history of the ring." Joe Louis claimed to have drifted off to sleep somewhere during the middle rounds, and Howard omits the deafening boos that poured from the stands amid the snooze-fest.

When the outpointed Bear loses unanimously, the opponents shake hands, which seems pretty sporting on the part of Baer's self-identified killer. (In truth, the two shook hands before the final round, when Baer's only chance at victory was a knockout.)

Upon announcement of the decision, the fighters embraced. "I have no alibis to offer," said Baer. "Jimmy won, and no better fellow deserves a break." Asked how long he thought Braddock would retain the title, Baer responded, "Until he fights someone else." He was right, and Braddock ceded the title two years later to Joe Louis. It was the worst beating of his career, leaving him with twenty-three stitches in his face and a tooth sticking through his mouthpiece into his lip.

But the Louis bout was still a long way off, and congratulatory telegrams immediately started to pour in following Braddock's victory. Among the first to arrive was a missive from Franklin Delano Roosevelt: "YOU REPRESENT AN ENTIRE NATION... YOU WILL BE A ROLE MODEL FOR SO MANY OTHERS WHO STRUGGLED THROUGH OUR GREAT DEPRESSION." But the majority of congratulatory telegrams and letters came not from politicians, sports or film stars, but from "men who," writes John D. McCallum, "had [felt] hopeless until this big guy had come swinging back from obscurity to show them how a losing fight could be won."

The final frame reveals three small turtles swimming placidly in a tank. The story goes that when Braddock left for the fight, he told his kids he'd be back after he got the title. As his Jersey tongue twisted the word into something that sounded like "toitle," he made good on his promise. Both of them.

Braddock hung up his gloves at thirty-two. It didn't bother him that he retired with such a poor record. In a labyrinth of corrupt boxing politics, he was handed a sweet (if somewhat shady) deal from the crooked promoter Mike Jacobs that brought in cuts from lucrative fights for a full ten years. He never cashed in on his fame with acting gigs like so many champions before and after him, though he did have a go in the restaurant business. Alas, "Inn Braddock's Corner" on West 49th Street failed due to Braddock's penchant for serving practically every drink on the house. With his faculties intact and his financial affairs in order, he returned to the manual labor he'd depended on throughout the most critical years of his career, including construction on the Verrazano Bridge.

Cinderella Man's outcome is clear from the start. While the film is not without feel-good thrills, it is best considered for its evocation of the more significant conflict of the Great Depression at a time when boxing's politics were inextricably intertwined with notorious criminals like Owney Madden.

W.C. Heinz wrote that "What happened to [Braddock]... happened to a whole country, and that is why I believe that no other fighter was ever as representative of his time." Howard's atmospheric depiction of the Depression is the film's strongest asset. To fully appreciate it means overlooking flagrant inaccuracies and setting the focus not on the kill, but on the slow and plodding chase that mirrors the fable of the hare and, as Braddock might put it, the "toitus."

7
THE PRIZEFIGHTER AND THE LADY

Directed by W.S. Van Dyke and Howard Hawks
(uncredited)
MGM Studios, 1933

A crowd stands around a full bar as one voice rises above
the others. "Where are the Sullivans, the Fitzsimmons, the
Ketchels... the good boys?" Meet Edwin "The Professor"
Bennett (Walter Huston), a washed-up manager who, by
his own admission, has been drunk since 1926. These days,
he usually shoehorns himself into throngs of bar patrons
and loudly bewails long-dead or retired fighters.

Despite the thinly drawn stereotype of a character that
practically fades into the ether by the film's end, the down-
at-heels manager is one of several genre tropes that was to
develop over the following decades. And *The Prizefighter and*

the Lady has them all: The manager who seeks a champion to redeem his fading career; the undiscovered bruiser's rise through the ranks; the love interest that unfolds under the duality of affection and destruction; even a gangster—four years before 1937's game-changer *Kid Galahad*.

The Professor's companions regard him with dismissive pity as he sags into his stool and his eyes sag into his cheeks. As his face sags into his hands, a fight breaks out at the other end of the bar. The barkeep, played by Max Baer, steps in and puts an expeditious end to the horseplay.

Breaking up brawls is just part of the job for Baer's Steve Morgan. But to a rapt public—mainly Jewish filmgoers and female admirers—Baer was the dreamboat Macabee Warrior who'd clobbered the German Max Schmeling, a favorite with the Führer and associated stateside with the Reich. While only a quarter Jewish, Baer wore the yellow Star of David on his trunks in solidarity. But to Josef Goebbels, twenty-five percent Jewish blood was enough to brand the fighter a full-fledged Semite. Despite confirmations that "he was no Jew" from fighters who'd seen Baer in the showers, the Reich Minister of Propaganda banned *The Prizefighter and the Lady* in Germany because "its chief character" was Jewish. Baer laughed it off: "They didn't ban the picture because I have Jewish blood. They banned it because I knocked out Schmeling."

Production got off to a shaky start. Howard Hawks (then of *Scarface* renown) was slated to direct what was initially titled *The Sailor and the Lady* to star Clark Gable as per his agreement with MGM. But like the prematurely aged Errol Flynn, Gable's star power was hobbled by a lack of athletic ability, and the actor refused any training to make him a passable screen pugilist (or, as the original script had it, sailor). When Max Baer's pretty mug, already plastered across the pages of *Boxing News* and the *Ring Magazine*, started to appear in gossip columns and movie magazine covers, MGM knew they had found their man. His good-natured, self-deprecating humor and an absence of ego—rare among film stars of the day—didn't hurt either, and the script was revised to a boxing story.

But even a giant like Hawks was at the mercy of the studio's whims. It was the 1930s, and directors had little control over the casting and production of their films. In his book *Max Baer and Barney Ross: Jewish Heroes of Boxing*, Jeffrey Sussman notes that directors "were little more than hired hands," interchangeable, and ultimately expendable. As Hawks began filming with characteristic obsession, the studio nixed Norma Shearer, his top pick for the female lead, in favor of Jean Harlow of *Public Enemy* renown. Hawks fumed, then fumed some more when the role was again passed to the prolific but lesser-known Myrna Loy. Upon commencement of filming, Hawks went over budget almost immediately. Now it was Louis B. Mayer, the vindictive MGM studio head and devoted Baer fan, who was fuming.

Unsympathetic to Hawks's objections over limited shooting time and more than a little irritated over his frittering of studio funds, Mayer replaced the director with W.S. Van Dyke, the filmmaker who was to turn Loy into a major star the following year in *The Thin Man*. Known as "One Take Woody," Van Dyke was a workhorse who shot fast and cheap. Despite Hawks's contributions to the film's early scenes, the original director remains uncredited. As for Baer, the ready-made box-office attraction was lauded on marquees as *"Another Clark Gable! A New Valentino! ...Heavy Lover - He's great in the clinches - All kinds of clinches - The Screen's New 'It Man!'"*

Despite Baer's cocksure demeanor around the studio lot (he purred "Hello, Baby," upon meeting an abashed Joan Crawford and slapped Mae West on the ass), he was nervous when it came to acting. Though charismatic in the ring, he had small faith in his on-screen abilities. Stepping in as a replacement for Clark Gable couldn't have helped.

Playing himself, the retired Jack Dempsey brought levity to the filming with his practical jokes. Even Loy got in on the fun, and upon learning of Baer's terror of mice, released one into the ring while the cast and crew had a good laugh watching the tanker scramble in fear.

When The Professor waddles out of retirement to offer the affable, two-fisted bartender a chance to make a few bucks, Morgan's all ears. The job? If Morgan can last three rounds in an upcoming bout, he stands to make a sweet little sum.

Through a confluence of circumstances inherent to fiction and Dear Abbey columns, Morgan makes the acquaintance of Loy's Belle Mercer. She's dreamy, alright, but what Morgan doesn't know (at least not yet) is that she's Willy Ryan's girl. One of the earliest examples of the gangster as a genre mainstay, Ryan (the collected, oddly sympathetic Otto Kruger) is a benign prototype for the cold-eyed fixers that were part and parcel to the boxing noir as crime and the fight game commenced their entwinement in earnest. Devoid of genuine menace, Kruger's affable businessman exhibits only the subtlest hint that he's not a guy you want to cross.

Morgan kayos his first opponent with playful ease, and as Belle watches from ringside, the seeds of love are sown. But off camera, and despite Baer's libertine lifestyle, Loy so intimidated the fighter that he grew dumbstruck in her presence and suffered fits of anxiety. Upon learning of Baer's consternation, Loy summarily put the cowing pugilist at ease and the costars developed a fast, plutonic friendship in which Baer confided his persistent torment over the deaths of Frankie Campbell and Ernie Schaaf as discussed in the previous chapter.

The Professor warns Morgan that if he wants to keep fighting, or breathing, he'd better stay away from Belle. Tongues are already wagging. Ryan's also getting suspicious, so when Morgan, wearing a white suit, saunters into the club, the gangster waves him over to his table to introduce his entourage, all clad in black. Ryan points out his right-hand man Sonny, of whom he remarks, "He has good aim with a fly swatter." When Belle walks on stage to sing a number with the band, Ryan detects a little too much admiration in Morgan's gaze.

Although Belle pleads with Morgan that there can never be anything between them, the viewer senses the inevitable first kiss a mile off. It was a kiss Loy later described as "simply delicious... it was like the first kiss of a boy who had never kissed a girl before me." Maybe Baer was a better actor than he supposed.

Having learned that Belle married Morgan the day after the fight, Ryan's pained stoicism speaks to an impotent lack of authority—it would be another few years before screen racketeers bared their teeth in earnest. Still, Ryan doesn't keep Sonny and his fly swatter around for nothing.

At a training camp in the Catskills, the viewer is first and foremost reminded that Baer was a great boxer who could easily command a dollar fee for the privilege of watching him train. Known for his lax approach, Baer took advantage of these sessions both onscreen and off for his upcoming title fight against the current World Champion Primo Carnera, who surprisingly plays himself in the role of Morgan's opponent. Morgan's eyes wander from the heavy bag to Belle, and as befits his real-life regimen, follows the shapelier of the two inside for a different cardio workout.

A former circus strong man from the Italian village of Sequals, Primo Carnera was uneducated, spoke poor English, and had little means of earning power other than his size. He was the ideal target for thugs like Owney Madden, and because so many of his early bouts were fixed, suspicions lingered over the legitimacy of his title win in 1933. He wasn't much of a boxer either. In his essay "Pity the Poor Giant," Paul Gallico wrote that "[Carnera's] entire record must be thrown out as one gigantic falsehood." Maybe, but few career arcs better chart the link between boxing and crime.

The Professor implores Belle to keep away from the camp: Eros and Thanatos, love and war, fucking and fighting don't mix. According to the abstinence rule, especially popular among the old-timers, coitus and its subsequent release saps the ferocity intrinsic to fighting (see Robert De Niro pouring ice water down his briefs in *Raging Bull*). Baer, known to have been caught more than once *in flagrante* only minutes before a bout, thought otherwise.

Baer didn't have to perform a role he was already living, and Morgan is soon distracted by another cute number wiggling her nose at him from ringside. Back at the club, he enjoys an overabundance of female adoration and phones Belle with the fiction of being held up by "business." His subsequent apologies ("She means nothing to me!") ring hollow. But for gossip-starved viewers, portrayals of adultery and infidelity scratched an itch akin to the scandals they read about in film magazines, tabloids, and gossip columns.

The headlines announcing the upcoming bout anticipate Baer's fast-approaching real-life title fight with Carnera in June of 1934. Morgan takes his show on the road with a hokey song-and-dance routine on the rigmaroles of training in an erratically quaint stage production with the refrain "Lucky fella on the make for love." This might elucidate why the film was retitled *Every Woman's Man* in England. (The Brits took a lot more interest in Baer's womanizing than his boxing.) Amid a troop of showgirls, the performance is a cheap shill by MGM to tout Baer's terpsichorean skills in a choreographed training montage wholly unlike anything else in the genre. Yet there's surreal pleasure in the vaudevillian detour as Max jogs in place with a bevy of dancers, skips rope, and extolls the virtues of exercise and a healthy diet. Like Loy's nightclub act, the insertion of musical numbers into the early talkies was an MGM hallmark. Having produced the first sound film to win an Academy Award for Best Picture (Harry Beaumont's 1929 *The Broadway Melody*), the studio that spearheaded the cinematic musical had a reputation to uphold.

To finalize Morgan's upcoming bout, Ryan contacts the production company of Jack Dempsey, a name that would have been as familiar with contemporary viewers as the president. An unstoppable juggernaut, Dempsey took the heavyweight title in 1919 with bone-crunching ferocity from Jack Johnson's dethroner Jess Willard. Now six years retired, he plays himself and sits behind the desk at his promotion company while sleepwalking through the role. Not that anyone cared about his acting: America's obsession with the "Manassa Mauler" was still strong enough to earn him top billing along with Carnera, second only to Baer and Loy. Injecting some on-screen editorial, Dempsey's prediction that Morgan will lose to Carnera echoes his real-life disappointment with Baer, whom he believed would have been a far better fighter had he spent less time "dilly-dallying" and more time training.

Originally written to include the requisite kayo by Morgan, the on-screen fight was revised to go the distance. Carnera hits the canvas like a fallen tree. Morgan's knocked through the ropes. A slugfest with more knockdowns than a bowling scorecard, there was a method to the madness. In a fiction that was dangerously close to reality (the real-life bout was just seven months away), it would have been unseemly to favor one boxer over another, and a draw is declared.

Boxing upwards of thirty rounds with Carnera during shooting, Baer studied his opponent's weakness firsthand, an opportunity Carnera biographer Frederic Mullally describes as "the best pay-off Max Baer would get in his life." Upon learning that he was an underdog with the bookmakers, Baer again laughed it off. "You saw what happened to Max Schmeling when I conked him, huh? Well, Carnera'll go the same way, but it'll be funnier."

Sadly, it was. The bout (briefly recreated in *Cinderella Man*) took place on June 14, where, throughout eleven rounds, Baer dropped Carnera as many times while teasing and humiliating his opponent before the referee stopped the fight. While the Italian lay in the hospital, Owney Madden split town for unrelated crimes. Indignant over his opponent's treatment, Baer paid for Carnera's medical expenses, and the two remained friends—only partly through their shared grief over their roles in the death of Ernie Schaaf.

The presence of The Professor is diminished to a weak breeze by the film's end as his character ultimately proves little more than a crude archetype and catalyst for Morgan's career. As for Ryan, he'd just as soon forget the whole affair. So much for the bad guy. The rote denouement is notable solely for the on-set chemistry that spills into Baer and Loy's playful burlesque capped with professions of love and a declaration by Morgan: "I'm tired of being a big shot." Two years later, life imitated art when the twenty-six-year-old Baer married Mary Ellen Sullivan in his second foray into matrimony, the first having failed due to one-sided infidelities. "I was watching a friend of mine... put a diaper on a baby and I thought it was the cutest thing I ever saw in my life." Having sown his bushels of oats, Baer remained with Mary Ellen until his death twenty-four years later. They had three children. Meanwhile, Carnera had returned to his birthplace of Sequals and took up professional wrestling to support his wife and two children while enjoying renewed adoration in his homeland. He'd earned it.

Baer's "ingratiating personality" and on-screen persona were universally lauded by critics. One can practically hear Kate Cameron's lusty sigh in her *New York Times* review as she describes his "clear, low-pitched voice that is pleasing, particularly to the female ear." The *New York World Telegram* called him "a movie natural."

After his taste of Hollywood, the stage and screen held

a far stronger pull for Baer, which contributed to his lax training regimen for his unsuccessful 1935 title defense against the Cinderella Man. Taking the loss with breezy insouciance, Baer made another twelve films after retiring from the ring in 1941. Signing up for service in 1943, he told the press, "After all, I started the whole business when I upset Mussolini beating Carnera, and I made Hitler mad when I knocked Schmeling out."

Bear was seized by a heart attack when he was fifty years old. A wag to the end, his last words to the medics, firemen, and staff that hovered over him at the Hollywood Roosevelt Hotel was a mock dramatic, "Oh God, here I go!"

Damon Runyan, whose quote on James Braddock opened the previous chapter, best summarized the whirlwind that descended upon the ring and Hollywood in the person of Madcap Maxie: "There have been many better fighters than Max Baer, but never a greater showman." Despite *Prizefighter's* lack of high-stakes drama, the viewer forgives and even delights in the fighter's hammy performance—even that silly song-and-dance number. After all, the guy was having the time of his life. That's hard to begrudge anyone.

8
THE HARDER THEY FALL

Directed by Mark Robson
Columbia Pictures, 1956

Nothing short of a wholesale indictment of corruption in the fight game, Mark Robson's *The Harder They Fall* addressed boxing's criminal ties with more antipathy than any film before or since. Writing in the *Independent*, Ken Jones observed that the film was "released when the newspapers were full of investigations into boxing." But the sport's criminal ties had been splashing the top folds for over two decades. *Kid Galahad* had been released a full nineteen years prior, and Robson had directed *Champion* in 1949. In 1950, mob control had come to a head as Tennessee Senator Estes Kefauver launched his televised investigations into organized crime. While boxing wasn't the focal point of what came to be known as "the Hearings" (see Chapter 14), it figured largely.

Budd Schulburg wrote the film's source novel of the same name in 1947, the same year "The Bronx Bull" (aka *Raging Bull*) Jake LaMotta botched a dive against Billy Fox for which he was to answer thirteen years later before a televised Committee hearing. Schulburg, who also penned the screenplay for the 1954 redemption tale of Marlon Brando's coulda' been contender-cum-dock worker *On the Waterfront*, called *The Harder They Fall*, his "black valentine to the sweet science of boxing." Both book and film (the latter adapted for the screen by Philip Yordan, a possible front for the blacklisted Schulburg) are equivalent to lifting a rock of corruption to reveal the squirming colony beneath: shifty vermin in double-breasted suits and cash boxes that are never quite full enough.

The archetypal strong-armed boxer Primo Carnera is blatantly referenced in the gawkish Argentinian Toro Moreno (played by professional wrestler Mike Lane). It's understandable why the ex-Champion was saddened by this story of a towering, half-witted pawn for the Syndicate (a thin euphemism that lent an air of corporate legitimacy to the mob), for no one could fail to recognize the "Ambling Alp" in the gullible Moreno.

Upon *The Harder They Fall*'s release, Carnera sued Schulburg and Columbia Pictures for $1.5 million. A judge dismissed the charges with the apologia that, as a celebrity, the fighter had relinquished "the right to privacy and [did] not regain it by changing his profession from boxing to wrestling." Carnera merely expressed regret over never having had the opportunity to speak with Schulberg directly. "It is all true," the fighter said, "but I wish he had come to me. I would tell him so much more."

The Humphrey Bogart-Rod Steiger combo drew audiences craving further exposés of fictional gangsters as stand-ins for the real deal: tight-lipped wise guys who'd graced their television sets every night amid the Hearings. Eddie Muller writes that the prototypical noir criminal is characterized as having "learned how to fold [his] rackets into the straining streams of the capitalist economy." This being the case, Owney Madden, with his ownership of Carnera (among others), was a first-rate professional. So too is Steiger's Nick Benko, a loose avatar of the criminal who, Carnera biographer Joseph Page writes, "had bled [Carnera] dry."

By 1956, Humphrey Bogart's world-weary cynicism had bottomed out. The actor's physical decline was conspicuous as he vented belligerence over the Hollywood blacklist. His skin and hair had turned grey. His teeth were yellow. Those debauched, alcoholic nights had taken their toll, and the icon known to mold his characters to accommodate his own taut charisma could no longer hide the misanthropy he carried under the weight of the House Un-American Activities Committee. *The Harder They Fall* was to be Bogart's final film. Nine months after its release, the actor died at fifty-seven.

HUAC kept a sharp eye on Bogart from the moment it turned its attention to Hollywood in 1947, and the heading "THE BOGART SITUATION" appeared regularly in government wires and memos. In a comment that earned him "Marxist status" with the conservative press, the fiercely liberal actor griped that HUAC would "nail anyone who even scratched his ass during the National Anthem."

Although he told the press, "I have absolutely no use for communism, or anyone who serves that philosophy," Bogart nevertheless adhered to the tenet that freedom of religion and party affiliation was an American birthright. His wife, Lauren Bacall, spearheaded the Committee for the First Amendment (CFA). Consisting of twenty-five Hollywood notables, including Bette Davis, John Garfield, John Huston, Ring Lardner, Burgess Meredith, Edward G. Robinson, and Robert Ryan, the Committee formed the same year HUAC set its sights on Tinseltown. Formidable in its membership, Bogart served as the Committee's public face only to grow increasingly disheartened as he watched once-trusted colleagues and leftist luminaries (notably the staunch Democrat Jack Warner) squeal under HUAC questioning. As the public face of the CFA, Bogart was tired. He was also ornery, with a button he wore on his lapel at parties that read, "No causes, politics, or religion discussed here."

Steiger's Nick Benko, his cadre of goons, and Moreno's handler, Luís (based on Carnera's French manager Leon See) stand around a ring. Outside the gym, a washed-out ex-sportswriter Eddie Willis (a washed-out Bogart) climbs from a taxi and ascends the stairs. He's come to hear out a proposition Benko has for him: how would Eddie like to make a few bucks by coming out of retirement to ingratiate the public to this behemoth who, like Carnera, was discovered in a traveling circus?

A wolf in lamb's clothes, Benko is characterized by Schulberg as having clawed his way to the top by the "constant application of the principal Do Unto Others As You Would Not Have Them Do Unto You." Benko's outer mien of altruism belies the greed and cruelty with which fighters had to contend in members of the mob—notably those that operated under the auspices of the organization aptly titled Murder, Inc. As their criminal activity came to light, public suspicion over dubious fight results—still integral to the decade's social, cultural, and ethnical zeitgeist—was confirmed.

Toro Moreno is sparring with the gym hand, Joe (the real-life ex-Heavyweight Champion Jersey Joe Walcott) as Eddie looks on with the same bemusement Schulberg uses to describe the reporter's initial reaction: "His hands were monstrous, the size of his feet was monstrous and his oversized head instantly became my conception of the Neanderthal Man who roamed the world some forty thousand years ago." The sportswriter laughs mirthlessly at Benko's offer of $250 a week as he pulls on a Chesterfield, the steadfast prop that Bogart wielded with more authority than most men could muster with a Smith and Wesson. Off-screen, Bogart's health was so diminished by nicotine consumption that he required regular breaks while filming to attend to the wracking coughs that would seize him for upward of five minutes.

"An old fighter who's been punched around, spilled his blood freely for the fans' amusement only to wind up broke, battered, and forgotten has got the stuff of tragedy for me," Eddie muses in the source novel. He has no interest in this lurching Argentine yokel swatting powder puffs, but Benko has a plan. All Eddie has to do is build the kid up with some ink in the sports section, and the Syndicate will take care of the rest.

Eddie's eyes narrow. This must be a joke. But if it isn't, five hundred could work. Five hundred bucks a week to convince the public that this human punching bag is the real deal. It won't be easy, it won't be honest, and working with a criminal is always a shady prospect. But for Eddie, it's also money in the bank. To Benko, it's pretty simple: "Forget your self-respect." Money's money, and Eddie has no reason to concern himself with what Schulberg calls "such mathematical problems as how to cut a pie into five quarters."

In *Shadowbox: An Amateur in the Ring*, George Plimpton wrote how a "fight can be over in a few seconds... [and] a couple of thousand words must be composed out of an act which very likely took place when the reporter was looking down." The prospect of a return to sports writing holds no attraction to Eddie. The love is gone, but he's good at what he does. That's why he was hired.

After a string of pre-arranged bouts, Moreno starts to believe that he can fight. But Benko's not ready to give the kid any cash just yet. He's got a few concerns of his own, namely an investigation into the egregious dive during Moreno's first fight. Eddie wonders if it's time to walk away, so Benko ups his fee. After all, someone has to smooth things over, and it can't be a prominent gangster.

Despite the shower drain that runs red with the blood of the boxer who flubbed the dive (courtesy of Benko's goons), the Boxing Commissioner seems amenable to wiping the slate. He can see Moreno's lack of prowess as well as anyone. Still, by way of discreet warning, he has Eddie watch a filmed interview with a punch-drunk ex-pug played with well-earned credibility by a real-life retired club fighter whose voice resonates with the smack of broken teeth and whose nose has seen more breaks than a gallery of Greek sculpture. Living in his car after a career of 220 fights, the once-noble pugilist bemoans the lack of retirement plans for fighters. But it's the only trade he's ever known. When the interviewer asks about his future plans, he thinks for a moment. "What future?" The message was not lost on contemporary audiences, fueling furor over the inside mechanisms of the game they had come to discover was a racket that destroyed its practitioners. "Very few fighters get the consideration of racehorses," wrote Schulberg, "which are put out to pasture to grow old with dignity and comfort when they haven't got it anymore."

A group of managers visits Benko to gripe about all

these dives their fighters have been taking for Moreno. Sure, they're well-compensated, but the losses are sapping their own guys' earning potential, and they respectfully ask for compensation. While the gangster hears them out, Eddie synopsizes the crux of their predicament via Bogart's characteristic, punctuation-free elocution: "All you do is spot a strong kid buy him a license for ten dollars rent him a towel for a dime and throw him in the ring. For that you grab a third of his purse grab another third by padding the expense account then cheat him out of half of what's left. You're the managers, that's for sure." The reproach is among the most concise summaries of the operations and shoddy qualifications the majority of managers held during the fifties. Even more telling is the rejoinder from one of the managers: "Fighters come and go. Managers are here forever. Fighters are dirt." Maybe, but not while they're earning.

Benko offers a $25,000 donation to a charitable organization to host a fight featuring Moreno as a contender for the heavyweight title. When a priest on the board objects to taking money from a hood, Eddie mollifies him with a bit of philosophy even the padre can get behind: "Money's not evil in and of itself. It's the way it's used that's the determining factor."

Life-size wooden cutouts in Moreno's likeness adorn the tops of buses as if ready to punch through tunnels—or get their heads ripped to shreds inside them. The fighter has officially "invaded" Chicago, and Louís again asks Benko for money for his boy. If Moreno's being groomed as contender, why can't he get a taste of the action, too? As with Leon See, who maintained what was euphemistically called a "partnership" with Owney Madden's associate "Broadway" Bill Duffy, Benko tells Luis it's still a no-go. They're still in the red. The manager balks, and Benko has his goons throw him out. Pretty simple business. As for See, Paul Gallico gingerly recounts the manager as having been sent back to France "for his health."

On the rooftop garden of a Chicago hotel, Eddie skulks behind Benko and his boys, who convene with Moreno's upcoming opponent, Gus Dundee. Played by ex-heavyweight Pat Comiskey (whose flawless record was broken by a loss to Max Baer in 1940), Dundee's type is epitomized in the broken, aging fighter of James T. Farrell's grim 1930 short story *Twenty-Five Bucks*. "His face had been punched into hash: cauliflower ears, a flattened nose... shifty with the fleeting nervous cowardice of a scared and broken man."

Dundee's neurodegeneration is woven into his movement, his speech, and, apparently, his memory. His headaches have worsened since his last fight, and he begs out of the Moreno bout. Doctor's orders. But a steely glare from Benko prompts a quick re-diagnosis: Maybe it isn't headaches after all. "Oh yeah," Dundee scrambles to change his story. "I'm allergic to Penicillin!" Benko doesn't give a rat's ass what it was so long as Dundee goes down, and the envelope containing $10,000 he hands him should be more than enough incentive. With a gate sure to bring in over a million bucks, what's a little chump change to give the old pug a warm send-off? For starters, it's a hell of a lot more than Madden or Broadway Bill Duffy would have done.

Eddie's apathy qualifies him as one of a small, select few who can berate Nick Benko without getting his ribs broken in the back room by five thugs and ten shoes. He tells the gangster that Luís needs to be bought off if he's being sent back, and it's not a request. Benko isn't comfortable being spoken to this way and darkly reminds Eddie that no one here is indispensable. "Then fire me." But Benko wants to keep everybody happy, so he throws the manager on a plane with five Gs. Maybe he needs Eddie more than he'd care to admit.

On fight day, Dundee can barely walk. His tired wrestler's movements harken to the age of lawless clandestine bouts when boxing was still illegal in almost every state, rules were more like suggestions, and fighters killed in the ring were quietly dumped in the river. But this is no basement brawl, and despite the sizable gate, Benko still hasn't given Moreno any money. If the kid loses, Benko can just write it off; most gangsters still considered boxing a secondary market anyway. It's a miracle that Benko intends to pay up at all.

Dazed by a series of clumsy blows from Moreno, Dundee staggers to his corner, turns to the center of the ring, and falls face-first on the canvas. Benko is disgusted with what looks like a poorly staged dive, and he's missing that ten large already. But Dundee, who dies from his injuries, won't have the chance to spend it. It was a sloppy fight and an ill-advised fix. Had Benko known the outcome, he'd probably have dumped Dundee in the river himself—dead or alive.

The passage is an apparent reference to Ernie Schaaf, long thought to have been so tenderized in his 1933 fight with Max Baer that it was only a matter of time before another trauma, however small, would finish him for good (as recounted in Chapter 6). Five months later, the fighter died following a flimsy blow in his bout with Carnera. But while Carnera and Baer sat vigil at Schaaf's hospital bedside, Dundee dies alone while a drunken Moreno parties back at the hotel.

The casting of Max Baer as Heavyweight Champion Buddy Brannen underscores his apparent role in the Schaaf tragedy. In an uncharacteristic, villainous turn, Baer's Brannen reminds Eddie of his previous bout with Dundee. "All your joker did was tap him. I did all the work." Even twenty-four years after his bout with Schaaf, it's hard to imagine Baer feeling comfortable playing the killer. He remains a minor character, at war not with Moreno but with the crooked dealings of Eddie and Benko.

The following day, Moreno goes to confession where the priest implores him to return to Argentina. But, as is often the case, money trumps the word of god, and a little false flattery from Benko convinces Moreno to stick around just a while longer. Why pull a gun on the guy when false flattery is a little less messy and a lot more profitable? But

Eddie knows Brannen won't take a swim for anyone. Benko knows it too, and business being business, bets accordingly.

Back at the gym, Eddie sits Moreno down for some straight talk: "You're what's called a bum." Rather than enumerate Moreno's litany of fixed fights, Eddie has the fighter double-check his skills in a little spar with Joe to prove that there's no way Moreno can win his upcoming bout. That being the case, he might as well lose with dignity. Joe shows him how to stay on his feet by moving around to give the crowd a show before Brannen inevitably drops him. He shows him how to keep Brannen at bay with his reach and to fall into a clinch when he gets too close. "Make it quick - just not too quick... go down and stay down," Eddie tells him. Nobody wants another investigation.

Over two decades after the release of *The Prizefighter and the Lady* and fifteen years after his retirement from the ring, the forty-seven-year-old Baer's goofball charisma had not diminished, nor had his capacity to navigate the ring like a twenty-five-year-old. As he sets about hammering Moreno, Benko looks on with contentment. That ten thousand he wasted on Dundee is starting to hurt less.

Moreno got off easy in his defeat at the hands of Brannen compared to Primo Carnera's loss to Max Baer, wherein the Italian endured an excessive dose of humiliation and several injuries into the mix. "Not one of [the gangsters] came to see me," Carnera recounted. Moreno is dispensed efficiently, emerging with ribs intact and a busted jaw.

His mouth a bloody hole with the guard hanging out, Moreno lies in the dressing room and asks Eddie for his cut so he can return to Argentina. The viewer never learns the amount of Moreno's promised purse, though Carnera's was set at \$122,057.08, of which he never saw a dime. Benko's money man adds sparring and training expenses, the towel, and the locker room. Then there are hotel fees for the gangster and his entourage, and they like to travel in style. Twiddling with his ledger and punching the buttons, Benko really can cut a pie into five quarters. Just not evenly. The adding machine finally spits a strip of paper to reveal Moreno's slice: \$49.07.

In a cab from the hospital to the airport, Eddie hands Moreno the envelope containing \$26,000 from his own coffers. "That's a lot of money in my country," says the fighter. Eddie stares at the buildings that whiz by outside the cab window and nods slowly. "That's a lot of money in any country." Even in this business.

Benko's golden goose still had a few fights in him. He could still be earning. At least until he ends up dead like Dundee. But now he's gone and Benko's pissed. That's not Eddie's problem anymore. The racketeer's business tactics and pie-dividing stopped cutting ice with the reporter some time ago. In fact, they never did. Eddie was hired for publicity, not as a middleman, babysitter, or emergency guidance counselor. His initial apprehensions were well-founded. He knew it from the start, but five hundred dollars a day buys a lot of rationales.

Eddie's decision to extricate himself from Benko outweighs any payday. Lying to the newspapers is easy, but advancing some innocent clod for the leeches to suck dry is something else. Eddie neither wants nor cares about his blood money anymore, and changing one's outlook on money can change their outlook on life.

To a vindicated public, the film further proved the Kefauver Hearings' findings. In the original script, Eddie sits at his desk and types, "Boxing must be abolished in America." But the raison d'être behind Schulberg's "black valentine" was not to vilify the sport but its criminal ties. The International Boxing Commission fumed at the film's perceived aspersion of the sport.

So follows an amended, freshly typewritten sheet: "The boxing business must rid itself of the evil influence of racketeers and crooked managers, even if it takes an act of Congress to do it." Eddie titles his piece *The Harder They Fall*, swivels his chair, and keeps banging the keys. It's a fair bet he'll be out of retirement longer than he'd planned.

9
REQUIEM FOR A HEAVYWEIGHT

Directed by Ralph Nelson
Columbia Pictures, 1962

Requiem for a Heavyweight charts the swift, heartrending ter-
minus of a fighter's career through his own epiphany that
he's finished, washed-up, damaged beyond repair. Whereas
The Harder They Fall approached the subject six years prior as
an exposé, *Requiem* confronts the vagaries and realities of
aging fighters who, having outgrown their earning power,
are cast adrift from society. For the viewer, there's nothing
to do but wait alongside them for a wind that will never
blow again.

Penned by a thirty-one-year-old Rod Serling for
Playhouse 90 (a CBS live drama that aired from 1956 to 1960),
Requiem's original 1957 teleplay starred a twitchy, slurring

Jack Palance. The following year, the BBC aired its own production featuring Sean Connery in his first starring television role. Four years later, Serling adapted the multiple Emmy-winner for the big screen.

Best known for probing the uncanny with 156 seminal episodes of *The Twilight Zone* (1959-1964) and forty-three episodes of *Night Gallery* (1969-1973), Serling also fought seventeen bouts as a flyweight in the military. His time in the Air Force helped shape his interest in the uncanny, unexpected, and frequently morbid (among other horrors, he witnessed a fellow soldier crushed by a box from an American supply plane). His first published work, a four-page short story about a boxer's suicide titled *The Good Right Hand*, appeared in the 1948 edition of the Antioch College literary magazine when Serling was twenty-three. He also wrote two episodes for *The Twilight Zone* devoted to the game (1960's *The Big Tall Wish*, notable for its Black cast, and 1963's *Steel*). He sold a more faithful adaptation of Ring Lardner's *Champion* to the CBS anthology series *Climax!* in 1955, six years after the release of Robson's film.

Professor Andrew Delblanco describes the "soul-killing loneliness" of Serling's characters as embodied in "voyagers stranded, astronauts marooned, spouses estranged, clerks doing mind-numbing work while dreaming of a larger life." In the boxing arena, Serling's attentions lay with the uncertain futures of lesser known-fighters or, as he wrote in his dedication to the play's novelization, "the punchies, the cauliflowered wrecks, the mumbling ghosts of Eighth

Avenue bars." To the writer, boxing was the ultimate stage upon which hopes were dashed, victories short-lived, and participants wore "the sorrow-etched face of a panhandler exchanging a fragment of dignity for a hot cup of soup." Unlike the zones of the fantastic for which he is best known, the writer considered *Requiem*'s pathos most representative of the stories that he wanted to tell. A heavy smoker and drinker, Serling died of heart complications at fifty.

In 1945 there were less than 10,000 television sets domestically. By 1952, that number had climbed to nearly twenty million. But Serling was disheartened at producers' formulaic approach to the medium, which ran contrary to his vision of encapsulated, stand-alone stories that spoke to a wide berth of the human condition and compared the network's demand for regular, reappearing characters and linear plot lines to "asking Arthur Miller to write about salesmen every time."

Requiem for a Heavyweight charts Anthony Quinn's piteous, punchy Louis "Mountain" Rivera, whose career ends as the film opens. In his day, Rivera was ranked number five in the heavyweight division, a piece of history the rest of the world has forgotten, though Mountain clings to it like a lifebuoy. Quinn's hoarse, naive articulation makes Rivera's desperate efforts to grasp life outside the boxing world palpable. Detached from Rivera's denial, the viewer can see that seventeen years in the ring has won the fighter no more than a pair of cauliflower ears, a string of broken noses, and a dangerous accumulation of scar tissue around his eyes. As patrons crowd an Eight Avenue dive bar, the announcer on the television confirms Rivera's tenacity as he cries in astonishment. "The old guy won't quit!"

Cinematographer Arthur Ornitz's lens sets on a bright-eyed Cassius Clay playing himself in the second year of his professional career. Filmed in distorted POV, Clay's face emerges as if through a lava lamp. When he drops Rivera, both camera and viewer fall a giddy ninety degrees with the fighter as the canvas slants and folds into a vertical strip where Rivera's head lands with concussive force. Somewhere overhead, the blurry ref finishes the count.

Rivera staggers to the locker room, where his battered visage is revealed in a cracked mirror that he studies with dread. Laurence Rosenthal's horror film score explodes, as imperious, angular typeface rises like towers from the bottom of the frame. Revived by his manager Maish Rennick (Jackie Gleason) and his trainer Army (Mickey Rooney), Rivera can't even remember what city they're in.

The fight doctor enters with his black bag and magnifying light and studies Rivera's eyes. "You see the pupil?" he asks the handlers. "You see the tissue? That's known as sclerotic damage... a detached retina." The Mountain's race is run. After seventeen years of accumulated punishment, "a couple of good rights and you can give him a tin cup and pencils." The doc cannot, in good conscience, allow the commission to renew Rivera's license. The plaintive simplicity with which the fighter tries to salvage his dignity is that of a rummy begging for a final nip. Without comprehension of the matter at hand, he tells the doctor that he never took a dive in all his 111 fights. He's an honest fighter and no pawn to the mob. Gleeson's Maish turns to Rooney's Army with hollow enthusiasm. "At least he walks away with his brain." Sort of.

Requiem is another film for which *Il Gigante Buono*, Primo Carnera, served as inspiration. Serling credited the Italian with directly influencing Rivera, even riffing on Carnera's sobriquet "Man Mountain."

Quinn was sixteen when he acquired his own boxing license. Two years under the legal age, he fought in several bouts. "I had no killer instinct," he later wrote, "I would never make a good fighter." By stunning coincidence, the young pugilist and future actor had an opportunity to spar with Carnera at a training session just after the latter took the title. Of the much-abused heavyweight, Quinn lamented, "Poor soul, one of the kindest men I have ever met in my life."

The dissimilarities between Carnera and Rivera are numerous: Carnera retained his facilities after his eighteen-year, 105-fight career and retired comfortably. By contrast, Rivera's seventeen years in the ring have left him a shadow of the fighter he was when he was ranked at number five. Carnera was nothing if not mob-owned and participated in numerous fixed bouts, but in Rivera's 111 fights, he never swam— "Not once!" In short, one would be remiss to view the fictional Rivera as a truthful reflection of his real-life progenitor the abundance of film critics, boxing historians, and biographers might have them believe. In fact, Rivera is more invoking of the ex-pug interviewed in *The Harder They Fall*, with no work experience outside the ring and a sixth-grade education.

In the history of the boxing film, no fighter epitomizes the tragedy of neurodegeneration like Mountain. "When your career is finished," wrote Serling, "the profession discards you. In terms of society, it discards a freak, a man only able to live by his fists and instincts." The doctor's warning of the accumulated blows that will eventually kill the fighter recalls the deaths of Frankie Campell, Ernie Schaff, and countless others whose brains were so primed that even a mild tap could spell the final count.

Rivera's damage is apparent in any situation outside the boxing circuit, appearing as he does like a dazed Rip van Winkle loping down the mountain after seventeen years out cold and rubbing scar tissue instead of a beard. If Serling's assessment of these ex-fighters as "freaks" rings as harsh, it's sadly applicable to Rivera's potential employers. Even the few that don't require experience won't hire him—if only because his arms are too long for the uniform.

Maish is convinced that Rivera still has a few more fights in him. It's risky and selfish, but Rivera's been the manager's seventeen-year project, and the boxer's not the only one out of work. Besides, for some reason, Maish seems to need the money.

The Mountain may be 86'd from boxing, but he could always work the wrestling circuit. A post-career fate adopted by countless fighters, wrestling was often an embarrassing indication of financial duress or an easy means of cashing in on name recognition. In its theater of pulled punches and rehearsed combat, it's a lot less dangerous than boxing, and there's money to be made. Just ask Primo Carnera.

As Rivera's would-be protector, Maish emerges like a pair of weighted dice that always lands on the side of greed. Like *The Harder They Fall*'s Willy Ryan or *The Set-up*'s Tiny, he plays both sides of the street. Ostensibly working for Rivera, the viewer learns that Maish bet against his fighter in his final bout. His rationale was purely financial. Now he has a lot of incentive to pay up.

With its near-singular focus on the fighter's decline, the film is also a haunted, adumbral boxing noir peopled with Muller's above-mentioned "predatory tribes of men" or, in this case, a formidable, rapacious woman. Ma Greeny (Bertha Levine, aka Madame Spivy) is one of the most unique racketeers the viewer could hope to meet. With short hair and eyes obfuscated by dark sunglasses, her ambiguous sexuality would have been more than a little unsettling to viewers in 1962. As a caricature, a cartoon, and a lost opportunity for a formidable Bond villain, she's too enjoyable to come across as wholly intimidating. But she's all business, her presence equally commanding, and her ultimatums just as serious as any slick boy counting the bills he's made off cheating malleable pugs. With steely detachment wholly at odds with the sex-soaked fatales whose villainy is born of seduction, Spivy's presence brings fresh discomfort to an already uncomfortable film. And right now, nobody's as uncomfortable as Maish.

The bet was a lock. The way Maish saw things, there was no way Rivera could have lasted more than two rounds against the twenty-year-old upstart. But he did: it took Clay six to put him down. Now Maish is into Ma to the tune of $1,500, and another characteristic she shares with her fellow cinematic racketeers is a lack of patience.

Ma's especially ill-tempered after putting down cash for a second-round kayo on Maish's advice, and now she's out to collect. Like Midge Kelley before him, the manager skitters through the stadium, down aisles and under the ropes to the center of the ring. Mired in washes of floodlights that gouge shadows into the stands and surrounded by Ma's goons, Maish breathlessly explains to Ma the plan that might save his hide. It would make everyone money if he could convince Rivera to take up wrestling. His boy would be a cash cow but he needs time to bring Mountain on board. It's not the worst idea, and Ma agrees to wait a few days for Maish to make it happen. But just a few.

Lumbering through the unemployment office, Rivera meets with a job-placement social worker named Grace Miller (Julie Harris, notably credited on the film's posters as "The Muse"). Grace is intrigued by Rivera's experience as a prizefighter, and it pains her to inform him that there are no jobs available.

Later that day, Grace finds Rivera at a corner table at the same bar from the opening scene. He buys her a beer, delighted that she remembers he was once ranked number five. He recounts his days in the ring and swings blows in the air, growing animated with memory. When other patrons eye him with concern, the light in his eyes dims as though the reality of his career's end has only now dawned on him. But Miss Miller has a proposition. What would Rivera think about working as a counselor for boys at an athletic camp in the Adirondacks? Rivera's puzzled at the idea, but he likes kids. He always has. Grace sets off to secure an appointment with the camp's directors.

The unctuous wrestling promoter Perelli (Stan Adams) bursts into the office with a voice that could wake the neighbors and a wily smile like a cartoon cat. Both a caricature and a fair embodiment of the crude counterfeit that was and is the world of professional wrestling, Perelli's head is already swimming with harebrained schemes. To wit: put Rivera "in one of those Indian costumes with those crazy feathers" and pit him against a guy in a cowboy suit. One night the Indian wins, the next night it's the cowboy. Night after night, ad infinitum.

Rivera has a hard time comprehending such an arrangement. Besides, he's lost his license. He can't fight if he wants to. With his detached retina, there's still the possibility of that tin cup and pencils. More importantly, he's never taken a dive, and he's not going start now by throwing himself over the ropes with some ersatz cowpoke.

Perelli erupts in rancid laughter. "All you need to do is learn how to fake it! Make it *look* real! How to land so you don't hoit yourself!" Maish looks on anxiously and finally speaks up: if the work pays, there's no dignity lost. Nobody cares or even remembers who wins or loses these burlesques anyway.

Army's eyes bore disdain at the promoter, but Maish can already smell the money. The sooner he can get Rivera into that monkey ring, the sooner he can pay Ma. But Rivera announces that he's going to be a camp counselor. He even has a meeting later that night with the social worker from the unemployment office and the camp's owners.

The hourglass is running out for Maish, but what can he do if Rivera "wants to sit around a campfire" with a bunch of scouts? For starters, he can pour him out three fingers of the hard stuff. Then another. He suggests they go to Jack Dempsey's restaurant, where the sixty-seven-year-old Mauler stops at the table for a moment. (Chalk up another paycheck for Dempsey and free publicity for his place to boot.) Here's to new beginnings.

Maish tilts the bottle for another round when Army approaches the table. Isn't Rivera supposed to be somewhere? Mountain's well into his cups, and no matter how hard he tries, he just can't remember.

A good trainer can spot a fighter's strengths and hone them into something closer to perfection, fomenting natural skills and bolstering individual styles. It's an intimacy that differs from the relationship with a manager, whose role is generally confined to financial matters and negotiations. Army turns to Maish with contempt, knowing the manager willfully diverted Rivera from his meeting to continue milking him, now in the wrestling circuit.

Mountain stumbles into the lobby of a nearby hotel and asks for Miss Miller. The room's on the tenth floor—that much he remembers. Weaving through the halls and calling out Miss Miller's name, a door opens to reveal Grace flanked by a wealthy couple and Rivera flees in shame.

Later that night, the broken pugilist sits at the edge of his twin bed with his head in his hands. When Grace Miller enters, a disquieting dread seizes the viewer that maybe Rivera hasn't hit bottom quite yet. Pressing her hand to his lips, he draws on its sustenance in hope and self-forgiveness, but when their heads move in to meet at the lips, Grace departs from the story and film for good. Only she knows why. Rivera's muse has fled, and once again he's alone in the company of venal men and one tough woman.

The post-career havoc wrought by CTE is difficult—maybe impossible—to assess. Former editor-in-chief of *Ring Magazine* Nigel Collins estimates that seventy-five to eighty percent of boxers suffer brain damage. Roughly five hundred fighters have died in the ring or in the hospital following a bout since the standardization of the Queensberry rules from accumulated concussions in which the brain is knocked through its protective cerebrospinal fluid and slammed against the skull. While these rarely spell the death sentence they did for Frankie Campell, Ernie Schaff, or poor Dundee from *The Harder They Fall*, they amass dangerously over time. Even more disquieting than Collins's appraisal is a 2013 study by the Association of Neurological Surgeons that estimates nearly ninety percent of boxers suffer brain injury "of some extent" in their career. In this instance, "some extent" means just one concussion, and every fighter amasses considerably more. With no rigid standards or set numbers, one thing is certain: the brain needs time—usually between three and six weeks—to recover. Without it, even a slight impact carries enormous risk. Since most boxers don't display symptoms until well after their career has ended, the onset and severity of damage is often difficult or impossible to track. With this (and the benefit of sixty years' hindsight) in mind, the spritely, twenty-year-old Cassius Clay from *Requiem*'s opening bout eerily foreshadows his degeneration over nineteen years and sixty-one professional fights.

Roland Barthes wrote, "A boxing match is a story which is constructed before the eyes of the spectator [while] wrestling presents man's suffering with all the amplification of tragic masks." Considering Barthes's likening of the wrestler's "excessive portrayal of Suffering" to "a primitive Pieta," Rivera's debilitation is far closer in temper to the plaintive *Boxer of the Quirinal* (dated roughly 300 BCE and noted in relation to the Douglas Tildon sculpture in Chapter 4). Like the spent, debased warrior forever frozen in shame and exhaustion, the lines of predestination engraved into Rivera's face denote a map with a thousand dead ends, each underscoring his "tragic mask." If boxing is primal theater, wrestling is the theater of the tragicomic where there is no glory for the warrior because there's no war. Just a short script, a little money, and in Rivera's case, a lot of humiliation.

Of course, sometimes the end-of-the-line lets off at new beginnings. Maish's been telling Rivera this for some time now. Although it's hardly possible to remain serene, the viewer's pity is neither triggered nor aroused amid the wrestling club's backstage din where men with flat noses bespeak a nobler past. Managers and promoters juggle desperate plays for a spot in tonight's fights, still the only game in town where an ex-pug with no education can put on a cape or a onesie, swallow the bitter pill that hopefully gets a less bitter with each dose, and make some money.

A pageant of cowboys, cavemen, Caesars, and centurions blunder through the dressing room as Perelli laughs and adjusts Rivera's headdress. When Army and Maish enter, Rivera is examining himself in the mirror—an act he performs three times throughout the film—as though questioning his very existence. He tears off the braided wig in horror as the manager's treachery is exposed all at once. Silence drowns out the floppy din of pratfalls from the ring. Rivera begins to understand. Why else would Maish need the money so badly, so *quickly*? In a cruel, impetuous appeal to reason, Maish levels with him. "You're not a winner anymore, Mountain... Why not make some money from the loser?"

His shredded maw pressed by Maish's metaphorical lips like Judas betraying Christ in an Italian fresco, Rivera's sad eyes confirm that despite the betrayal, he'll honor his debt to his manager. His last shred of pride finally stripped away, the warrior's capitulation implies what he only now discovers is the worst fate of all: shame.

Rivera dispatches the first wave of Ma's goons who enter the dressing room with fists like old rubber mallets. Ma follows with more men in tow. Taking aim at Maish, her black, round lenses are like a shark's eyes as she prepares to take care of the welsher herself.

Rivera dons the wig with its wiry braids as his eyes search the room for the headdress with the "crazy" feathers. "Put me in next." Pirelli lays it out: eight fights with an option of sixteen more. After that, they'll evaluate, though Pirelli's optimistic that "Big Chief Mountain" will be a smash.

Rivera picks up the peace pipe and Maish looks up at him. "We don't have to break up now." But they already have.

"Big Chief Mountain" climbs under the ropes like a cigar store Indian come to life while the crowd leers with demented glee. In primal, spasmodic caterwauls, he thumps his chest, hoots, yowls, yips, jumps, and invokes a torrent of hellfire. His morbid war-whoops sound the void of a future the viewer will never learn. For everyone but Rivera, the story's over.

Paul Gallico wrote of Primo Carnera's wrestling years, "There is nothing left for this man but reflections upon his humiliations." But Carnera earned a lot more wrestling than he ever made in the fight game. Conversely, Rivera has joined the ghoulish pageant of Barthes's tragic masks not as a warrior but as a pratfall actor.

It didn't have to happen like this, but Maish's dishonesty has forever marred Mountain's legacy; his brain and his future are just fallout. "Tell me," Army asks in Serling's original teleplay, "Why is it so many people have to feed off one guy's misery?"

10
MONKEY ON MY BACK

Directed by André De Toth
1957, United Artists

André De Toth's ashen fever-dream *Monkey on My Back* applies the visual asperity of noir to a hard-nosed, anti-drug film that plays out like a ghoulish PSA. Merging traditional biopic with hallucinogenic horror, the discord in *Monkey*'s plot, style, and ham-fisted message defies classification. If the unmitigated noir motifs that run through most of the Austro-Hungarian director's filmography are diluted here with a gently moralizing coda, it's a rough ride nonetheless. Set against a dark and muggy Chicago teeming with para-noid hop-heads, junkyard dogs, and funereal alleys, *Monkey on My Back* eschews clichéd moralizing and leaves viewers wondering if its happy ending can last.

A borderline-exploitative portrayal of Barney Ross, who dominated the light and welterweight divisions during the thirties, *Monkey on My Back* largely passes over Ross's time in the ring, focusing instead on his post-career heroin addiction. Boxers afflicted by drug dependence are legion, counting such luminaries as Joe Louis, Sonny Liston, and Mike Tyson among their ranks. Drugs of choice may change with the years, but addiction has always occupied a shadowy corner on the sidelines of the sport. Hard drugs were another racket on which the mob had a stranglehold, but there weren't any racketeers skulking around alleys infested with burnouts looking for a piece of the action in an upcoming fight. Just dealers, and they have to make a living, too.

Born Beryl Rasovsky in 1909, Ross was affectionately dubbed "Berchik" by his Orthodox Jewish family. A variation on the diminutive "Little Bear," it was an apt moniker for his youthful ferocity. Scorning the anti-violent tenets upheld by his strict Jewish upbringing, the small, undernourished Berchik spent most of his childhood in street brawls. Weighing in at twenty pounds below the national average never deterred him. His father, a Talmudic Scholar, told his son that "the religious man prizes learning above everything else... Let the goyim be fighters."

A lot of second-generation Jews thought otherwise. In a 1991 interview with Dick Cavett, renowned trainer Ray Arcel (who honed Jim Braddock's jab—see Chapter 6) recounted an incident in which the father of the great

Jewish lightweight Benny Leonard berated his son for pursuing a career in boxing. When Benny threw down thirty-five dollars one evening, his father, who made eight dollars a week as a presser, gasped. "You made this in one night?" When his son answered in the affirmative, his father asked, "When do you fight again?"

Despite Rasovsky Senior's imprecations, little Berchik was to become one of the all-time great defensive boxers. With the levelheaded understanding that brawn rarely trumps calculated patience, he exhausted his opponents and tested the patience of newspaper writers with their affinity for knockouts, winning mainly by decisions. Throughout eighty-one bouts, Ross put just twenty-two opponents down for the count. He was never knocked out.

Between 1881 and 1924, a third of European Jews immigrated to the United States—roughly 2.5 million. By 1930, Jews comprised twenty-five percent of New York City's population. In Brooklyn alone, their number rose from 100,000 to over 800,000 between 1905 and 1930. While first-generation Jews scorned boxing (and all sports, for that matter), second-generation Jews dominated the game during the late 1920s. By the end of the Second World War, as Jews began to turn to education opportunities and business ventures, their place within the sport was largely relegated to the white-collar roles of managers and promotors. By 1950, Jewish boxers had vanished almost entirely from the ring.

Allen Bodner, author of *When Boxing Was a Jewish Sport*,

writes, "To most Jewish participants, boxing was simply a means to earn money and had no other social overtones." To the fans, however, it was a source of religious pride and validation that their representatives in the ring were looking out for them. "The knowledge that one Jew is on trial when he fights," wrote the 1920s-30s promotor Jimmy Johnson (briefly portrayed in *Cinderella Man*), "gives him an incentive for training more faithfully and taking greater pride in his work."

Ross's parents escaped the pogroms in Brest, Belarus and immigrated to Chicago during the Depression to settle in the Jewish ghetto known as the Bloody Maxwell district. As the young Beryl matured, he embraced his Judaism as a badge of honor, and woe unto the Italian, Black, or Irish punk that came looking for trouble in Maxwell when Rasofsky was around. He dropped out of school in his early teens to work brothels and craps games and even had a brief stint as a delivery boy for Al Capone, who after a short while, gave him twenty dollars and told him to shove on back to school. Instead, Ross prowled the streets with a neighborhood watch group called The Nails. On the lookout for outsiders trying to shakedown Jewish businesses, they kept the peace with baseball bats.

With no money to study or teach rabbinic text, Ross's father opened a grocery store, where he was killed in a botched robbery when his son was fifteen. In his 1957 autobiography, *No Man Stands Alone*, Ross wrote that he lost faith in god and man when the soul witness to the murder refused to testify. When a friend brought him to Kid Howard's Gym as an outlet for his impotence in the face of failed justice, Beryl Rasovsky renamed himself Barney Ross and lied about his age to compete as an amateur before turning professional three years later in 1929.

From a young age, Ross contrived various means of rebellion against his father, including an indulgence in tobacco and alcohol, a refusal to attend Shul, and even a taste for pig's knuckles. While his father's death never curbed these habits, Ross daily recited the Kaddish (the Jewish prayer of mourning) to honor the old man's memory.

As a rule, Ross's handlers refrained from making his religion a selling point or, if possible, mentioning it at all. As the country adjusted to the massive migration of English and Irish immigrants into its cities during the second half of the nineteenth century, the climate remained chilly to foreigners. Jews, conspicuous in their worship and dress, were no exception. While antisemitism was virtually non-existent in the fight game, it was a different story when it came to the fans.

Antisemitism fanned the blacklist's paranoia where, in 1957 Hollywood, *Jew* was a transparent euphemism for *Commie*. Accordingly, *Monkey on My Back* avoids Ross's religion, including the pigs' knuckles, the Kaddish recitations, and the mezuzah over his door. Yet Ross was vehement and vocal in his anti-Nazi politics and, in the interest of creating a Jewish state, even drew upon old mob connections to run guns for the region. The wise guys, with whom he was always a favorite for helping them rack in tens of thousands in bets, were happy to help facilitate the operations. With the film's absence of religion and a boxing career relegated to a sidebar, *Monkey on My Back* homes in on another of Ross's causes: one that is in no way confined to religion or boxing.

Ross took the welterweight title from Jimmy "The Jew Beater" McLarnin in 1935. (The Irish boxer had bestowed himself the moniker upon his 1932 defeat of the above-mentioned, aging Benny Leonard.) The film opens in 1938 at the cusp of Ross's title loss. Played by a husky Cameron Mitchell, Ross is the biggest celebrity Chicago has seen in years, and at a swank club on the South Side, his attentions fall to a dancer and widowed mother named Kathy Holland (Dianne Foster) who tells him she plans to attend his upcoming bout against the featherweight Henry Armstrong. It was to be Ross's final fight, and while his corner begged him to throw in the towel, he absorbed fifteen rounds of relentless punishment without hitting the canvas.

Retiring at twenty-nine, Ross had already added a gambling habit to his vices that bordered on degeneracy, landing him in perpetual debt to a bookmaker the film dubs Big Ralph (played by a sleepy-eyed Larry Kelly). Handing over his entire purse from the Armstrong fight to his bookies for monies owed, he was also forced to give them a twenty-five percent share of The Barney Ross Cocktail Lounge, a club the fighter had opened to *eliminate* his debt.

In December of 1941, Ross enlisted as a marine after the attack on Pearl Harbor. He requested combat, and the film depicts him composing swooning letters to Kathy from his training camp. Call it young love, limerence, or the heart growing fonder with absence, but not until they are married does the film's paranoid desperation begin to edge and slice across the screen from any and every corner.

Ross was sent to the front lines on the South Pacific, where he suffered severe depressive episodes that served as fodder for his imminent addiction. Haunted battle scenes shot through gray and black leaves reveal the glinting enemy eyes of Japanese soldiers hiding in the trees. On his fifth and final tour of duty, Ross singlehandedly defended his troops for thirteen hours in a foxhole during the Battle of Guadalcanal. Administered morphine for chronic pain, he pleads with the ship's doctor on the return home to keep it coming but is firmly rebuked. "You think it can give you a lift," the doctor tells him. It isn't a question. "All it can do is give you a lift straight up to hell." But Ross can't think that far ahead. Journalist Thomas de Quincy described his first taste of Laudanum twelve decades prior in his tell-all *Confessions of an English Opium Eater* as "a panacea... for all human woes: here was the secret of happiness." And for a while, it was. Soon enough, Ross didn't just want more; he needed it.

Awarded the Silver Star for his heroism, Ross told the Marines to "give it to my company, this is no one-man show." He was a war hero, but he was also a junkie. Thirty pounds lighter and with hair that had turned white almost overnight, he wangled morphine from doctors who initially couldn't bring themselves to deny a decorated veteran. But it was only so long before the tap ran dry. Forced to the streets to maintain what had become a $500-a-day habit, Ross mastered boiling over-the-counter paregoric medicine to expertly shoot up on his own. As in other early addiction films, including *The Lost Weekend* (1945, in which booze is the poison of choice), *The Man with the Golden Arm* (1955, heroin), and *A Hatful of Rain* (1957, opium), *Monkey on My Back* emphasizes the addict's dissemblance of their habit from loved ones and the crippling guilt that follows.

With frantic attempts to hide his dope use and ever-mounting debt, Mitchell's Ross elicits the viewer's sympathy, but in lying to Kathy, he's digging his marital grave. Excursions to his dealer-cum-bookie Rico (a bored, nasally Paul Richards) grow increasingly frequent as his tolerance climbs. He trades his diamond-encrusted watch for a fix. He gets fired from his office job. And Kathy's beginning to wonder who this Rico guy is that keeps coming around.

$27,000 in the hole, Ross asks Rico to extend a little credit, but Rico's not a bank. Besides, the dealer's got his own worries. He could wind up in prison, explaining that with each transaction, "I'm risking ten years of my life... I wanna get paid for it." He suggests Ross knock over a liquor store to come up with the cash, but Ross never recovered from his father's shooting, and robbery is out of the question. But

Rico's impatient. He even considers sending a few guys over to snap Ross's wrists. "It'd be so hard to give yourself a shot with two broken flippers."

Kathy discovers her husband rummaging through drawers and scrounging for any bit of loose change he can get his hands on. She assumes he's looking for money to pay off gambling debts and points to a fifty cent-piece under the counter that he's overlooked. She also gives him the twelve dollars from her purse. Then she gives him her wedding ring and a divorce.

With a fistful of loose bills, Ross steals into a cheerless lot where a well-dressed man with a white pocket square materializes like a genie out of the fog and studies his eyes. His scrutiny is well-practiced. "You ain't got a monkey on your back, you got a gorilla."

Ross makes off with needle and product into the most dismal alley in Chicago. Slum dogs whine and stick their snouts in clanging garbage cans as the discordant screech of cats bounces around oppressive brick walls. The spoon is bent and Ross clamps his teeth on the tie-off. Under the heat of the flame, the smack rises with buoyant effervescence. Then the needle's plunge, the transfusion of de Quincey's sweet "panacea for all human woes."

Kathy agrees to remarry if her husband dries out at the Federal Narcotics Farm in Lexington, Kentucky. Established in 1935, the hospital, which became a prison in 1974, counts Chet Baker, Sammy Davis Jr., and William S.

Burroughs among its former residents. Ross arrives at the clinic with eyes spinning like wheels and the jerking legs of Saint Vitus, terrorized by hallucinations of the ceiling crashing in. While Ross wrote that it was the specter of his father that haunted him during detox, De Toth envisions flashbacks to the war and apparitions of Kathy. "The first week is always the hardest," the doc tells him.

As Ross's health improves, the cravings abate. But nothing comes for free. "The hell of withdrawal was the easiest because I was fightin' something," his voiceover laments. "I had somethin' to lick. But now the craving's gone, and all that's left is fear." The exact nature of Ross's fear is never wholly defined, and the soliloquy is cut short as the strings swell and he's released into Kathy's waiting arms.

Hollywood's interest in the story lay with the prize-fighter as soldier-turned-hophead. But Ross wanted a film version of *No Man Stands Alone* that would help make strides toward the de-stigmatization of drug abuse, especially among doctors and other addicts. Despite remonstrations from friends over writing the book in the first place, Ross was never ashamed or embarrassed. Besides, advancing the case for narcotic addiction as a medical illness rather than a criminal-justice problem would have rung hollow had he not openly discussed his own former sweet tooth.

Released the same year as the book, Barney and Kathy were caught off-guard by the film's marquee, where a wild-eyed Mitchell, a needle sticking from his arm, hovers over the tagline: *"The Barney Ross Story! Junkie! It means DOPE-FIEND! The HOTTEST HELL ON EARTH! SHOCK by SHOCK... It Jabs Like a Hopped-Up Needle!"*

Ross dismissed the film as "rubbish" and sued the producers for $5 million. Although the lawsuit was ostensibly for defamation of character, Ross's main concern was that the film's marketing portrayed his addiction as ongoing, which he claimed, "defeats the whole purpose of the picture." In 1960, he settled out of court for ten thousand dollars (one percent of his asking price) and began to lecture publicly on addiction and antisemitism. The text that fills the final frame as Barney and Kathy emerge arm-in-arm from the Farm tritely reads, *"The Beginning,"* implying that the real work is yet to come. It's cloying, but it speaks to De Toth's depiction of the addict in a hopeful and unabashed light in marked contrast to the studio's publicity department.

While newspapers and radio announcements revealed Ross as a junkie in the months leading to the film's release, the ex-fighter was busy touring the country, delivering gratis lectures at schools, recreation centers, and prisons. He used his own money (far more than he could afford) to devote the rest of his brief life to spreading his message of hope in conjunction with his vocal politics.

Ross might have been "clean" in the parlance of 1957, but that doesn't mean he was drug-free. A binge drinker and chain-smoker to the end, the vices he'd taken up in his teenage years to provoke his father had become lifelong habits that proved as deadly as the gorilla he'd managed to shake.

Vodka was his poison of choice on nights before training so as not to show up stinking of booze in the morning.

Diagnosed with throat cancer in his fifties, Ross decided that it no longer mattered what he did to his body. Much like Bogart during the filming of *The Harder They Fall*, the fighter seemed resigned to an early death—both men died at fifty-seven. With headlong surrender to fate, Ross continued to drink heavily while chain-smoking from birdsong to bedtime. With cancer's rapid advancement, a "celebratory send-off" was held in his honor in 1967. In truth, it was a means of assuring Kathy's security after her husband passed, which he did the same year.

Milton Gross of the *New York Post* wrote, "He was born Beryl Rasovski, but he should have been named Job." Ross may have suffered excruciations on a biblical level, but his real demons came from within. His achievements in combat and recovery demonstrate the intrepid fortitude that kept him on his feet throughout his eighty-one fights, especially his final bout with Henry Armstrong. As his legs grew rubbery that night, it was the moment that—in Ross's estimation—he became "old." The nineteen years that followed are a testament that his life's work was just beginning.

11
BODY AND SOUL

Directed by Robert Rossen
United Artists, 1947

A heavy bag swings pendulously, its shadow swaying above the canvas of an outdoor ring in the dead of night. Behind it, a house with an open window emerges through a tangle of gnarled oak branches like black claws. Inside, Charlie Davis (John Garfield) wakes in terror with a chin that bears the white streak of an old wound. He'd be able to tell you where he got it—his scars crisscross the country. His forehead sports a fresh, open gash. He cries out the name "Ben" and rushes to his car.

Three in the morning and the action's just picking up. The coat-check girl at the nightclub calls Charlie "Champ" as couples fill the dance floor while Alice (the sultry Hazel Brooks) fairly fellates the microphone. Charlie's pretty tight, and Alice takes a break to tell him he should be resting for tomorrow's fight with Marlowe. Besides, his manager and trainer have been looking all over for him.

The next day, Charlie's first on the scale for the weigh-in. Right on the nose. "Whiskey fat," the Marlowe kid cracks, "Thirty-five-year-old fat." He's asking for it, and deserves the slap Charlie gives him when he steps off the scale. But as the manager said, the boxing business is "all addition and subtraction... the rest is conversation." Marlowe's just building hype.

At the approach of the crooked fight, moral torments run off the rails and leave Charlie with few choices: swallow his pride and make a fortune or endanger his career and physical well-being by refusing. These agonies of ambivalence separate *Body and Soul* from the abundance of morality parables that generally culminate in unequivocal triumph or tragedy. There are no blacks or whites here—just endless swaths of gray.

The film's emphatic motif—that opportunity comes with the sacrifice of principles—resonated with the film's cast and crew, many of whom came to Hollywood on the heels of left-leaning, communist-affiliated theaters in New York on the cusp of Hollywood's darkest chapter under McCarthyism. The timing of the film's release, coinciding as it did with an abundance of newspaper accounts of escalating Senate probes into racketeering in the boxing world and the nascent Hollywood blacklist, could not have been more auspicious.

It was 1938 when Martin Dies Jr. of the United States House of Representatives and Supreme Court Justice Samuel Dickstein formed the House Un-American Activities Committee to target and weed out communist infiltrators and sympathizers, particularly those with governmental ties. In 1944, Congressman J. Parnell Thomas of New Jersey took the helm and, with priggish gravitas, set HUAC's sights on Hollywood to oust any suspected reds hiding in plain sight on studio lots.

"Every great campaign in American history," wrote journalist H.L. Mencken, "however decorously it started with a statement of principles, has always ended with a pursuit of hobgoblins." With J. Edgar Hoover's blessing, Thomas announced that this was no "quickie investigation." Hollywood turned into a hornet's nest of paranoia and recriminations practically overnight as Thomas advanced his crusade. Some, like Humphrey Bogart, rolled their eyes and spoke their minds. Others, like Kirk Douglas, took advantage with revisionist accounts. But John Garfield, an East-coast Jew with a background in communist theater, stood at the epicenter of the blacklist as one of HUAC's most vehement detractors and hounded victims.

Fomented amid the so-called second Red Scare under Senator Joseph McCarthy, the House Un-American Activities Committee started to subpoena film industry members in

October of 1947. Released the following month, *Body and Soul's* credits read as a virtual who's who of suspected sympathizers.

New York's Group Theater (aka the Group) was considered an axis of mid-century communism. Governmental investigations painted such theaters as free-love orgies crawling with anarchist agitators "shot through with the philosophy of communism." They weren't far off. While they never could produce any hard evidence, their soon-to-be-scapegoat arrived in the form of a young actor with the birth name Jacob Julius Garfinkle.

Garfield absorbed the Group's philosophical approach developed by the Russian actor and stage director Constantin Stanislavski—whose book *An Actor's Work* was translated into English in 1935—as if by osmosis. "The System," or "the Method," rejected the rote, empty recitations inherent to early twentieth-century theater's stiff pomp by turning its focus to actors' complete embodiment of their roles through delivery, reaction, and the accessing of emotion. "One of the most important creative principles," wrote Stanislavski, "is that an actor's tasks must always be able to coax his feelings, will and intelligence, so that they become part of him." In the 1980 film *My Dinner with Andre*, playwright André Gregory specifies the questions the actor should constantly ask themselves when applying Stanislavski's Method: "Who am I? Why am I here? Where do I come from, and where am I going?"

When Garfield biographer Larry Swindell described the actor's performances as "un-actorly," it was not a criticism: "He didn't recite dialogue," Swindell writes, "he attacked it until it lost the quality of talk and took on the nature of speech." Cementing his place as the prototypical ur-method actor, Garfield blazed a trail for disciples including Marlon Brando, Robert De Niro, and others to follow.

In 1946, Garfield's affiliation with the socialist-leaning Warner Bros. ended. Eight years prior, the decidedly un-antisemitic Jack Warner had taken on the young Jacob and given him his new name. But even the most liberal studios came to regard Garfield with unease. The actor started his own production company, The Enterprise Studios, to obviate negotiations with studios that did not permit stage work (Garfield's original passion) to actors under contract. More importantly, it gave Garfield greater control over his projects that made him a free agent in Hollywood.

Charlie is a thirty-five-year-old fighter unable to escape the clutches of the poker-faced racketeer Roberts (played with imperious composure by a soon-to-be-blacklisted Lloyd Gough). With a face that conveyed the cocksure ambition of youth or the weariness of a man grown old before his time, Garfield could speak volumes with little more than the twitch of an eyebrow or a pulse of the jaw. In his introduction to *Body and Soul* screenwriter Abraham Polonski's 1948 film *Force of Evil*, Martin Scorsese describes the actor's face as "a landscape of moral conflict." It was a conflict that extended far beyond Garfield's cinematic roles.

Despite (or because of) the inherent nihilism of film

noir, its themes are frequently anti-capitalist. To filmmakers, the free market was the bailiwick of racketeers,
extortionists, and cheats. But when it came to politics, the
message that social justice brings moral redemption didn't
always jibe with HUAC's tenets where free enterprise, even
when carried out by the same hoods the blacklist sought to
punish, could be read as tacit approbation of communism.

Jack Warner was among the first to be called upon
to divulge names which, to his immediate remorse, he
did. When *Body and Soul*'s would-be hobgoblins Garfield,
Polonski, director Robert Rossen, cinematographer James
Wong-Howe, and producer Bob Roberts were subsequently
called to testify, their refusal to name names precipitated
their undoing. In 1960, Rossen spilled no less than fifty-seven names. Like Dalton Trumbo following his work on
Spartacus, Polonski kept under the radar by writing under
pseudonyms while Roberts fled to England.

Meanwhile, the government continued to badger
Garfield, as did the famously anti-communist tabloid
gadfly Victor Riesel, who repeatedly bad-mouthed the
actor in damning exposés. Despite a half-assed attempt at
back-peddling in a piece for *Look* magazine titled "I Was
a Sucker for a Left Hook" (written at the height of his
persecution), Garfield remained tight-lipped as regarded
his "fellow travelers," or non-formal party members. As to
himself, he denied his inquisitors outright: "My life is an
open book.... I am no red... I am a Democrat by politics, a

liberal by inclination, and a loyal citizen of this country by every act of my life."

By the early fifties, the Committee's aggressive inquiries reached a pitch. Although Garfield never made the Hollywood Ten, accusations of communist sympathies saw HUAC label him "a very dangerous citizen," exacerbating his already-weak heart. Although Garfield surrendered to his impending death with similar tobacco-fueled, alcoholic abandon as Bogart or Barney Ross, the blacklist is widely cited as his final mortal straw. In May of 1952, at the age of thirty-nine, he was dead. In a 2017 *New York Times* op-ed, his daughter Julie wrote that his family "were all convinced that it was the witch hunt of the House Committee that had killed him." Polonski wrote that Garfield had "defended his street boy honor, and they killed him for it."

Polonski penned *Body and Soul* after Garfield approached him with an idea for a film about a Jewish fighter along the lines of Barney Ross. "I want to make pictures," said Garfield, "with a point-zing, spit, fire," and Ross fit the bill as someone to whom Garfield, a Jewish gang member in his youth, could relate.

As noted, Ross's Judaism is never touched on in *Monkey on My Back*, and Garfield and Polonski were subtle in their insertion of religion into *Body and Soul*, which is conveyed almost entirely through a Jewish delivery boy's toast to the champ. "Over in Europe," he trumpets, "the Nazis are killing people like us just because of our religion. Over here, Charlie Davis is Champion."

It was the first instance in which the actor's Russian-Jewish heritage was made public on screen. (Two days after *Body and Soul*'s release, Elia Kazan's *Gentleman's Agreement* hit theaters, where Garfield starred as the persecuted Jewish soldier Dave Goldman.) Just as Hollywood turned a tacit blind eye to Jewish cash cows like Edward G. Robinson, nor did they advertise it. While antisemitism could be suspended among the public when it came to the cinema, De Toth's exclusion of the fighter's religion in *Monkey on My Back*, made ten years after *Body and Soul*, nevertheless spoke volumes.

After winning a local amateur bout, Charlie Davis is bewitched by the refined and self-assured Peg (Lilly Palmer). Who is this West Side bohemian with an apartment full of canvases and sketch pads? And where did she pick up that patrician inflection and big words like "symmetry?" As she sketches the restless fighter, she asks if he plans to turn professional. His reply is vague, ambivalent, and open-ended: "I just want to be a success." Peg amends his words. "You want everyone to *think* you're a success." Isn't that the same thing?

The finished portrait reveals a boyish, gloved boxer from whose head emerges a single horn like a displaced lock of hair. Dressed in boxing trunks, the rest of the body appears covered in fur with soft, vertical graphite hatching. Maybe it's just a hasty shading job, but that doesn't explain the cloven hoofs that replace Charlie's boxing shoes.

Charlie's mother (the avowed communist actor Anne

Revere) expresses indignant disgust at her son fighting other men: "knocking their teeth in, smashing their noses, breaking their heads in." As was the case with countless Jews as discussed in the previous chapter, Charlie's mother is reluctant to see her son take up a game antithetical to first-generation Jewish non-violent ideals. (Notably, Garfield's father, a presser in their Lower East Side tenement neighborhood, steered his son away from organized religion with atheistic, righteous posturing.)

Charlie's father quietly slips him a tenner for equipment. He knows a good fight will bring in a lot more money than the Sugar Daddies and Pixie Stix they sell at the family candy store. When the next-door speakeasy is bombed in a gang attack, Davis Sr. is killed in the fallout in a direct reference to the shooting of Ross's father.

Prizefighting's a dirty business, but it doesn't stop the dollar signs that flash in Charlie's eyes like numbers on a cash register. In turning pro, his apostasy causes his mother to hiss, "I'd rather you shoot yourself," to which Charlie responds, "You need money to buy a gun."

Garfield knew his way around a ring from his early pursuit of prizefighting. It was short-lived, and after a particularly well-placed blow to the face, he opted to stay down in his last bout. His training is nevertheless evident, saving cinematographer James Wong-Howe the trouble of drawing chalk marks on the canvas to guide the actor during his fight scenes.

Charlie and his trainer Shorty (the jaunty, squeaky Joseph Pevney) visit a sordid pool room seeking out a manager named Quinn (William Conrad) who, jaded from a lifetime of managing fighters, wears his apathy on his sleeve. Good boys come and go, bad men keep business moving, and there's no room for half-assed hopefuls. Sinking balls and sermonizing on the countless fighters he's managed, watched, discarded, and ignored, Quinn tells the boys that "one out of a hundred goes professional, one out of a thousand is worth watching, and one out of a million is worth coffee and donuts." Pretty shabby odds.

When Charlie puts his fists to use in a barroom brawl, Quinn brings him on board. Charlie and Peg fall in love in a swooning, smoochy montage featuring a string of Charlie's knockouts interspersed with Peg's tender, trembling lip. As fight posters swirl and flap like flat birds in the wind, a bill pins itself to a brick wall to reveal Charlie's rise: nineteen kayos in twenty-one fights. But he's getting antsy. "We've been fighting for peanuts, and we been eating them too," he complains to Shorty. Maybe it's time to let Roberts call the shots. The gangster knows the game, and a bigger pie—even when cut unevenly—means "more to eat for everyone."

Charlie's slated for a championship bout with a waning fighter named Ben, whose head suffered an ugly collision with a corner post in the ring during his last fight. Already spoken of in the past tense since the doctor detected a brain clot following his previous bout, Ben must not fight again.

Roberts's philosophy is more direct: "It wouldn't be business if debts didn't get paid," he tells Quinn, who's into him for $40,000. (Such was the capitalism HUAC so ardently defended.) Ben steals to the manager's aide and tells Roberts he'll take the fight. In turn, Roberts assures them that Charlie will take it easy and let it go the distance. However, as Roberts and Quinn stay behind, Roberts advises the manager to keep mum. If he's going to finance the fight—and no title bout goes down unless he has a hand in it—Roberts wants a knockout. Because *that's* good business.

Besides Garfield, the film's foremost presence is the gentle pathos of professional welterweight and civil rights activist Canada Lee as Ben. Another HUAC target during the forties, the fighter-turned-actor was blacklisted in 1952 but died before he could testify. He was forty-five, and never divulged a single name. Two years after *Body and Soul*, Robert Wise wanted to cast Lee in the role of Stoker in *The Set-up* (recall Pansy, the fighter of the poem on which the film is based, and Howard Hughes's refusal to cast a Black actor). When casting *Body and Soul*, a Warner Bros. executive asked Garfield, "Why don't you just avoid any trouble and make the champion white?" The actor's reply was laconic. "Fuck you."

Charlie's perception of success has altered since last he spoke to Peg. Where once it was a vague word filled with promise, now it's a concrete yardstick measured in hard cash—fifty percent under Roberts. To further rattle his moral bearings, Charlie gets cozy with the willing, vampy Alice from the nightclub of the film's opening. She may be Quinn's girl, but these days, she's been hanging around Charlie's camp, cradling, cuddling, and mounting the heavy bag.

Despite playing the sex-kitten stunt to the hilt, Brooks's allure withers under the plain-spoken, refined charisma of Lilly Palmer's Peg. Alice doesn't see any conflict of morals in Charlie's actions. Money never pronounces judgments. Earned or stolen, it's worth about the same, all of which is to say that Charlie may as well enjoy the ride.

Ben's lost the fight before he answers the first bell. Unaware of his opponent's fragility, Charlie pummels at his head throughout several rounds before bullying Ben down for the final count, where he remains out cold for hours. When Charlie learns of the brain clot, he confronts Roberts with cocksure aggression. Wholly composed, the gangster advises Charlie to be happy. After all, he won. That's money in the bank. As for Ben, it's with a cold indifference that Roberts reminds Charlie, "Everybody dies." The new Middleweight Champion, Charlie is learning that money (or is that success?) can make even the cruelest aphorism palatable.

When Roberts passes Ben in the locker room, he drops a wad of cash at his feet by way of disingenuous apology for allowing him to get clobbered. Ben's headaches are getting worse. He lets Roberts's "blood money" lay on the floor. He's not taking handouts, but Charlie grabs the folded bills and holds them like an old friend. "It's not like people," he tells Ben. "It's got no memory. It doesn't *think*." It's a familiar sentiment that Garfield would echo a year later in Abraham Polonski's *Force of Evil*: "Money's got no *moral* opinions." It also recalls Eddie's plea to the church in *The Harder They Fall*: "Money's not evil in and of itself. It's the way it's used that's the determining factor."

Charlie's dubious rationale prompts Ben to ask if he sold the fight. In a stunning POV, Ben's gentle, sad eyes lock with Charlie's. Under Ben's stare, the fourth wall collapses to entangle the viewer in his ruination. It is one of cinema's more challenging moments in its implication of the viewer in a lie about which Charlie knew nothing.

Charlie's moral equivocating betrays his willful refusal to acknowledge the correlation between Ben's fate and his expanding connection to the Syndicate. He may have been ignorant of Ben's affliction, but his affiliation with Roberts makes for de facto complicity. With his gift for assuaging strained superegos, Roberts situates Charlie in a luxury suite. That's living. Back at Charlie's camp, Ben dies of a stroke brought on by his blood clot.

Charlie could make himself a pile betting on a 2-1 underdog like that cocky young up-and-comer Jack Marlowe (played by professional welterweight Artie Dorrell). But as always, there's a hitch: this time, Charlie's the one who's taking a swim. He's been with Roberts for over a year, blissfully ignorant of any machinations cooked up to advance his career. But one thing's certain: Charlie's never taken a dive, and he's not planning to start now. But that stack of bills Roberts shows him, in all its lack of moral judgment, looks pretty tempting.

Charlie insists he can put Marlowe down in the second, but it's too late. The bet's are in, and Roberts wants a dive. But for a pal like Charlie, maybe there's a compromise. What if Charlie were to carry the fight and lose by decision? It sounds good in theory, though recalling the bout with Ben, there's an uneasy sense of deja-vous and double-crossing. Still, considering the sixty thousand he stands to make, it seems his mind is already made up.

Rossen leaps from the film's extended flashback and back to the house, still painted in a rictus of shadow, where Charlie's form is again revealed through the window. His mouth moves. He tries to speak before rising in terror and remorse.

Underslept but sizzling like a firecracker ready to pop, Charlie laces up in the dressing room. Enter Roberts to go over things one last time. Nothing rough: carry the fight, go the distance, lose by decision, and everyone's richer. He again offers his guiding tenet with cool consolation: "Everybody dies, Charlie... even you." But there's a new ring to Roberts's well-worn platitude that sounds like a threat, and by now, Charlie's fully complicit in the corruption. There are no more excuses, and tonight's fight could require much more degradation than he's prepared to take on. "The fates close inexorably in," wrote Bosley Crowler in his *New York Times* review, "until the wraps are ripped from his allusions and [Charlie] finds himself owned, body and soul."

Filmed in Garfield's Enterprise Studios, ground zero of communist sympathizers and Hollywood Bolsheviks, the Marlowe bout is a textbook lesson in the meticulous collaboration of director, cinematographer, editor, actors, choreographers, and trainers. Despite the frenzy of flurries and tangle of flesh, the immediacy of Wong Howe's lens never strays from Garfield's face for long. With grass-roots ingenuity, the cinematographer was pushed along the perimeters of the ring on roller skates to follow the fighters and accentuate the hysteria. Combined with editors Francis Lyon and Robert Parrish's relentless cuts, a spinning slug-fest unfolds with choreography that remains some of the best in the genre.

Body and Soul cleaned up at the Oscars. Despite the film's cast, crew, and anti-capitalist posturing, the Academy didn't allow HUAC much wiggle-room for their politics regarding nominees, including Polonski's screenplay and Garfield as Best Actor in a Leading Role. However, it was Lyon and Parrish, both clear of HUAC scrutiny, who took home the award for Best Film Editing. (Perhaps there was a slight degree of trepidation among Academy members after all.)

Garfield's "landscape of moral conflict" grows bloodier as Marlowe comes on hard. It's evident to Charlie that his opponent's not here for a fifteen-round decision, and it doesn't take him long to figure out the real set-up here.

Roberts has double-crossed him again, and while Charlie might be able to drop the kid early, he can't carry him the complete fifteen rounds. Roberts knows this all too well.

"The audience loves a killing," the gangster once told Charlie. Well, if Charlie's the patsy, the least he can do is give the crowd their money's worth and go out with a bang—even if the bang comes from the pistol tucked inside Roberts's jacket. The old, dubious axiom that revenge is the best motivator prompts Charlie to put Marlowe down in the twelfth. Held against playing chump for the mob, maybe that $60k has a "moral opinion" after all.

Roberts's sage words on being "business-like [because] businessmen keep their agreements" was the American way, and HUAC interpreted Charlie's rejection of the fix as an indictment of Robert's capitalist principles despite their blatant corruption. Maybe it was the way the camera rested on those bills whipping in the air, flapping around as if trapped in a giant bingo blower. Maybe it was the spread of diamonds the lens lovingly caressed in the same montage. Or perhaps it was the envelope of cash Roberts slipped Charlie in that empty office with the bare lightbulb—capitalism at its best.

Emerging from the fight in his robe, Charlie's nihilistic gamble has restored his honor, but other matters are at hand. Roberts just lost a lot of money, and men have come to a lot of grief over lesser things. Maybe this isn't over yet, but as Charlie stares down the racketeer, his stockpile of fear is depleted.

Charlie's capitulation to death's inevitability declaws Roberts of his favorite catchphrase. Money (or is that "success?") has finally lost out to pride. Will Roberts get his revenge? Maybe. Maybe next week. Maybe tonight or maybe not at all. Where's the fun is in offing a fellow who's not afraid to die? But Roberts needn't worry. Charlie will die. Someday. Everyone does.

12
KID MONK BARONI

Directed by Harold D. Schuster
Realart Pictures, Inc., 1952

The first reel of Harold D. Schuster's lighthearted, immensely watchable *Kid Monk Baroni* dispels any concerns that its fighter might meet with a bad end. Monk (Leonard Nimoy) is too sensitive. Although his short fuse wields all the menace of a kid playing hooky, he'll slug anyone who looks at him sideways when it blows. And a lot of people do. Despite his cultivated air of intimidation, Monk's contempt for humanity stems from a facial deformity that's convinced him that life's just god's idea of a spiteful joke.

"Monk" Baroni serves as an unofficial leader to a scrappy posse known, albeit briefly, as *The Billy Goat Gang*. Even the film's primary cast members couldn't say what happened to this gaggle of benign scamps: Were they simply a one-off for the film, or—as the credits suggest—being groomed to bring a *Dead-End Kids* levity to further productions? The most likely scenario is the hasty filming under the tight fist of producer Jack Broder, who scrapped the gang halfway through the shoot to move things along. Such vanishing acts perfectly encapsulate the B movie master's fast, cheap, sometimes nonsensical approach to saving money. Meanwhile, screenwriter Aben Kandel (author of the 1936 novel *City for Conquest*, on which the 1940 James Cagney boxing film was based) patiently cut, pasted, and deleted from his script in accordance with the producer's whims.

Busting up a tenement stairway for firewood, the Goats encounter the kindly Father Callahan (Richard Roper), who chides them gently for destroying what doesn't belong to them. But if they're cold, they can stay in the church basement. It's warm there. There's even a boxing setup, which Monk studies dubiously. As he blathers about his street cred, Monk is silenced when the Father suggests they lace up the gloves and test his grandstanding first-hand. Warning him that he won't hold back, even on a guy in a collar, Monk's put on the floor in short order. Father Callahan removes the gloves and offers a makeshift Christian aphorism: "Sometimes, in anger, one forgets the Lord, but never the knack of throwing a left jab."

As discussed in the previous two chapters, Barney Ross, Benny Leonard, or the fictional Charlie Davis's rejection of their non-violent Jewish upbringings speak to a decade when impoverished, second-generation Jews dominated the ring. But the first domestic practitioners of the sport under the Queensberry rules were comprised of devout British and Irish Catholics, whose bare-knuckle predecessors flouted their working-class crudity and thumbed their noses at Victorian theological stringency.

In her essay *Why boxing was the most Catholic sport for almost 100 years,* Amy Koehlinger correlates physical suffering with spiritual redemption. Both are intrinsic to Catholicism, and boxing is its archetypal expression. Noting turn-of-the-century Catholic periodicals that featured boxing columns, the incorporation of boxing lessons into parish school curricula, and priests who acted as trainers, she writes that "a boxing match enacted the central spiritual mysteries of the faith—the *imitatio Christi* [imitation of Christ] personified in a boxer's willingness to endure suffering for a greater cause."

Father Barry almost takes a bullet for Brando's Terry Malloy before convincing him to take the non-violent path of revenge in Elia Kazan's *On the Waterfront* (1954). The titular pugilistic priest of *The Leather Saint* (1955) hides his profession and his scars from the church to raise money for a children's hospital, and the family priest's interest in the Irish brothers' scraps in *Gentleman Jim* is notably prurient. Rosalind Ross's 1922 *Father Stu* saw Mark Wahlberg portray a onetime-boxer-turned-priest, and even Father Miller takes his Catholic guilt out on the heavy bag in 1973's *The Exorcist.* While the chances of a Rabbi lacing up the gloves are slim, it's not hard to find a priest willing to go a few rounds, especially when recalling Roland Barthes's likening of wrestlers' "excessive portrayal of Suffering" to "a primitive Pieta."

The 1930s boxer Max Schmeling writes of his priest's account of St. Bernardine of Sienna, who, in 1201, encouraged boxing matches as an alternative to the knife fights that plagued the walled city. This less deadly alternative might have poised Bernardine as boxing's patron saint. Alas, the honor had already been claimed by the fourth-century bishop Saint Nicholas, whose mission was the abolishment of fistic combat altogether. Stories of religious guidance in boxing are without end and replete with famous examples. In the 1930s, the young ne'er do well Rocky Graziano (the basis for the 1956 film *Somebody Up There Likes Me*) left the Coxsackie Reform School to hone his skills in a Catholic protectory before turning pro. In the 1940s, the sixteen-year-old delinquent Jake LaMotta was introduced to boxing by Father Joseph, another priest at Coxsackie. The Roman Catholic and Heavyweight Champion Floyd Patterson volunteered at his parish and dispensed holy Communion at a local nursing home, where he described himself as "the eucharistic minister with the biggest hands." His dethroner, the functionally illiterate Sonny Liston, traveled to Denver in 1962 to undergo Father Edward P. Murphy's educational rehabilitation program. A Jesuit, Murphy preferred the word "reorientation" to "rehabilitation" and proved instrumental in lifting Liston's suspension from the ring. Muhammad Ali, who also began his training in a church basement, sparked fear and furor among White Christian America when he adopted the Muslim faith in 1964. In 1977, his hard-hitting opponent George Foreman turned born-again. Although Mike Tyson converted to Islam in prison, his Pascal's wager covers all bases: "I'm a Muslim... I got a rabbi. I got a priest. I got a reverend... I got 'em all."

Whatever Nimoy's doing in the ring, it isn't boxing, despite a two-week crash-course under Mushy Callahan (who, as noted above, doubled for Errol Flynn in *Gentleman Jim* and trained Kirk Douglas for *Champion*). Under Broder's prohibitive time constraints and nonexistent interest in the sport, Nimoy failed to mimic the game's most fundamental techniques. It was the best thing to have happened to the film, and Monk's illegal, primitive violence carries a cathartic seduction in its primeval brutality.

Monk hones that left jab, all the while wearing his shame like a literal mask. At nineteen, he approaches the mirror with trepidation and loathing. Father Callahan's consolation—"If you call yourself ugly because some ignorant man called you ugly, you're just as guilty as he is"—fails to convince. The prosthetics also affected Nimoy: "Instinctively, my emotions began to respond to my new appearance. I could begin to identify with the internal life of this face—the insecurities, the retiring shyness, the bursts of anger, the paranoia."

Prosthetics may turn Nimoy's nose into a bumpy,

winding slope courtesy of make-up artist Gus Norin (who made a pulpy wreck of Kirk Douglas in *Champion*), but the rage and despair that burn in his eyes are his own. The best Father Callahan can do now is to remind Baroni that "a human being can protect himself without killing his opponent." It's a start. Under the Father's tutelage, Monk's tough moves from street fighter to something not much more skilled. But he also joins the church choir and purchases 78s of fugues and hymns to blast Baroque cantatas while he trains.

In a weaponless ambush, Monk learns that once you're a Goat you're a Goat all the way. In his choirboy robes, the inner savage takes over to permanently cancel his membership with his brand-new jab. When he accidentally strikes Father Callahan, he flees. At least there's still the fight game: "With this face and these fists, what else can I do?"

The boos that Monk endures upon stepping into the ring empower him like cheers, spurring old insecurities and fomenting a hatred he hones like a dagger to his advantage. A string of six more first-round knockouts follows his debut bout, but the fighter's growing impatient with the penny-ante purses in the form of cheap watches. (The term "prizefight" derives from these long-obsolete "pawnshop fights," so named for the watches and medals given to small-time amateurs in lieu of cash.)

Monk is accompanied by his ersatz manager, another reformed ex-Goat, played by Jack Larson, who went on to star as Jimmy Olsen in the 1950s television show *The*

Adventures of Superman. Together, they seek out the jaded, tired manager Hellman, played by Bruce Cabot, who saved Fay Wray in 1933's *King Kong.* (With its trio of *King Kong, Star Trek,* and *Superman* leads, the cast jointly identified *Baroni* as "the ultimate sci-fi film.") In a narrative that betrays his lazy apathy, Hellman explains that the Syndicate pays him to scout new talent despite his contempt for the sport and the "punch-drunk gargoyles" he manages. Recalling Eddie's discourse on managers in *The Harder They Fall,* where fifteen bucks "entitles you to ruin a kid's life, maybe end it." Hellman's commodious office and Savile Row suits are tangible proof of fifteen dollars well-spent.

Hellman studies Monk's face using primordial adjectives like "atavistic" and "prehistoric." Monk is a derivative of "monkey," and the name suits him perfectly. ("Fight like a man, not like an ape" is among the Father's instructions.) An inexplicable penchant for the simian runs through an impressive number of Broder's films, with titles that include *Bride of the Gorilla* (1951), *Bela Lugosi Meets a Brooklyn Gorilla* (1952), and *Women of the Prehistoric Planet* (1966). So when and where was the word "monk" used as slang for "monkey?" Aside from its common usage to denote male members of pious orders; uneven inking that results in dark areas on a print; and a "Floridian slang for vagina," searches come up dry.

Given Broder's penchant for cutting scripts the way he cut down on time and budget, it's not unlikely that he discarded reams of Kandel's script. In keeping with the producer's affinity for the prehistoric, Kandel followed up *Baroni* with schlock like *I Was a Teenage Werewolf* (1957), *Black Zoo* (1963, complete with a deified gorilla), and *Trog*. Short for "troglodyte," the 1970 film is remembered solely for Joan Crawford's final performance.

Like the producer and screenwriter, the Syndicate wants someone in the ring who's "primitive... an animal." Handing Monk twenty dollars for expenses, Hellman sends him out to buy gloves and shoes and schedules a four-round preliminary. Although still an amateur, expository headlines indicate that Monk's already piqued the public's attention.

Browsing Gregorian chants at the record store, Monk runs into Father Callahan and is again touched by his Christian forgiveness. But the fighter's heavy brow darkens when he's invited to an upcoming dance at the church, no doubt recalling Hellman's words: "In this business, you got no friends." But the church isn't the racket to which Hellman was referring, and so Monk attends, where he meets the young Emily Brooks (Allene Roberts). Emily might be unfazed by his appearance, but that doesn't make it any easier for Monk. As long as his "curse" remains in plain view, so will his spite, with resentment that expands and contracts like a bloody sponge.

The Syndicate decides to give Monk his first professional fight, where boys are carefully paired according to style, background, ethnicity... even scruples. Mix them up, and the public gets a show where they can identify with one or the other. More diversity means larger gates, and right now, the Syndicate needs a "dirty fighter:" an eye-gouging, head-butting brute who's not afraid to hit below the belt. Considering the inefficient, illegal punching style with which Monk clobbers opponents like he's hammering nails, the role suits him fine. Upon hearing that his first opponent is "good-looking," he growls, "I'll fix that" And he does, recalling Marvin Hagler's anticipation of his 1987 bout with Sugar Ray Leonard: "I like those pretty boys. I like to smash in their faces."

When Monk admits to Emily that he's more comfortable with his face covered in gauze, his voice silences the crickets and stills the evening wind: "It's like putting a gorilla into a slaughter fest!" Emily suggests that it can be fixed if that's what's holding him back from who he wants to be. "Just look at what they've been doing with war veterans." As the post-surgical bandages are removed, the mirror reveals Monk's handsome new face.

Monk's newfound confidence veers into vanity like a foreign language he takes to like a native. Spurred to a flirtation with a coat-check girl (Mona Knox), Monk justifies his infidelity as making up for lost time. But in *Baroni*'s persistent avoidance of pretense to high-stakes drama, Knox's presence serves as no more than confirmation that Monk can attract women. But this no longer applies to Emily, who's driven away by his constant preening. "Do you think this new face matters to me?" she asks in exasperation. But that's not the point. It matters to Monk, and he wants to protect it. After months of welcoming blows to his mouth, eyes, nose, and head, he's suddenly found himself stuck in the wrong profession.

The success that drives the fighter to self-destructive choices is so prevalent in the boxing film as to seem mandatory. Monk isn't the first fighter whose side-action proves detrimental, and his paramour's penchant for expensive things sucks him dry. In a backhanded plea for gratitude and expression of indifference, she lets him thank her for "breaking in [his] new face" before shutting the door in that same face for good. So much for the fatale. She got what she wanted.

Hellman tells Monk that he liked the old face better. What happened to that primal allure? Monk might have grown sick of playing the scary ape, but the ghost of his old face still serves as a half Janus head that allows full reign to ongoing aggression born of a life of insecurity and hard luck. Now his face holds little more than sneering conceit, an affectation much uglier than his old deformity.

Monk wants out. Hellman shakes his head. What other job qualifications does he have? Another impassive reminder: "When you leave the stadium a night after a fight, who sells you the morning papers? A blind ex-pug... When one laces up those gloves, he's already made a life-long marriage to the game." Of course, Hellman won't beg—dirty fighters are a dime a dozen. But there's still money to be made.

The gorilla once celebrated for welcoming blows to his

face steps into the ring with desperate attempts to protect it. Along with Hellman, the two Syndicate boys flanking the manager fast realize that deformity was Monk's only asset. Their motives are purely financial, but so are Monk's, who, despite his newfound arrogance, is raising funds to complete the new church recreation center. Having estranged himself from Emily and Father Callahan, he knows that a return to the church won't come from a financial gift alone. A literal stranger in his skin, he reshapes himself back into the reformed (or, per Sonny Liston's Father Edward P. Murphy, "reoriented") choir boy who found peace training to oratorios and singing in church. His desire to make pretty guys ugly having vanished with his old face, his upcoming bout means taking some punishment to his new one. Knowing this, his opponent's trainer tells his boy to work Monk's new Achilles heel: his eyes, his nose—all of it.

Released during the apex of the boxing noir, no one could call *Kid Monk Baroni* a crime film. The imperative doom exuded by the quotidian noir racketeer is downplayed to allow for the implication that Monk's real enemy comes from within, his fortitude less the product of individual agency than the greater wish to reattain his piety amid corruption and the burden of pride.

Monk reverts to his old tactics in the scheduled ten-rounder that emerge like burnt offerings through self-flagellation. Koehlinger's Christian ideal of the "boxer's willingness to endure suffering for a greater cause" sees Monk's face systematically pummeled until the ref stops the fight. But handsome or ugly, his real purse comes as a return to the church.

No noir racketeer worth his salt would let the situation with Monk die out so quickly, but the fighter's clean break with the goons underscores the innocent zeal laced into the curious script in all its twisting and vanishing loose ends. (One wonders how things would have played out under a different producer who favored art over excessive frugality.)

Monk's defeat means five dimes that Hellman won't see again, plus another five of the Syndicate's, who summarily issue the manager his pink slip instead of filling him with holes. The mob's finished with the manager, the manager's finished with Monk, and, having found meaning in what might be called a higher calling, Monk's done with the lot of them.

Fifty years after *Kid Monk Baroni*'s release, Father Callahan's worthy successor can be found in Father Dave Smith, the world record-holder for continuous boxing: eight hours and sixty-six opponents over the course of 120 rounds. At thirty-four, he had his first professional bout in 1996 to fund the construction of a boxing gym in Sydney, Australia to rehabilitate gang members and addicts. Two years later, in the spirit of St. Bernardine of Sienna, he developed the Order of the Fighting Fathers for the instruction of boxing for priests and other religious leaders as a means of drawing young members to the flock and getting them off the streets, out of gangs, and on their feet. Ex-Champion Joe Frazier said of his own gym in Philadelphia, through which some of the greatest heavyweights of his day had passed, "I keep it here for the boys." As gang activity ran rampant in the nineties, Frazier continued, "One gym like this does more than a whole squad of cops."

The newlyweds Monk and Emily will go on to live as happy, good-looking churchgoers. Sadly, the tightwad Broder cut the ten-day shoot to nine in an act of penny-pinching that leads to the conspicuous omission of the lovebirds from the film's last act. Broder's work may have been done, but Father Callahan's is far from over. Just as Monk won't be the last kid he takes off the cold streets, Callahan won't be the last man of the cloth to take a punk and give him some dignity in the comfort of the ring (and sometimes the church).

More than the thrill of victory, it's probably the leap of faith inherent to redemption that prompted songwriter Nick Cave to write, "Everyone loves a good boxing story, especially God." In its lack of sanctimony or preachiness, *Kid Monk Baroni* is a boxing story that even the man upstairs can get behind.

13
KILLER'S KISS

Directed by Stanley Kubrick
United Artists, 1955

Two bodies dance and flit like albino bats swooping and diving in a dank cave where no one else has ever been. Teetering between chaotic imbalance and lingering stagnation, Stanley Kubrick explores more compositional variations in his second film than in the entirety of its genre predecessors. Considering its sixty-seven-minute running time, the young auteur's film might have collapsed under its own stylistic disparities. What emerges is a seamless collage of technique and storytelling.

Kubrick's original title, *Kiss Me, Kill Me...* (ellipsis included) was abridged to *Killer's Kiss* from the same noirspeak grab-bag—as generic and misleading as the director's initial choice. Yet the film's fidelity to noir's moody atmosphere of the soulless city and the pervasive, simmering threat of violence remains among the genre's great apotheoses punctuated by the merciful, rewarding bruises of victory.

Released a year prior to *The Harder They Fall* and two years before *Monkey on My Back*, *Killer's Kiss* nevertheless comes off as a premature requiem to film noir's golden age, anticipating a new wave of 1960s and seventies American arthouse directors among whom Kubrick was both an outsider and willfully arcane *pater familias*.

When film writer Gene D. Phillips told Kubrick he'd never seen *Killer's Kiss*, the director said he was lucky. Asked of his first feature, 1953's *Fear and Desire*, Kubrick dismissed it as "embarrassingly pretentious." An autocrat of the highest order, Kubrick's disdain for his early work speaks less to quality than to the budgetary and authoritarian constraints that hobbled his exacting conceptions and lead him to scorn whatever praise the work garnered with contemporary critics.

Kubrick received a Graflex single-lens high-speed camera from his father for his thirteenth birthday. Having sold his first photograph to the Iowa-based general interest magazine *LOOK*, he was made the magazine's New York correspondent when he was seventeen to become the youngest employee on the payroll. Assigned to cover all of New York's grit and glamor, the young photographer had a gift for teasing out the tension, loneliness, and luridness in subject matter ranging from dockworkers to uptown hair salons. "The pathos of ordinary life," explains curator Sean Corcoran of the Museum of the City of New York, "inspired [Kubrick] and fit so well with the magazine's populist perspective."

A friend and admirer of crime-scene photographer Arthur Fellig (better known as Weegee, who had an uncredited cameo in *The Set-up*), Kubrick never shied from violence and seized the opportunity to shoot intimate portraits for *LOOK* featuring boxing A-listers Rocky Marciano and Rocky Graziano. But it was the middleweight Walter Cartier, the subject of a photo-essay titled *Prizefighter* in the January 1949 issue, who inadvertently launched the photographer's career as a filmmaker.

Lacking formal education, Kubrick used books to teach himself editing and the operation of different cameras. On the conceptual level, Vsevolod Pudovkin's *Film Technique and Film Acting* (1929) made a deep impression on the soon-to-be director in its assertion of film as a wholly unique artistic medium. "After four years of seeing how things worked in the world," Kubrick said of his years at *LOOK*, "I think if I had gone to college, I would never have been a director." Shooting on assignment for Jules Dassin's 1948 procedural *The Naked City*, the future filmmaker observed first-hand how film noir's visual and cinematic elements jibed with the disquiet to which he aspired in his photography.

A regular filmgoer, Kubrick was stunned at the preponderance of dreck being churned out by the major studios. "I was aware I didn't know anything about making films, but I believed I couldn't make them any worse than the majority of films I was seeing."

Using *Prizefighter* as a springboard, Kubrick made his first delve into cinema with a documentary for *LOOK* titled *Day of the Fight* in which he followed Cartier to battle over a single day. April 17, 1950: the boxer wakes, shaves, and goes to church to pray before he heads to the arena for his fight with Bobby James, set for ten p.m. The anticipation of bloodshed is underscored as his hands are wrapped in bright white cloth with slow and deliberate care.

For a moment, Cartier is shown resting in his corner, ingeniously filmed through the back of James's stool. The frame is fast abandoned to allow for evermore visual divergence within the short bout, by turns centered, cockeyed, but always yielding to image over action, form over function.

Kubrick's obsession with carefully staged, arresting compositions and plodding shots that often take on the quality of stills numbers him among the rare directors whose films reside in the realm of the visual arts as much as the cinematic. (Indeed, how many other filmmakers boast a bibliography with as many photo-art books as Kubrick?)

Even the documentary retains a fidelity to noir's obliterating darkness and deliberate tonality, further incorporating the unexpected perspectives that Kubrick honed during his days at *LOOK*. Old habits die hard, and while the title was not uncommon in the fifties, it is pertinent that the director credited himself not for "Cinematography" but "Photography."

Sometimes the spontaneous and unexpected is a welcome wild card, even for a director as exacting as Kubrick. So when a *carpe diem*-opportunity presented itself to the twenty-two-year-old neophyte, the director dove under the ropes to shoot the fighters from below. Whether re-shot for clarity or the real McCoy, it's among the earliest instances in which a boxing film portrayed a bout as shot from *within* the ring—let alone from an angle where the man with the camera was in danger of being crushed by a fallen boxer. As to the fight itself, Cartier kayoed his man in the first.

Two versions of *Day of the Fight* were assembled from the footage. The original weighed in at roughly twelve and a half minutes. The second, purchased by RKO, was turned into a seventeen-minute newsreel puff-piece overlaid with hectoring yet disinterested narration. Kubrick wasn't thrilled with the additions but was glad to recoup the $3,900 budget.

Although he took out a forty-thousand-dollar loan from relatives to finance *Killer's Kiss*, Kubrick still called an early wrap each Friday to pick up his unemployment check. Burning through the budget and lacking additional funds to hire a sound editor, the lengthy post-production required the director-photographer to meticulously post-synch dialogue and insert the music himself. It was here that the director got his first-hard lesson in editing. In Michael Ondaatje's 2002 book *The Conversations*, Walter Murch, sound editor for films including George Lucas's *THX 1138*

(1971) and *American Graffiti* (1973) as well as Francis Ford Coppola's *The Godfather Part II*, *The Conversation* (both from 1974), and *Apocalypse Now* (1979), explains that "sound is really half the experience of this medium." Kubrick griped "I had to spend four months just laying out sound effects footstep by footstep." Nevertheless, his use of lightweight, portable equipment led him to note "with what little facilities and personnel one could actually make a film." With this in mind, Kubrick was freed from "any concern... about the technical or logistical aspects of filmmaking," an observation that echoes 1970s heavyweight Floyd "Jumbo" Cummings assertion that "all [boxing] is, is street fighting with a little polish."

In the aftermath of *Killers Kiss*'s single bout, Davey Gordon (Jamie Smith) paces the departure gates at Penn Station: the brooding, chain-smoking portrait of resignation. The viewer knows Davey's problem the moment he enters the frame—this guy has to skip town ASAP. Davey reflects on how seriously he'd taken life before the fight in a voiceover steeped in calm, nihilistic pathos. A lot can happen in a few days.

While the plot doesn't require the protagonist to be a fighter, boxing's brutality helps underscore Kubrick's vision of a New York steeped in lawless apathy as it tugs at the strictures of civilization. The violence that unfolds in the square trap of the ring is both microcosm and mirror to Manhattan as a labyrinthine prison hissing with vipers and crawling with creeps. But it's not the game that gets Davey in trouble. After all, not *every* goon in New York has a hand in boxing.

"A filmmaker," wrote Kubrick about newer, smaller, and less expensive equipment, "has almost the same freedom as a novelist has when he buys himself some paper." Boxing afforded the director endless experimentation in hand-held filming, including a return to the canvas to again shoot the fighters from below, this time with full control over choreography to avoid the risk of being fallen on.

While the short running time doesn't allow for much agonizing over principles in Kubrick's Escape from New York, there's a backstory to Davey's agony. In a déjà vu recalling *Day of the Fight*, preparations are made in Davey's locker room as the wraps are again applied. The ring is centered like a diamond on the screen to create a series of symmetrical triangles and parallelograms. Squint, and the frame resembles an eight-pointed star or the flying geese pattern on a nineteenth-century quilt.

In another part of town, a man stands by a television in a comfy pad that smells of leather club chairs, cigar smoke, and ill-gotten wealth. The carefree but sadistic laugh inherent to almost any first-rate lowlife is the giveaway, and this one swirls the ice in his glass as he watches the set and delights in Davey's slaughter. The man nods in sober agreement when the announcer recounts Davey's career as "one long promise without fulfillment." The kid may be "clever," but a veteran at twenty-nine, he's "plagued by a weak chin." He always has been.

Twenty-five seconds in and Davey's put down only to bounce back up. Another twenty and he's nearly knocked through the ropes. Felled a third time, he stares up in a POV recalling Mountain's kayo in *Requiem for a Heavyweight* (which also opened inside the ring seven years later). Coruscating overheads blur his vision, and, rising one last time, Davey swipes at the air as a left jab finishes him off. The man at the television chuckles and pulls at his cigar.

Davey knows he's washed-up, and he's already made arrangements to move back to Seattle and leave the chaos of New York behind for good. Looking out his kitchen window, he witnesses a woman being assaulted in the building across from his. He rushes to her aid to find her assailant—the same fellow who was having such a good time watching him get butchered on TV—has escaped. As to the woman, her name is Gloria. Played by the barely known Irene Kane, the actor quipped that taking the role "might [have been] better than getting a real job at Dunkin," leading Kubrick to express surprise at how cheaply actors were willing to work for the chance to practice their trade.

Davey stays on to keep vigil while Gloria sleeps. He runs a hand down a black stocking and studies her unmentionables drying on a string in the bedroom. A doll looks on without blinking.

The following day, Gloria explains that her attacker

is the unsavory nightclub owner Vinnie Rapallo (Frank Silvera). Part-time businessman and full-time criminal, he's also her ex, and Gloria's made it clear that whatever they had is finished. It also remains vague, leaving open the possibility that they'd never commenced or consummated a relationship to begin with. Nevertheless, Rapallo's made it his mission to hold onto her, and there's the easy way or the hard way.

Gloria descends into a dreamy voiceover recounting her family history with erratic verbal panache and a twang of upper-crust elocution. It's the film's most extreme, surreal transition. From a black void not unlike the ring that hovered in infinite space at the film's opening, the pale specter of a ballerina leaps into the frame like a ghostly mezzotint scraped, burnished, and polished to a white glow.

The Viennese eyes that smolder on the whirling dancer (played by Kubrick's second wife, Ruth Sobotka) belong to Gloria's sister Iris. Was it because their mother died giving birth to Gloria that Iris was always their father's favorite? Having renounced her promising dance career to marry a wealthy suitor, Iris continues to twirl and leap as her sister recounts how, soon after the wedding, Iris tucked herself in bed and slashed her wrists.

A proclivity for one-point perspective is one of the director's most distinct visual hallmarks and a key element to the pervasive symmetry that runs through his films. The spherical view down the airlock tunnel in *2001: A Space Odyssey* (1968); the droogs flanked by white plastic statues in *A Clockwork Orange* (1971); and the centered banquets in *Barry Lyndon* (1975) are miles from the slanting *Look* photos or the rote, sleek assembly of *Day of the Fight*. But for the time being, the director was still experimenting, opening *Killer's Kiss* with the protagonist placed in the middle of the screen's centered credit text.

Iris whirls like a spinning doll with a phantom stare that opens like a Rorschach card. Not so far away, the banisters of the vertiginous stairway to Rapallo's nightclub tumbles to a vanishing point where floor tiles continue to recede. A large sign centered overhead reads, "Watch Your Step." The words might have served as a warning to the director about his break with modern composition, but he wasn't worried.

Still, the verboten framing device rubbed against the grain of contemporary stylistic edicts within the realm of the visual. By 1955, New York had been the center of the art world, of which Kubrick, as a photographer, was an active if reticent figure, for over a decade. His symmetry became a recurrent rejection of the aggressive imbalance and intentional distortions inherent to noir's paranoid lens and modern art in general. Such distortions were part and parcel of Kubrick's methodology as well. Still, if variety was the order of the day, the director was ready to take his chances on reinventing *all* manner of presentation, including Classicism's staid self-restraint.

Kubrick's long-format shots, in all their perpetual movement, are noted as having distinguished the director from his contemporaries. The three-and-a-half-minute opening of Orson Wells's *Touch of Evil* (1948) is dazzling in its swooping view of the city. Alfred Hitchcock's ten-minute take in his stage-play-style *Rope* (1958) is tense and staid. But in both cases, the camera itself remained stagnant. In 1975, twenty years after *Killer's Kiss*, the American inventor Garrett Brown contrived the Steadicam, first employed in Hal Ashby's Woody Guthrie biopic *Bound for Glory* (1976). To a director known for extending imagery until it feels like art on a gallery wall and bores its way into the viewer's skull, Brown's invention was a godsend. Kubrick's interest in dolly and long tracking shots culminated in 1980's *The Shining*, where, with DIY ingenuity, he altered the device to what has come to be known as a "low mode." Mounted to a post, the camera was set below waist level and attached to a giant wheel moving through the winding halls of the haunted hotel. *Raging Bull* director Martin Scorsese, a long-time admirer of Kubrick's use of constant movement punctuated by long periods of inertia, immortalized the Steadicam's fluidity in the three-minute, four-second Copa Cabana sequence for 1990's *Goodfellas*. He also credited *Killer's Kiss* with what he found indispensable to filming a boxing movie: shooting from inside the ring.

When the inevitable romance sparks between Davey and Gloria, the two decide to leave the city together. Of course, Gloria has her own reasons for skipping town, and now Davey's made Rapello's list too.

The club owner pours out some brandy and admires

a painting of a boxer in turn-of-the-century street clothes who just laid some poor gent out on a pool table. It's not the most honorable setting for a match, and probably not an especially honorable fight. But the piece also foreshadows the careful interior staging and fine, sometimes perverse art to which Kubrick was drawn. It speaks of Rapello the way the modernist paintings betray the "cat lady's" predilection for the erotic in *A Clockwork Orange*, the Navajo and Apache décor in *The Shining*'s evocation of the hotel's malign roots, or the poker table that doubles as a stage for war planning in 1964's *Dr. Strangelove*.

Davey brings a gun to go after Rapello upon learning the club owner has kidnapped Gloria. When he tracks him down, Rapello's quick to cave: "She's in a loft on 24th Street!" The freight elevator takes its time to ultimately reveal Gloria tied to a beam. Davey turns his gun on the welcome party and puts them against the wall. He can hold them at bay for a while, but these guys are pros, and Davey's dented hands and glass jaw won't help him much in a bare-knuckle scrap. Outnumbered three to one by adversaries who only know how to play dirty, Davey leaps through a window and crashes into a gray and lifeless daylight devoid of all promise.

Rapello and one of the boys scramble to the back of the building where, under the same grungy sun, their pitch-black silhouettes zip across vertical white furrows outside an alley's devouring maw. Chasms and rooftops slant, come apart, and reassemble like moving tangrams that recall Kubrick's ensconced *Look* compositions. In another moment of stasis, the camera vertically dissects the network of pipes and water towers like mechanical guts and disused organs to splay across the city ceiling. "Watch Your Step" is indeed sound advice for Davey as he climes a fire escape that appears to recede twenty-six miles upward in a panic-filled inverse of the club stairway's steep, sobering drop.

Manhattan's stone arches, ridged entablatures, and carved door jambs are reduced to meaningless veneer twenty stories above the staid pretense of civilization. There's no id suppression up among the lifeless whir of centrifugal fans, monstrous ventilators, brick stacks, and humming wires over which Davey is pursued. Through an inimical mist rising from the East River, The Queensboro Bridge hovers like a prison wall.

The dankest loft in all of Manhattan is a storage house for mannequins, and it is into this clearance that Davey and Rapello tumble. Maybe there isn't a ring, but nor are there any Queensberry rules. Outside of gravity, few strictures are enforced six hundred feet above ground.

Composer Gerald Fried's ghostly *Murder 'mongst the Mannequins* starts with a haunted drum march snuffed by a braying of low brass and the insistent bleating of strings. In its attendant choreography, Fried's score anticipates the director's exacting synchronization of music and image, a winding, craggy link between psychedelic vaudeville, panicked Loony Toons, and MTV. As Kubrick was to gain complete control over his material by the early sixties, his merging of sound and vision converged into a storytelling device that elevated Pudovkin's assertion of film as an independent medium to a new level.

Limbs, feet, and rows of torsos cover tables and lean on walls. Hands hang suspended from the ceiling with fingers pointed down. If W.C. Heinz's assertion that "every fight is in front of an audience" is true, then the two men are goaded by an unblinking crowd of fiberglass in a macabre mirroring of the doll's wide-eyed nocturnal vigil. Davey and Rapello commence an impromptu duel that quickly escalates from hurling plastic hands and feet to employing detached arms and legs as epees.

Back at Penn Station, Davey continues dragging at his cigarettes until the final call for Seattle is announced. With seconds to spare, Gloria darts from a cab and into Davey's arms in a happy ending straight from the playbook. It's pat, but they deserve it.

Dragged through the rubble of Davey's travails, the viewer is mercifully spared the bitter nag of uncertainty that's threatened to extend beyond the final reel. Unlike the industrious skirt-chasers who meddle with gangsters' girls, Gloria and Davey were a pair from the moment they met. There are no fixes or set-ups to add to Davey's strife—he's had enough on his plate. Nor is there a demimonde fatale to distract him with her pointy breasts. He's too broke for that set anyway.

Impatient, stringent, and jaded from the get-go, Kubrick never got the ending he wanted. Screenwriter

Howard Sackler (who was to publish his play *The Great White Hope* twelve years later) rejected the director's wish for an ambiguous denouement in favor of closure that resonated hope and optimism, even ensuring it as a condition of the film's release. There wasn't much Kubrick could do but abide by the authorized version while mining whatever existentialism he could find simmering under Sackler's script and assimilating it with visuals suited to the bleakest breed of urban parables.

The following year, Kubrick achieved commercial success with his racetrack-heist noir *The Killing*. It was the first time the director accepted his due praise. In 1957, Kirk Douglas hired him to direct the war film *Paths of Glory*, which starred the actor and was produced by his own Bryna Productions. Three years later, Douglas called on Kubrick to helm the sword and sandal epic *Spartacus* after firing the original director.

Based on the novel by the full-blooded communist Howard Fast, *Spartacus* was Universal's top-grossing film for the next decade. Kubrick may have struck Hollywood gold, but Douglas's micromanagement hobbled the director's autocratic tendencies, and the sword of Damocles the actor had tied over Kubrick's head during filming indicated the director's role as expendable. Moving forward, Kubrick insisted on complete authority over his future projects, writing in the MGM contract for his next two-films, "I must have complete final annihilating artistic control."

The film that opened with Davey kayoed in the inky

void closes with the more permanent stoppage of Rapallo. As Davey waits on the platform, his resolve is rewarded with a kiss from Gloria and not a shot to the gut from Rapello's pistol. The warring forces of death and love are the bookends that demonstrate the symmetry inherent to the film's arc as a whole; by turns unraveling and coming together again.

The protagonist of the boxing film is never in for a comfortable ride, but sometimes they deserve a pardon courtesy of an auspicious finale tied neatly with a ribbon and bow. For Davey, new beginnings don't just commence with a kiss, but with the termination of a hard-luck sentence in that pulsing, living penitentiary called Manhattan.

14
RAGING BULL

Directed by Martin Scorsese
United Artists, 1980

In what sounds like an academic panel on reprobates rather
than two guys drinking in a corner booth at P.J. Clarke's
saloon, Pete Hamill recounts a conversation with Frank
Sinatra during which they fell to deliberating who the
worst person in the world was. A silent moment of reflection, another round of Jack Daniels, and the verdict fell to
ex-middleweight Jake LaMotta. "Lower than whale shit,"
The Chairman hissed. Boxing writer W.C. Heinz put it
slightly more gingerly: "Jake LaMotta will go down into
the books as one of the most unpopular figures of all time."
Sportswriter Jimmy Cannon wrote that the fighter was
"probably the most despised man of his generation."

Bully, thug, woman-basher, sociopathic powder keg. LaMotta fit every bullet-point. Martin Scorsese's *Raging Bull* sees a transformative Robert De Niro assimilate, masticate, and spew forth the caustic jealousy and grotesque masochism that isolated everyone within the boxer's life. At the film's premier, LaMotta watched a hard-hitting recreation of his fraternal bond and doomed marriage systematically dismantled by the pathological jealousy of a man whose only means of expression is violence. "I don't like that person. He's a bad man, and I know he's me."

LaMotta's 1970 autobiography, from which the film takes its title, doesn't attempt to whitewash the fighter's criminal past. Coauthored by his friend Pete Savage and anonymous contributor Joseph Carter, LaMotta paints his life in black and blue strokes to convey an excess of violence that far surpasses De Niro's embodiment of the fighter. In its break with nearly all of its genre predecessors, the absence of a hero worth rooting for indicates a refusal to cave to viewers' hard-wired confidence in the retribution most boxing films bestow like indulgences upon even the worst antiheroes.

The *New Yorker* critic Pauline Kael characterized *Raging Bull* as "a biography of the genre of prizefight films." Charging Scorsese with creating "a movie out of remembered high points [from classic boxing films], leaping from one to another," the allegation is rendered anemic when she betrays her regard for the genre by criticizing *Bull*'s renunciation of "the low-life entertainment values of prizefight films." Unlike its predecessors, the film's personification of this "bad man" is concerned less with *what* the fighter did than the senseless, paranoid motivations as to *why*, suspending the audience not in "lowlife entertainment values" but the shadowy realms of art and psychology. For all its sweaty dressing rooms, bloody rings, and smoky mob fronts, *Raging Bull*'s darkest territories reside within.

For a film widely considered the apex of the genre, *Raging Bull*'s focus on a marriage and brotherhood laid waste by compulsive self-loathing and unfounded suspicion renders LaMotta's career almost incidental. "Anyone who thinks it is a boxing film is crazy," Scorsese told the *New York Times* of an antihero whose gluttony for punishment inside the ring ran parallel with his abuses outside. A lot of ink has been spilled by writers who characterize *Bull* not as a boxing film but under the vague denotation "character study." (This being the case, one may freely regard *Star Wars* not as science fiction but a sweeping character study of aliens and droids.)

De Niro read LaMotta's book in 1973 while shooting *The Godfather Part II* in Sicily. Struck by the precarious balance of raw confession and suspect narration, he contacted his erstwhile collaborator Martin Scorsese about a film version. The director was less than enthused, and as he lay detoxing from a coke overdose five years later, the actor approached him again. Scorsese balked. "I didn't know anything about boxing." Televised fights were "always from one angle... I didn't know what the hell was going on." To the filmmaker most recognized for pushing the boundaries of mainstream cinematic violence, "the idea 'let's get two guys into the ring and let them hit each other' was something... I couldn't grasp."

But maybe there was a way he could. 1973's *Mean Streets* was a cathartic love letter to a childhood spent among mafiosi, petty thieves, and wannabe hoods in New York's Little Italy. In his 1974 documentary *Italian American*, the director's parents recount their own immigrant experience. Like LaMotta, they were both New York-based second-generation Italians and roughly the same age as the fighter.

Boxing has always been violent with a flair for the theatric, and Thanatos runs deep throughout Scorsese's work. To the future director who was booted from Catholic seminary school as a teenager, love is fleeting, but violence is forever. The collision of these opposite forces led the director to cultivate his unique take on a sport that he described as "primal as you can get in a 'civilized' world... I think it's through [boxers] that we live out those worlds." As to Thanatos's inverse, nowhere is the failure of Eros more conspicuous than the unhinged jealousy with which Jake destroys his marriage.

Few films are so discernibly confident and self-aware of their narrative style when turning their focus on such an unpredictable, unknowable lead. As to production, it's impossible to deny *Raging Bull*'s visionary potency in its action-fight sequences as contrived by cinema visionaries Scorsese, De Niro, cinematographer Michael Chapman, and editor Thelma Schoonmaker. If veracity suffers in the ring, it's not for lack of skill but the director and editor's unfathomable vantage points and flash-cut assembly that draws them closer to the protagonist.

With an output that includes *Mean Streets*, *Goodfellas*, 1995's *Casino*, and 2006's *The Departed*, Scorsese built his reputation as the consummate mafia director if not through quantity, then certainly in quality. For this reason, perhaps the best case for *Raging Bull* as a boxing film is its portrayal of mobsters as smiling, genial chums trying to help a fighter climb to the top while padding their own wallets. As the reader has learned, no boxer gets his back scratched without reciprocation, and *Raging Bull* reads as a swan song to old-school criminal control of the sport. By the mid-seventies, the politics of the fight game had undergone a complete reorganization as fixers and racketeers adopted more legitimate, less risky ties to the game. Jake's fighting years, on the other hand, were set amid the most corrupt decades in the sport's sordid history, the demise of which LaMotta himself was to play a crucial role.

It's 1964, and a bloated, forty-two-year-old ex-pug practices his schtick in the dressing room of Manhattan's Barbazon Plaza next to a cheap sign that reads "An Evening with Jake LaMotta." At 220 pounds (fifty pounds over his fighting weight of 167) and ten years retired with a nose like a root vegetable, he muses on a career via mangled Shakespeare and autobiographical stanzas before ending on a note of finality: "That's entertainment!" With a ringmaster's grandiose bluster, De Niro's LaMotta promises the viewer that they're in for a showstopper on stage, in the ring, and onscreen. The ding of the bell brings the action to 1941.

Cleveland, September 21. LaMotta shakes off a succession of blows to the face from local boy Jimmy Reeves. Too far gone on points to clinch a decision, his only hope is a kayo. As Jake advances in a crouch, a woman's scream from the stands initiates another melee, this time among the crowd. Reeves goes down and gets up to be floored once more. Then again. A fourth time and he's down for good, but when the final bell sounds, the count's only reached nine. By the skin of his busted teeth, Reeves clinches a split decision that marks LaMotta's first loss.

Reeves knows he was kayoed. So do the fans, who throw popcorn and whoop their disapproval. Jake's brother and manager, Joey (Joe Pesci), drapes Jake in his signature leopard-striped robe as the fighter raises his arms in smug victory. Like *The Set-up*, the bloodlust among the crowd comes in greater measure to that of the boxers'. A chair sails into the ring followed by a body tossed over three rows of seats. The organist starts in with the National Anthem to quell the angry stampede, presently trampling a woman underfoot in their dash for the exit. Popcorn rains like confetti.

In 1978, Scorsese was still wavering when director Jonathan Demme gifted him a folk painting of the fighter scrawled with the words, "fought like he didn't deserve to live." It was pure coincidence, but hard to ignore what was starting to feel like fate. (The original quote comes from a 1970 interview with boxing writer Peter Heller.) Newly sober, Scorsese secured the book rights, and in his haste to get the project moving, De Niro gave a copy of the book to Scorsese's former NYU classmate and *Mean Streets* collaborator, Mardik Martin. While Martin's two years of research yielded several jumbled scripts, they were rejected by the actor, director, and producers Robert Chartoff and Irwin Winkler (fresh off the first two *Rocky* films). Martin handed off his notes and screenplays to writer-director Paul Schrader, who both contrived and penned Scorsese's 1975 *Taxi Driver.* Schrader molded the surfeit of material into a tour-de-force of barbarity while smashing the boxing film's new template set by *Rocky* its 1979's sequel.

As to the fighter himself, De Niro found La Motta at a Manhattan strip club where the ex-fighter was "in charge of security." After a year of sparring in the 14th Street Gym, La Motta remarked that the actor would have made a formidable middleweight. But his interests were purely financial. "[If] I make money I couldn't care less," he told *Vanity Fair*. "They can make me a fag if they want."

Set chiefly in Pelham Parkway in The Bronx, Scorsese envisioned a period piece that invoked a lost age when second-rate hoods officiated on street corners, neighbors held conversations by yelling from tenement windows, and The Ink Spots spilled from every kitchen radio. So critical was the director's fidelity to time and place that it bordered on the obsessive and, in some instances, irrational (most famously when he threatened Winkler with pulling his name from the directorial credits because the drink order "Cutty Sark, please" was inaudible in the final cut).

Scorsese embraces noir's stylistic visuals and nihilism while excising the salvation and resolution that unfold as moral parables. Visually, *Raging Bull*'s pervasive soft, tonal grays are broken only occasionally by jolting blacks and burning whites that reference cinema of the 1940s and 50s. Speaking of the film as a period piece, the director noted that, in Jake's day, "[boxing] was always [filmed] in black and white—on television, in *Life* magazine...." But eschewing color also underscores the film's fealty to the era through hints at the documentary format via freeze-frames and expository text to denote date, location, and opponent.

As noted, the standard approach to shooting boxing films had been carried out through setting cameras outside the ring to capture multiple angles as needed. However, Scorsese's wish to bring the viewer as close to the fighters as the medium could support required multiple handheld shots from inside that allowed for infinite close-ups and radical shifts in framing. It follows that the director who remembered boxing as "one angle on TV" strove for such variegated style and frenetic edits. The director duly credited Kubrick's use of the technique a quarter century prior in the opening bout of *Killer's Kiss*, and the documentary-style text recalls the early short *The Day of the Fight*. Like that other famously obsessive director, Scorsese required multiple shootings that lasted days before Schoonmaker cut them down to a mere few seconds. No method or approach was rejected. On rare occasions when the shooting was done from outside the ring, Scorsese updated James Wong Howe's roller skate-contrivance with the newer Stedicam. In *The Conversations*, Murch describes the editor's job of creating fluidity from shot to shot as "a dot moving around the screen... If the dot is moving up to the right-hand corner of the frame... make sure there's something to look at in the right-hand corner of the next shot." With Schoonmaker in mind, he continues, "If you're cutting a fight scene, you actually want an element of disorientation... you abuse the audience's attention."

Despite the film's containing less than ten minutes of boxing within its 129-minute running time, ten weeks of the four-month shoot were allotted to filming fight scenes. While certain bouts maintain a modicum of fidelity to the originals, Scorsese's unexpected angles and close-ups often render his recreations unrecognizable when set beside contemporaneous footage. (The DVD and several YouTube offerings provide split-screen enactments of the film fights juxtaposed with the originals.)

Giacobe LaMotta was born in The Bronx in 1922. When he was eight, his father forced him into battles royale to earn rent money, setting the boy's life path. The older man, who beat his wife and Jake's four siblings with ferocious abandon, once pulled young Giacobe's ears so hard that it left the boy thirty percent deaf in one ear and seventy percent in the other.

LaMotta dropped out of school in the second grade to move from fighting for spare change to muggings and hold-ups, once crushing in a local bookie's skull with whom, by all accounts, he was otherwise quite friendly. He learned to box during a stint upstate at the Coxsackie Correctional Institute under the tutelage of one Father Joseph (as touched upon in *Kid More Baroni*). Upon release, Jake garnered a reputation as a 5' 8" juggernaut who used his diminutive height to his advantage as a charger and an inside fighter. Aptly dubbed "The Bronx Bull," he turned professional at nineteen and fought 106 bouts over a thirteen-year career.

Jake met Beverly Rosalyn Thailer, known as Vikki around the neighborhood and portrayed by Cathy Moriarty, as she's introduced at the Castle Hill swimming pool where they originally met. Leaving her friends (local, low-level hoods all), she moves to sit by the pool where her feet kick under the silent water in sensuous slo-mo, and for the moment, nothing exists outside the dazzling sexuality of the milk-white fifteen-year-old (Moriarty was twenty when filming commenced). Vikki recalled the scene in which Joey introduces her to Jake through the chain-link fence that bounds the pool as faithful despite the actors' laconic improvisation: *"How you doin'?" "Alright, how you doin'?" "Alright, what are you doin'?"* With dialogue so elemental, gesture, tone, inflection, and movement become a primary means of storytelling. (De Niro even cocks his head to indicate Jake's partial deafness.)

De Niro discovered Joe Pesci in a nightclub act, where he was performing with his childhood friend and partner Frank Vincent, who costars here as the gangster Salvi. (Vincent's immortality was sealed ten years later in *Goodfellas* when he told Pesci's Tommy DeVito to go home and get his shine box.) De Niro had to coax Pesci, who'd just released his first album, *Little Joe Sure Can Sing!*, to take a hiatus from the song-and-dance biz to play LaMotta's brother Joey.

While Joey is absent from the book, Schrader fashioned a composite of Jake's brother and his friend Pete Savage. If Jake's omission of Joey was a snub to his brother, his admission—in print—to forcefully deflowering Savage's fiancée while Savage was in jail was worse, and Schraeder wisely chose the more rational-minded Joey to further root the film in the inner sanctum of the familial.

A North Jersey boy, Pesci was pally with the Italian Bronx crowd and knew Moriarty from around the way. "She was the wet dream of every kid in the neighborhood," recalls a neighbor, and Scorsese cast her on the spot. She had no acting experience, but she was a dead ringer for the young Vikki.

Vikki Thailer grew up as a punching bag at the hands of her father, and Jake didn't treat her any better. Throughout their marriage, he confined her to the home where she would ostensibly remain ignorant of the outside world. "In a way, you can say Jake kidnapped me," she wrote in her 2010 memoir *The Vikki LaMotta Story: Jake, Raging Bull, Playboy, Sinatra, and the Mob*. The rationale put forth by LaMotta reads like a textbook definition of antisocial personality disorder, still referred to in medical circles under the classification of Psychopathology: "I wanted to train you, so you only knew what I wanted you to know." More importantly, closing her off from the outside world deprived her of contact with other men. As his career exacerbates his paranoia (or is it the other way around?), love and work, "the cornerstones of our humanness" (per Freud) blur and merge into a singular nightmare of maltreatment and masochism.

Freud's so-called Madonna-whore complex, touched upon in *Kid Galahad*, illustrates the impossible quandary of a man's wish to marry a virgin who screws like a pro. Although raped as a teenager, Vikki fit both requirements, and it's unlikely that Jake knew of her early defilement. Yet her apparent, natural skills in the sack only fanned his suspicions and accusations.

Scorsese had explored similar themes in *Who's That Knocking at My Door?* (1968) and *Mean Streets*, in which male leads struggle with female sexual experience and volition. But he dismissed psychoanalytic readings of *Raging Bull*, asserting, "You can't explain any human being with one Freudian term." To the director, psychoanalysis in cinema had its heyday in the 1940s and 50s in films like Hitchcock's *Spellbound* (1945), Curtis Berhardt's *Possessed* (1947), and

Raoul Walsh's Oedipal-centric *White Heat* (1949). Yet despite its intentions, *Raging Bull*'s psychoanalytic constructions are too conspicuous to ignore. Jake's litany of neuroses checks every bullet point on psychoanalyst Karen Horney's list of "Neurotic Personalities" and confounds all of Erik Erikson's "Eight Stages of Man." Still, one should take care to avoid a singular psychological reading lest they vanish down any one of countless rabbit holes.

LaMotta was already an established middleweight with over seventy professional fights when he met Vikki in 1946, five years after the film's introductory bout. (As with many of the fights depicted, and in deference to *Raging Bull* as creative nonfiction, chronological and factual nitpicking will be clarified only when pertinent.) When Vikki became pregnant by Jake, he summarily left his first wife, Lenore. Of the short-lived marriage, two things may be noted: Jake and Lenore had one child together, and Jake once struck her so hard he was sure he'd killed her.

Like *Cinderella Man* and *The Great White Hope*, *Raging Bull* commences with an established fighter whose career is already in its middlescence. When Joey enters to mitigate a fight with Lenore, Jake sits him down to complain about his small hands, of which LaMotta once said, "I should have been an artist, or a fag." (According to Savage, he once broke down in tears and cried, "I'll never be big enough to fight Joe Louis!") In a sport where glamor has always favored heavyweights, Jake's "little girl hands" were a constant reminder that he could never get a shot at "the best." Well, maybe he's not big, but he's tough as hell, and to prove it he has Joey wrap his fist in a dishrag and punch him in the face. It takes some goading, but calling Joey a fag moves things along. So follow several blows, shot by turns from both viewpoints.

"You throw a punch like you take it in the ass," sneers Jake in further accordance not only with the subject's rampant homophobia but the esprit de corps of his ilk. Released twelve years after the lifting of the Hayes Code, *Raging Bull* allows for language verboten during noir's heyday, and for anyone counting, the word "fuck" is used 114 times.

The blows Peschi metes out on De Niro's face are the first indication of the obscene levels of pain to which the actors subjected themselves. In an arduous introduction to the Method, Peschi nearly fractured his hand as De Niro continued to taunt him.

Speculation as to whether today's psychopharmacology would have quelled LaMotta's rage as generated by his obsessive, circular thinking is tempting, and of course, pointless. In an interview with ESPN, Heavyweight Champion Tyson Fury addressed boxing's correlation to depression. "Most of us who suffer from mental health problems, if we knew, we'd fix it. But we don't know. That's where it spirals into darkness."

Conversely, Mike Tyson's much-diagnosed depression was exacerbated by over-prescribed mood stabilizers like lithium. Following the nature-nurture paradigm, it's possible that the blows administered by Jake's father to his son's rock-hard head fostered Jake's predisposition to anti-social behavior. As Alex Williams of the University of Kansas explains, "People who are experiencing chronic pain or chronic medical conditions also experience clinical depression at a much higher rate." And Jake had been taking punches from the time he could walk.

LaMotta took the sexual abstinence method to extremes as he's shown quelling his arousal in the bedroom sink with a pitcher of ice water. "I would go a month, two months, without having sex," he told *Penthouse* in 1982, "...it made me a vicious animal." In a practice absent from the film, LaMotta would suit up, close the windows, blast the radiators, lay on top of Vikki, and administer dull, missionary thrusts before quashing his erection just as he was about to come. To Vikki's exasperation, the ordeal was repeated several times, further elucidating Jake's restive, combative ring style and all-around bad mood. "Try a little more fuckin' so you won't... pick on me and everybody else," Joey tells him. But the only sexual interest Jake appeared to have lay in unfounded suspicions that Vikki was having it behind his back. In a 1981 *Playboy* interview in which she posed nude at fifty-one, Vikki described herself as a "sexual animal" and Jake as a hopelessly inattentive partner. He could, however, drop eight to ten pounds in one four-hour session of *coitus prolongata*. Vikki recalled that when he finally did come, "You could hear it all over the Bronx."

LaMotta was usually too busy watching for any of Vikki's would-be admirers (or Vikki herself, lest her eyes wander) to enjoy himself, and their entrance into the Copa exacerbates his vigilance. When the top capo, Tommy Como (Nicholas Colasanto), waves in dreamy, gently menacing slow motion to summon Joey and his brother to his table of wise guys, Jake's reluctance is palpable. LaMotta never hid his contempt for small-time hoods like Frank Vincent's Salvi, but heavies like Como require some finesse.

Tommy Como is based squarely on Owney Madden-protégé Frankie Carbo, boxing's top fixer during the late 1940s. With a charm exceeded only by his vicious homicidal streak, Carbo was linked to the murders of several prominent mob contemporaries during the gangland wars of the 1930s, including posthumous speculation that he ordered the 1947 hit on West-Coast associate Bugsy Seigel. Having muscled in on Madison Square Garden, Carbo was instrumental in establishing the mob-owned sanctioning body benignly dubbed the International Boxing Club (IBC), through which he developed a stranglehold on the welterweight and middleweight divisions. He also officiated over Murder, Inc., carrying out the operation at a Brooklyn candy shop where, among other dealings, he threatened fighters and managers for a percentage of their earnings. Anyone looking for a title shot had to move through a series of fixes in which promoters were forced to pay enormous shares to Murder, Inc. Between 1949 and 1956, the IBC promoted forty-seven out of fifty-one championship bouts and took in every dime of advertising from the television boon. (The number of domestic TVs had jumped to 52 million by 1960, and paid advertising brought in even more than fixes.) In 1961, Carbo was sent to Alcatraz, then the McNeil Island Federal Penitentiary, where he later controlled the maligned heavyweight Sonny Liston. He died of a heart attack in 1976 shortly after his release.

Unlike Scorsese's ruthless, psychopathic gangsters of the 1990s, Tommy Como is presented as an avuncular peacekeeper. But as *Raging Bull* illustrates, LaMotta tested the gangster's patience in his refusal to play ball. Joey was the only manager he'd accept in this world of corruption. But there was nothing Jake could do when mobsters showed up to watch him train. They were as woven into the fabric of boxing locales as leather and cigar smoke. Joey was cozy with them from the start and urges Jake to take up their offer. In retaliation, Jake humiliates his brother to the canvas in front of his friends. De Niro's enthusiasm earned Peschi another injury, this time a broken rib.

1943 moves to '47 through expository text denoting a succession of bouts via dates and opponents. When LaMotta showed the director a series of contemporary home movies he'd shot with a color 16-millimeter camera, Scorsese recreated them using the cast and the same model camera before "aging" the film by scratching it with a nail. These passages nearly perfectly bifurcate the film's focus on Jake's early years with Vikki, the mob's mounting pressures, and the disintegration of his family. Five soundless color sequences (the brothers' weddings, poolside antics, and family barbecues) are interspersed with six fights. For a director so mindful of fidelity to the original bouts, the lion's share of recreations amounts to a few stills featuring Jake in action, often shown by himself. Unlike the incidental, almost interchangeable opponents, the contentment expressed in the color passages recalls the fighter's own likening of the film to "watching an old black-and-white movie of myself." But life's happier moments fade from memory faster than the bad.

Back at the wise guys' table at the Copa, Como tells Jake he'll be betting a lot of money ("and I mean a *lot* of money") on the upcoming fight with the formidable Tony Janiro (Kevin Mahon). Jake tells him to bet everything he's got: "I don't know whether I should fuck 'im or fight 'im." The film omits a $100,000 bribe Carbo offered Jake for a shot at a career-advancing dive that the fighter rejected out of hand. Considerably gentler than his real-life avatar, Como makes Jake feel at home throughout the tension. So at home that maybe Jake should be sitting at his table.

When Vikki offhandedly refers to Janiro as good-looking (a common term for promising up-and-comers, though in reality Janiro had already fought sixty bouts), Jake turns the fight into a slaughterfest of transference, his tyrannical jealousy exteriorized in the blood that spews from his opponent's face. Moving in on Janiro like a horror-film slasher, he gores his invented enemy as Vikki looks on stone-faced. Among the most violent images in the genre, makeup artist Michael George Westmore recalls flattening actor Kevin Mahon's nose as "a genuine plumbing job." But facts are again swapped out for histrionics: the fight was no one-round annihilation. Janiro wasn't even knocked out. Instead, the scene serves as a composite of Jake's violence in and out of the ring by skirting depictions of physical violence toward Vikki. Jake won the fight by decision, later remarking that Janiro "ain't human" for the punishment he absorbed.

On a rainy day at the Debonaire Social Club (a stand-in for Carbo's candy shop front with a sign that reads "Members Only"), *bravi ragazzi* play cards over espresso and grappa. At the same time, Joey sits with Como and Salvi to settle a beating he administered to the latter. Salvi's crime? Hosting Vikki at his table of gangsters without Jake's knowledge. The slapstick drubbing evinces Joey's mounting vigilance in shielding his sister-in-law from the company of other men. His motivations are not without logic, though it pains him to explain them to Vikki. "He'll be alright just as soon as he gets his shot," he tells his sister-in-law. But for now, keeping Jake ignorant of Vikki's comings and goings protects them both from inciting his rage.

Como spells out the cold reality that Joey's been waiting for. Echoing the real-life Carbo who said, "You don't get anywhere alone," Como gripes of Jake, "He ain't gonna get a shot at that title, not without us he ain't." The kid's an ATM waiting to dispense, and one dive is all they ask. It was 1947, a year widely considered to be the apex of corruption in the sport.

The American light-middleweight Billy Fox was notorious for doing what he was told. Owned and managed by

Murder Inc. affiliate Frank "Blinky" Palermo, he earned millions for the mob before being discarded in 1950. With corruption rampant among managers, it was easy for the likes of Carbo and Palermo to cherry-pick opponents, and, like Max Baer, LaMotta was among the rare fighters who all but told them take a walk. But things had changed in the fifteen years since the Carnera days: why force a fighter to comply when the mob could hamper his career by not giving him a title fight?

The odds for the Fox bout were well in LaMotta's favor but swung drastically on fight day. Rumors were spreading. A fix was at hand. Jake and Joey walk through the bowels of the stadium when a member of the State Athletic Commission asks for assurance that the fight will be legit. LaMotta tells the Commissioner to bet on his victory right there.

In the film, LaMotta isn't told that he was to pay Carbo and Palermo an additional $20,000 to fight Fox. "Jake is an elemental man," remarked Scorsese, so it's little wonder that the director skips over these numerical intricacies. Figures, odds, and ledgers have no place in this primal interpretation.

The fight occurred on November 14, ten days before the House of Representatives cited the Hollywood Ten with Contempt of Congress. While it consumes less than a minute of screen time, Schoonmaker's edits convey the bout's full arc with imperceptible fluidity. LaMotta was fully prepared to tank, but Fox proved so stiff that Jake couldn't help but bully him mercilessly throughout the first round, later writing, "I don't even know how we got through [it] without me murdering him." So followed the most transparent fix in the sport's history, candidly described by LaMotta biographer Lew Freedman as "bad theater." Bored and glazed, Jake dropped his defense to let Fox have at him throughout the following three rounds until the ref finally called it. He never hit the canvas.

"The art of pretending," wrote the *Daily Mirror*, "is one of the most difficult for an honest fighter to master," and Jake was a hopeless case. No showman, he freely admitted that "if there was anybody in the Garden who didn't know what was happening, he must have been dead drunk."

Suspended for his bald-faced dive, LaMotta waited eighteen months to face the Middleweight Champion Marcel Cerdan. The camera rests above four stark-white arms extended to form a black leather clover before an abrupt cut explodes to the fighters' hammering each other furiously from below in a quiet nod to *Killer's Kiss*. Schoonmaker parsed the fight down to slightly over fifty seconds of screen time. When Cerdan refused to rise for the tenth, Jake was declared the new Middleweight Champion. Tragically, there was to be no rematch as Cerdan—the greatest fighter to have come out of France and paramour to Edith Piaf—was killed in a plane crash just four months later.

As touched on previously, the wildly unpopular Tennessee Senator Estes Kefauver, fresh off a probe into the

U.S. pharmaceutical industry, commenced an investigation into organized crime, still known as "the Syndicate," in 1950. The boxing racket was just one facet of the Committee's larger crackdown on organized crime. The Hearings were well-timed in coinciding with the rapid sales of television sets that allowed millions to watch the man boxing writer Kevin Mitchell described as "the first reality television star." Carbo even agreed to serve as a compliant witness. The only caveat was that his face did not appear on television. His pleas for non-exposure honored, only his impeccably manicured hands were visible. In 1954, the IBC, along with their monopoly on boxing, was dissolved.

In 1960, LaMotta, who served as the Committee's key witness, confessed to the Fox dive before a U.S. Senate subcommittee investigating Blinky Palermo's ownership of Fox at the time of the fight. It took the Committee several months to locate Fox, who'd spent most of the thirteen years since the LaMotta bout languishing in a mental institution. While the investigations didn't put an immediate stop to the old-school gangsters' chokehold on the game, the writing was on the wall. The mob had grown increasingly loud and conspicuous. Mitchell writes that Carbo and Joey had become so lax in their attempts at keeping their business on the down-low that they had the chutzpah to "consort with Jake" even as the "officials of the New York State Athletic Commission were near enough to smell them."

LaMotta didn't sweat the proceedings. Carbo was in jail, the statute of limitations on the fix had elapsed, and

Sports Illustrated had offered him a neat sum for the sordid details. All of these would become a fixture in his nightclub anecdotes years later. "I'd do it again." wrote LaMotta in 1982, "The DA couldn't touch me." Carbo may have taken fifty percent, but "fifty percent of a lot" was "better than a hundred percent of a little bit." As Jake sang the Committee a blow-by-blow account of his dealings with Carbo and his cohorts, Arthur Daley of the *New York Times*, who described boxing as "the slum area of sports," wrote that "LaMotta's whistleblowing [was] a start" toward cleaning it up.

Jake's inability to pinpoint the nonexistent man (men?) that Vikki's been screwing compels him to invent one. Could it be Salvi? Tommy? One of the other hoods? And what about Joey? Before filming commenced, De Niro and Peschi took an apartment to live together in character in preparation for their rhythmic, spontaneous exchanges. But as with the kitchen scene, sometimes Peschi needed coaxing. Upon accusing Joey of fucking Vikki, De Niro asked if he'd fucked their mother—later overdubbed to "wife"—to elicit a more (in)credulous facial reaction.

LaMotta's most consistent and frustrating rival was born Walker Smith Jr., better known as Sugar Ray Robinson. Considered by many to be the sport's greatest pound-for-pound practitioner, Ray's calculated science and smart defense were the perfect foil to Jake's taurine brawling. The Bull's opposite in almost every regard, Robinson was handsome and outgoing. A sharp dresser, he'd roll through

Harlem in a Caddy he'd switch out every year for the newest model, trailed by children and no shortage of women. He danced alongside Gene Kelly and Fred Astaire, appeared in films with Richard Burton and Marlon Brando, clinched the divisional World Middleweight Championship no less than five times, and, like LaMotta, was never knocked out.

LaMotta and Robinson fought no less than six times; "so many times," LaMotta quipped, "we were close to getting married." Their first bout featured here depicts their second meeting—the only one in which Jake was victor. Shot from above, a right to the body and a left to the head send Ray out of the ring in the eighth. Jake adjusts the waistband of his trunks and watches like a bull pawing the dirt. The unanimous decision marked Robinson's first loss, though when they met again three weeks later, Ray took the decision. Speculation of favoritism among the judges lingers as Ray was to be deployed for service twelve days later. Although LaMotta had been declared 4-F ("Unfit for Service") for his partial deafness, fans booed the biased decision. Within the brief reenactment, their displeasure is apparent.

In a spectacular act of misguided violence, Jake beats his brother—the scapegoat for his torments—senseless in a surprise visit to the family dinner table in a veiled reenactment of the far more traumatic shellacking Jake gave Savage for kissing Vikki on the cheek. As Vikki places her clothes neatly into a suitcase, Jake pleads with her to stay, and she does—for now. But that doesn't mean she isn't devising a means to escape the marriage she dreaded before she even cut the cake.

On February 14, 1951, LaMotta again met Robinson in what's been dubbed "The Saint Valentine's Day Massacre." A nod to Al Capone's gunning down seven men twenty-two years prior just a few miles from Chicago Stadium where the bout took place, it remains debatable as to which massacre was bloodier.

Scorsese's films had already demonstrated the director's obligation to cave to—or lift above—the profane in the service of something approaching the sacred, and his various martyrdoms manifest as slow rivulets on the path to salvation. In *Mean Streets*, Harvey Keitel's Charlie holds his hand over a candle to envisage the eternal flames of hell. *Taxi Driver*'s Travis Bickle smiles with lunatic rapture as he points his pistols at either side of the viewer in a mock, defiled crucifixion. 1988's *The Last Temptation of Christ* fairly fetishizes the cross itself along with the attendant spikes and hammer.

Amy Koehlinger's *Why Boxing was the most Catholic Sport for almost 100 Years* (see Chapter 12) maintains that Catholics consecrated the sport as "a path to religious purity and bodily mortification; a tool for spiritual edification." In this way, "the central spiritual mysteries of the faith—the *imitatio Christi*," manifest "like the Stations of the Cross in [the boxer's] perseverance through round after round of punishment." Koehlinger equates the "stigmata in the gashes and abrasions that collect on [the boxer's] body" with the issue of the savior's four wounds. But the blood that jets from LaMotta's head holds no promise of redemption, as reflected in the above-mentioned 1970 Heller interview, wherein LaMotta added, "I didn't realize it, but subconsciously I was trying to punish myself."

In the eighth, Jake's arms begin to drape over the ropes. His head lolls like a dead Christ in a tortured Northern Renaissance altarpiece with blood pouring from the crown in translucent tempera and oils. "In that final fight with Sugar Ray," Schoonmaker contends, "... it's as if [Jake] is being given the last rites. ...as if he is the dead Christ being anointed." But Jake had another sixty-six years left in him and the loss didn't change his temperament. As depicted here, the massacre is a culmination of Jake's long, calamitous moral demise in which he begs for the punishment he knows he deserves, even if he doesn't know why. Though the actual bout was a true massacre, it wasn't nearly as gruesome or utterly one-sided as the film's recreation, in which Jake drops his defense and hollers at Ray to keep pounding.

The thirty-five discordant shots within the fight's final twenty-six seconds commence with Jake staring forward as steam rises as if from an inferno. Like Popeye winding up to conk Bluto, Ray holds his fist comically high before landing the punch that brings Koehlinger's *imitatio Christi* to life.

Bert Sugar recalls overhearing an unidentified man's response to the referee's hesitance to stop the fight:

"LaMotta's knocked out enough helpless guys in his time. Let the bum take it himself for a while." With one of LaMotta's eyes closing up and the other blinded by blood, the fight was stopped in the thirteenth.

Blood drips from the ropes like thick black rain, an image that registered with Scorsese during the matches he attended in preparation for the film: "I saw the blood dripping from the ropes. I said to myself that this sure didn't have anything to do with sport!" Yet the gruesome aftermath suggests it had everything to do with the sport, and as Jake ambles across the butcher's floor of the canvas, he reminds Ray, "You never put me down." (Contemporary accounts both confirm and rebuff the veracity this exchange.)

The screen reads 1951 as, all at once, the viewer is confronted with a bloated, wheezy, washed-up pug. Yet the Saint Valentine's Day Massacre occurred that same year. Like Schrader's composite of Joey and Savage, the streamlined compression continues to create fluidity that allows for complete immersion in what has now become—per those loath to label *Raging Bull* a boxing film—an unmitigated character study.

In 1956, Jake opened "Jake LaMotta's Club" in Miami. To the ex-champ, the nightclub-cum-package store served as a respectable, if self-aggrandizing, spotlight: *"a stage where this bull here can rage."*

In chilling adherence to the Method, De Niro suffered serious respiratory ailments after packing on sixty pounds during a three-month break in production where he binged his way through Northern Italy and France. The weight gain is among the film's most discussed and written-about elements, though aside from the physical transformation, there's little to add. As to his stage act, De Niro interprets LaMotta's approach to comedy much like he fought: with aggression, malice, and bad intentions.

Scorsese's decision to omit the pervasive physical violence Jake administered on Vikki wasn't just to appease the censors, for whom the persistent punching of a woman far exceeded blowing a guy's hand off as in *Taxi Driver*. Such depictions would be unwatchable to all but the most sadistic, and Scorsese had no desire to push his arthouse drama into the realm of grindhouse. Still, one should never lose sight of the fact that Jake's beatings were very real. "He's just punched the love out of me," Vikki said six years into the marriage. She was twenty-two. "I'm afraid... he really will kill me." She began packing in 1947, but upon learning that she was pregnant with their third child, further put off her plans for divorce.

Vikki left Jake for good when the family was living in Miami. With deliberate resolve, she delivers the news from her car window, keeping it open just a crack lest he makes a grab at her. Her escape from her husband also marks her flight from the film as she vanishes as swiftly (and a lot more decisively) than she appeared. As to Jake's demented jealous streak, it's fair to question its disappearance upon her departure. In the Scorsese-Catholic barter of blood for salvation, it's as though Jake's final bout with Ray served as the sacrifice that freed him of his demons. The reality was that his vigilance had yet to abate. Even after Vikki moved out, Jake paid her regular visits and battered her senseless while Miami's finest turned a blind eye.

Working his club and stage routine, Jake accepts Vikki's departure without further comment. There's no indication of sorrow or tragedy in the split on either side. Far sadder is the loss of the fraternal bond that provided Jake the most stable relationship he'd ever known and a flip-side to his thuggish frenemy Pete Savage. But Jake does reencounter his brother. It was the first time the actors saw each other since the filming of Jakes's attack on Joey.

While De Niro plodded around Europe packing on weight, Peschi grew thin and sunken. As Jake's girth envelopes his brother's fragile frame, Joey's lack of reciprocation confirms the ex-boxer has destroyed his only outlet for meaningful human contact. So how did LaMotta feel about the estrangement? The answer is best deduced in Joey's complete absence from the memoir. Brother, trainer, and protector are wiped away in a clear indication that, for reasons unknown, LaMotta wished to imbue his life with some historical fiction of his own.

Jake's intransigence toward authority again reared its head in his refusal to kowtow to the cops, for whom kickbacks from the club were an unspoken policy. When a fourteen-year-old girl was found working the place in 1958, Jake was nailed on charges of running a prostitution ring out of the club. (Again, liberties are taken with the timeline: the incident occurred three years after the film's denouement.) Although negligent when confirming customers' ages and expansive in making introductions, there's no evidence that LaMotta served in the capacity of a pimp. Nor did he engage the services of the girls who used the club as their base. As Vikki noted, he took little pleasure in sex. But Jake's virility didn't interest the DA, who could only confirm that, knowingly or otherwise, the ex-fighter was introducing underage prostitutes to would-be johns. It was more than enough to put him away.

Sentenced to six months of hard labor, the film throws Jake in the can for one long Dark Night of the Soul, where he pounds the walls of his eight-by-ten cell. The dull thuds of his fists build to percussive speed, drowned out by his wails of *"I'm not an animal!"* Maybe, but he's not the boss anymore either, a title he vocally bestows upon himself throughout the film in his refusal to cave to outside pressure. LaMotta said of his imprisonment, "With all the really bad things I've done in my life, I'm being punished for something I didn't do." The less sympathetic viewer—and sympathy is in short supply here—will recall the spectator overheard by Bert Sugar: "Let the bum take it himself for a while."

A sign that includes Budd Schulberg and Rod Serling among the evening's recitation material adorns the club entrance. Meanwhile, the forty-year-old, six years-retired thespian-raconteur rehearses the famous monologue from *On the Waterfront* in which Terry Malloy scolds his brother for coercing him into a dive. De Niro models his impression not on Brando but on the washed-up LaMotta, whose impression of the fictional fall guy comes through as a veiled requiem to the loss of his brother Joey.

Raging Bull's rejection of the pomp and grandeur of Winkler and Chartoff's *Rocky* and its first sequel grants free rein to "the worst person in the world" by providing a far more encompassing "stage where this bull here can rage." In a market where contemporary fight biopics demonstrate that studios would opt to send people home on a *Rocky* high, *Bull* is a nihilistic gut punch far closer to the realities of the game. Schrader could have wrapped up on a high note (*i.e.,* Jake winning the title), but it's hard to justify a happy ending for such a lout. And to create one would be a lie.

LaMotta died in 2017 at age ninety-five. An all-time top ten middleweight per *Ring Magazine*, he would be forgotten by all but the boxing cognoscenti if not for the film nominated for Best Picture with Oscars for Best Actor and Best Editing going to De Niro and Schoonmaker. His legacy already tarnished following the Hearings, it took another hit upon the film's release. But Jake made his money, and isn't that what he wanted? Turning to Vikki at the film's premiere, he asked, "Was I that bad?" It was their first encounter since their breakup twenty-three years prior. "Worse," she replied.

The friction from the collusion of the best talent in the business as they tackle their despicable subject makes for a film both action-packed and arthouse, where God's presence is conspicuous not on rosaries or church altars but among the riffraff that haunt bloody rings and sordid nightclubs. Stagnant Catholic overtones promise no salvation or atonement granted by only the most forgiving (*i.e.,* God). Everyone else is apt to side with Sinatra in bestowing their Final Judgement.

Scorsese defends the film as having "work[ed] on an almost primitive level... [that] may be closer to pure spirit." Considering the fighter's animalistic drive, there's a ring of truth in the assessment, though sadly, the spirit under discussion embodies the polar opposite of Christian purity. Still, Scorsese remains guardedly optimistic: "God is not a torturer. He wants us to be merciful with ourselves. And Jake gets there."

But not really.

15
ALI

Directed by Michael Mann
Columbia Pictures, 2001

In 1962, *New Yorker* journalist A.J. Liebling described Muhammed Ali's (then Cassius Clay) fighting style as "skittering...like a pebble over water." Similarly, Michael Mann's *Ali* skips and flits across the fighter's most celebrated, beleaguered decade of 1964 to 1974 to touch upon historical bullet points without context or explanation. The final product is a vague, shiny biopic that demands extensive familiarity with Ali's place amid the decade's social and political upheavals. Like his jab that traveled from shoulder to target and back again at 0.19 seconds (literally within the blink of an eye), *Ali*'s biographical bullet points vanish as fast as they materialize in their haste to forward the narrative.

While this may confuse some viewers, it also establishes a template for the fighter's singular place throughout the tumultuous sixties and seventies.

Conceding that Will Smith was "pretty" enough to portray him, Ali chose the thirty-two-year-old actor himself. In turn, Smith appointed Mann to replace Spike Lee as director, despite Lee's contention that "only a black man could do justice to the story of Cassius Clay." Columbia Pictures was relieved, having feared that, under Lee, the project would devolve into "a narrow, militant movie" lacking broad appeal. But Mann was a mainstream director whose 1999 film *The Insider* had just earned five Golden Globe awards. Pretty easy math for both the studio and the actor.

Cassius Clay was raised in a relatively integrated suburb of Louisville, where his father's income as a sign painter allowed him to buy his son a new bike. It was summarily stolen, and the young Clay bawled to a White police officer, Joe Elsby Martin, that he wanted to "whup whoever it was who stole [his] bike." Well, advised Martin, he'd better learn to fight first, and invited the boy to train at the boxing club he'd opened to keep kids out of trouble. Little Cassius was a fast learner. His moves were even faster. Largely self-taught and resistant to instruction, the show-off who learned to walk before his first birthday turned pro in 1960. He was eighteen.

Throughout the film's eleven-minute credit sequence, Sam Cooke (David Elliott) croons under a twinkling haze of floodlights at Miami's Hampton House Hotel where a sea of adoring Black women in jaw-grazing bobs bat their lashes in a swoon. Fourteen hundred miles away in Chicago, Sonny Liston (Michael Bentt) wrests the title from Floyd Patterson in a full-on slaughter. Clay, already boxing's biggest attraction, jogs through his newly adopted hometown of Miami, narrowly skirting a hassle from the cops as a cruiser slows to amble beside him. Leaning behind the back rows, he attends a sermon by Malcolm X (Mario Van Peebles), where the minister evangelizes the Nation of Islam (NOI). Sitting in his backyard, the fighter is approached by Drew Bundini (Jamie Foxx), who was to become a staple of Ali's entourage, and introduces himself to the fighter by telling him that he was sent by "Shorty" to serve as his "motivator." "Who's Shorty?" asks Clay, to which Bundini cocks his head toward the sky, though whatever god he's looking at, it isn't Allah. "I call 'im Shorty 'cause he like 'em circumcised," adds Bundini of a practice that's nevertheless de rigueur among Muslims. Flashback to Clay as a boy, watching his father paint a White Christ surrounded by his equally pale followers. Why, the fighter later protested, does his race continue to worship a man whose skin color continues to fuel Black oppression?

Among the progenitors of the so-called "neon noir," Mann's glitz is best demonstrated in snazzy crime films like 1981's *Thief* and 1995's *Heat*. In stylish pastels, white-hot neon, and sun-soaked violence, his palette and pacing conjure the icy polish of the best 1980s music videos that ran contemporary with his *Miami Vice* television series from 1984 to 1989.

As noted, biography in any medium is dubious when the subject is still alive. However, Mann depicts Ali as a universally beloved luminary, and his DVD commentary track suggests he'd put him in the same light twenty-two years later. However, the fighter's racial agitation, Muslim separatism, and draft dodging made him enormously unpopular during most of his career. Only when his motor functions began to deteriorate did he become the poster boy for what Joe Flaherty of the *Village Voice* referred to as "the Dylan left and the older lib-labs." Such were the original exponents of so-called white liberal guilt fomented on college campuses at the height of the Black Power movement and opposition to the war in Vietnam. In his book *I Fight for a Living: Boxing and the Battle for Black Manhood, 1880-1915*, Louis Moore writes that it was only "when he could no longer speak [that] white America celebrated Ali for his independence."

In 1961, Clay appeared on the radio with the wrestler known as Gorgeous George (*aka* "The Human Orchid"). In ringlet curls, painted nails, and a sequin gown, George infuriated crowds who, in turn, shelled out their cash in hopes of seeing the preening wrestler destroyed. "Boxing, wrestling, it's all a show," George said of his vilification. When Dick Cavett told Ail that "shaving must probably be an orgasm for you," the boxer explained how George alchemized psychology into money: "They *paid* to see him whipped. I said this is a go-oood idea." In a 1966 piece in *Esquire* titled "In Defense of Cassius Clay," Floyd Patterson recounts an abusive Ali leaning over during a press conference to whisper in his ear: "You want to make some money, don't you, Floyd?"

"Where do you think I'd be next week," fumed the young pro, "if I didn't know how to shout and holler and make the public stand up and take notice?" Some agreed. "I don't care if this kid can fight a lick," said Jack Dempsey with approval, "things are alive again." Others, including James "Cinderella Man" Braddock, disagreed: "He should have people liking him. Instead, they hated him. That don't help boxing."

Clay was attracted to the NOI by age seventeen and, under Malcolm X's tutelage, fully embraced the sect by his twenties. Like many Black activists, the NOI considered boxing a means of exploitation by Whites for financial gain. But Malcolm, who joined the NOI while serving time in prison, saw Clay as a high-profile means of garnering converts. Mann is vague but sedulous in his depiction of the relentless FBI surveillance Malcolm endured, though no explanations are offered as to just what they're investigating. (Hint: Malcolm's recruitment of new NOI members and the incitement of Black separatism.)

In 1934, the nascent NOI fell under the control of the self-proclaimed "Minister of Islam," Elijah Muhammad (born Elijah Robert Poole and played by an austere Giancarlo

Esposito). Established in 1930, the fringe Muslim offshoot was more akin to Scientology than the original teachings of Allah. This was not because of its wanton antisemitism or homophobia, already present in the Quran, but its prophecy of a "battle of Armageddon" stipulating that the Black race would be lifted, Rapture-style, to a half-mile-wide spaceship called "The Mother Wheel." Whites, believed to be the invention of an evil scientist with a giant head, would be destroyed. Under the impossibly charismatic Clay and Malcolm, members proliferated exponentially in ghettos and prisons. The film depicts the NOI as a benign spin-off rather than a perversion of the Muslim faith.

Planting his flag of controversy on the national stage, Clay embraced blind devotion to Elijah. As the great-great-great-grandson of the Kentucky politician and slave owner General Green Clay, Cassius's wish to drop his "slave name" was intrinsic to NOI ideology. This was best reflected in Malcolm's declaration, "I have no last name. Just a name a white man gave one of my ancestors a long time ago. I'd rather be called nigger." When Elijah forbade NOI members from attending Martin Luther King Jr.'s March on Washington in 1963, Clay told Pete Hamill in a *New York Post* interview that he had "no use for the NAACP... I believe it's human nature to be with your own kind." King publicly responded: "When Cassius Clay joined the black Muslims... he became a champion of racial segregation."

"Float like a butterfly, sting like a bee," Clay announces as he enters the weigh-in for his title bout against Sonny

Liston. The catchphrase was coined by Bundini, the scribe of Ali's celebrated "poems." While recent years have recast these rhymes as forerunners to the hip-hop movement, Smith apes Clay's rhythm and rants with impassive disinclination and little screen time. A former hip-hop artist who recorded the 1989 single, "I Think I Can Beat Mike Tyson," the film's limited employment of Smith's lingual chops is among *Ali*'s most wasted opportunities.

To portray the lithe, 215-pound heavyweight, Smith packed on thirty-five pounds of muscle to outweigh his subject-in-his-prime by ten pounds. In a misguided application of the Method, he also abstained from sex during filming, calling into question communication between the actor and the ex-fighter—the latter known to have frequently sneaked in a quickie minutes before battle.

By age fifteen, Sonny Liston had a rap sheet longer than his eighty-four-inch reach. Feared and reviled for his felonious past, his fists measured fifteen inches around. He knocked heavy bags from their chains. "He hurts when he breathes on you," bemoaned an early opponent. Worried that a Liston victory would hamper the civil rights movement, the NAACP attempted to prevent him from fighting Floyd Patterson—*aka* "The Gentleman of Boxing"—for the title in 1962. President Kennedy contacted Patterson with the same plea. By contrast, James Baldwin wrote that in Liston, "...I sensed no cruelty at all... He reminded me of big, black men I have known who acquired the reputation of being tough in order to conceal the fact that they weren't hard."

Among history's most mob-controlled champions, Liston was "acquired" in 1962 by Blinky Palermo and Frankie Carbo, the latter of whom owned him while serving time. In 1960, Edward W. O'Brian wrote in the *Philadelphia Inquirer* that "Kefauver warned Liston to 'shake off' racketeers... and other leaches if he wants a shot at the title." Although Liston managed to take the belt from Patterson in 1962, ridding himself of the "leeches" proved easier said than done. His mysterious death at thirty-eight from a heroin overdose is widely acknowledged as the mob's handiwork.

Clay presented the public a Hobson's choice between Liston's brooding menace and his own insufferable braggadocio, including threats to turn the champ he'd dubbed "the Ugly Bear" into a rug. Mann passes over Clay's psychological warfare on Liston as the bout approaches, including the bus he drove to Liston's house in the middle of the night with a swarm of hangers-on and a megaphone.

Prior to the bout, Robert Lipsyte of the *New York Times* mapped the fastest route to the hospital, where he assumed he'd conduct his post-fight interview with Clay. Instead, the knockout artist known for ending his fights early was dazed and befuddled by his opponent's speed, his ability to vanish and reappear, and those blink-of-an-eye jabs. Refusing to rise for the seventh, the exasperated Liston spit out his mouthpiece like a banner of defeat. As reenacted from existing footage, the sequence culminates in the camera's flash that immortalized the new champ lunging toward Liston's corner, eyes full of manic fury. Not many fans cheered his victory as he screamed, "I am the greatest! I shook up the world!" On the contrary: while not portrayed here, shouts of "Fix! Fix! Fix!" rained from the stands.

Clay's anti-civil rights stance, call for racial separatism, and disparagement of Christianity had already alienated much of the Black population, and two days into his role as the newly minted Champion, he announced that he had officially joined the NOI.

Within a matter of days, Elijah Muhammad bestowed Clay his new name: Muhammed (meaning "worthy of praise") Ali ("elevated" or "champion"). It was an honor that fell to only one percent of NOI members, the rest of whom replaced their "slave names" with an X. Even Malcolm—born Malcolm Little and thus far the NOI's most valuable asset—retained his vacant surname. But Elijah sensed Clay's fame and potential to attract new members. Despite detesting what he called "sport and play" as "the pleasures of the idle rich," the NOI leader fast-tracked the fighter to a full Muslim name in order to increase their own visibility.

(For an extended examination on this pivotal moment in the Aliverse, Regina King's 2020 *One Night in Miami*, based on the play by Kemp Powers, presents a focused narrative of Ali's conversion and Malcolm's apostasy to provide a

contained, manageable delve into this singular chapter of
Ali's career.)

Clay's name change sparked a national riff that doubled
down on the racial divide. His ongoing diatribes—especially
on Black nationalism—were in full force in 1965, when he
told Alex Haley in a *Playboy* interview, "A black man should
be killed if he's messing with a white woman." When asked
if the same applied to women, he answered, "Kill her too."

Malcolm became a pariah almost overnight as his
stance on racial separatism abated. Ousted from the NOI
in 1964, he met Ali for the last time in Africa during his
pilgrimage to Mecca. The two men, wearing dashikis, face
each other affectionately before the fighter walks away. "You
shouldn't have turned your back on Brother Muhammad."
Almost fifty years later, the seventy-one-year-old Ali wrote
in his memoir *The Soul of a Butterfly: Reflections on Life's Journey*
that "turning my back on Malcolm was one of the mistakes
that I regret most in my life."

Lecturing at Manhattan's Audubon Ballroom, Malcolm
is gunned down by an NOI operative from the Newark
mosque. It was February 21, 1965. Despite the momentous
ramifications for Ali and the NOI, the film's competent
recreation of the assassination amounts to just another
perfunctory bullet point. Ali hears the news on his car
radio. A tear curls down his cheek. He puts his car in gear
and drives on to the next chapter.

Although the Muslim faith forbade extramarital

affairs, Ali was a notorious bounder who divorced his first wife, Sonji Roi, for her lax adherence to Muslim law. At the Tiger Lounge in Chicago, Mann recreates their introduction by Elijah's son Herbert Muhammad (Barry Shabaka Henley).

Roi (Jada Pinkett Smith) had been a barmaid, a model, and, in all likelihood, a prostitute for Herbert's private harem. Like his father, Herbert considered himself above Muslim law—a godlike entity with a sacred duty to spread his holy seed. What he didn't anticipate was that Ali and Roi would become engaged the night they met. "She was a date," Herbert tells Ali of the woman he'd coerced into participating in his homemade pornographic films. "You don't *marry* this girl."

Roi's refusal to adhere to Muslim law spurred the NOI to seek divorce proceedings. "The onliest reason I married her," Ali said of their seventeen-month marriage, "was because she agreed to do everything I ordered her to do." But aside from Ali's displeasure over Sonji's manner of dress and a scene in which he calls her to change the baby's diaper (sources indicate he didn't know how), scant reference is made to his adherence to outmoded Muslim gender roles.

The circumstances behind Ali's May 25 rematch with Liston could stand alone as a four-hour conspiracy epic. For starters, rumors of an NOI hit on Ali began to circulate for his suspected friendship with Malcolm X following the minister's expulsion and before his assassination.

There were murmurings that the Nation had threatened to kidnap Liston's nephew to ensure their show pony would retain the title, as well as a mob order on Liston to take a dive in exchange for making a 1953 rape allegation disappear. Wary of Liston's criminal ties, the city of Boston pulled out of hosting the bout, which was hastily relocated to a five-thousand-seat youth center in Lewiston, Maine, where Liston hit the canvas in under two minutes.

No one knew what to think. They didn't even know what they saw. Or if they saw it at all: the overhand right dubbed the "phantom punch" not just for its speed but for the ongoing debate as to how it could have felled a 215-pound colossus like Liston. The ongoing consensus of a Liston dive is highly unpopular in many circles. "Any objective observer," writes Rob Sneddon in his 2015 book *The Phantom Punch: The Story Behind Boxing's Most Controversial Bout,* "would have had to concede that Ali's counterpunch had landed, and landed with enough force to turn Liston's head." But if it was so effective, why didn't Ali employ what he referred to as his "anchor punch" in his future bouts? Other sources indicate a dive: "I didn't want anything to do with [Ali]," Liston told *Sports Illustrated*'s Mark Kram. "And the Muslims were coming up.... so I went down." Even Ali, believing he had merely tapped his opponent, told a fellow NOI member, "He laid down."

If Liston did tank, he was a worse actor than LaMotta in his swim with Billy Fox. Landing on his back like a cock-roach, Sonny pushed on his wrists and gloves in an attempt to rise, only to fall back pitifully on his elbows. Although an enraged Ali refused to retreat to a neutral corner, the referee, former Heavyweight Champion Jersey Joe Walcott (Joe from *The Harder They Fall*) began the count all the same. By the time Liston rose, the fight had been called.

The film cedes twenty-three seconds to history's most controversial sporting event. Sonny lies on his back as the flash from Neil Leifer's camera blinds the screen to capture what has become boxing's most iconic photograph: Ali standing over the fallen giant, right arm cocked and, depending on the source, screaming, "Nobody will believe this!" or "Get up and fight sucker!" In line with the boomers and Flaherty's above-mentioned "Dylan lib-labs," Mann's blind faith in the knockout is unequivocal. Nor is any contention acknowledged among the fans, and the director coyly hints that he's among the handful of experts, or as he says on his commentary track, "most of the other people I've talked to," that are wholly in the know.

It was the first time Ali had fought under his new name. His prayer to Allah at the commencement of the bout substantiated his standing as the world's most controversial and recognizable figure. Of the living icon, Dick Cavett wrote, "In the most far-flung regions there was only one face pointed to by the Bantu tribesmen and farmer's wife in rural Tibet," and it wasn't Sinatra, Liz Taylor, or Mickey Mouse. Yet for all his fame, Ali had usurped Liston as White America's new Black menace.

Jon Voight's Howard Cosell follows Ali with a microphone, faultlessly mimicking the legendary announcer's un-re-*mittably* staccato iteration. With a cautiously amused mien and prosthetics that render the actor unrecognizable, Voight is the film's crown jewel—right up to the tip of that precarious hair piece that Ali plays with like a chinchilla.

Born Howard Cohen in 1918, Cosell grew up in Brooklyn. "Arrogant, obnoxious, vain, persecuting, distasteful, verbose, a showoff," he readily conceded as he elbowed his way from law into sportscasting at the advanced age of forty-eight, "I have been called all of these. Of course, I am." He was also a natural sportscaster for the television age who broke with the old-school anonymity of previous announcers. Not everyone took to his style. "He makes the world of fun and games sound like the Nuremberg Trials," wrote sportswriter Larry Merchant.

A visionary who helped conceive "action shots," wherein boxing was filmed from several angles for television, Cosell was also the first sportscaster to conduct clubhouse and post-fight interviews. These innovations, paired with his on-air, politicized Punch and Judy act with Ali, launched televised sports into the realm of showbiz.

Cosell and Ali met in 1962. As the first broadcaster to call him by his adopted Muslim name, the film introduces Cosell mid-interview. His authoritative intonation is directed not at Ali, but at the viewing public: "You have a right to be called whatever you want," he tells the fighter.

A Martin and Lewis combo replete with childish razzing, their affection was genuine and mutual. As their exchanges rose to variety-show status, Cosell was deluged with hate mail, where the most common salutation was "Nigger-loving Jew bastard."

On April 28, 1967, Ali publicly refuted his draft notice. He'd already flunked the exam once: "I said I'm the greatest, not the smartest." When Cosell calls to tell him test standards have been lowered to the fifteenth percentile to meet the need for more soldiers, the fighter was not only eligible to serve but was required to.

As one of history's most politically active athletes, Ali was bullishly incurious when it came to details. This was especially conspicuous when it came to a war ten thousand miles away in a place called Vietnam. "I know where Vietnam is," he tells Tom Fitzpatrick of the *Chicago Daily News* on the phone. "It's on TV." Then follows the boxer's most quoted proclamation on America's new war: "I don't have no quarrel with those Viet Kong." The pronouncement quickly became a rebel yell to dissidents of all colors and a middle finger to conservative America's attempt to silence them. But Ali's plea for conscientious objector status—a prerequisite that requires opposition to *all* war—fell flat when he declared that he would go to war if it were "declared by Allah." (Elijah had served four years for his refusal to fight in World War II, as had his son Wallace for skirting Vietnam.) Elijah, who saw the war as a catalyst for the destruction of American morals, was content to hang back as the country laid the groundwork for its imminent race war.

Ali arrives at the induction ceremony with Herbert and an entourage of NOI officials who watch on like hawks. After refusing to answer to his former name, the fighter is stripped of the title, handed a $10,000 fine, and given the maximum sentence of five years in prison. Worst of all, he was suspended from boxing from March of 1967 to October of 1970.

A year and a half after his divorce from Roi, Ali married the seventeen-year-old Belinda Boyd (played by the twenty-nine-year-old Nona Gaye). The child of Muslim parents, a graduate of the University of Islam, and a congregant of South Side's Temple #2 in Chicago, Boyd was also a virgin—a prerequisite for a Muslim bride. Although the meeting is presented here as a chance encounter, Ali deliberately introduced himself at the behest of Herbert. At the bakery where she worked, Boyd reminds him that they met when she was ten when the young Cassius visited her Muslim school. Ali squints hard, but he's not looking at her hair. "You had a braid." The marriage was held in strict accordance with Muslim tradition. Then, in a 1969 appearance on *The Tonight Show*, Ali told Johnny Carson that he needed money. His public display of impatience to return to the world of "sport and play" cost him indefinite ostracism from the NOI.

When the opportunity for a $100-million-dollar-gate

championship bout against world Heavyweight Champion "Smokin'" Joe Frazier (who had assumed the mantle during Ali's absence) arose, the Supreme Court, spurred by the NAACP, granted a reprieve. With the suspension lifted, Ali receives the call from Cosell. (He hears a lot of things from Cosell, who serves as a merciful composite of numerous ancillary players in an already overpopulated film.) The vote was unanimous: 8-0 in Ali's favor. The fighter, who'd just lost three and a half prime fighting years, was about to enter the most celebrated phase of his career.

Ali and Frazier were on friendly terms when Ali and Belinda moved to Frazier's hometown of Philly in 1970. "You look like the heavyweight champion of pimps," Ali chides his future opponent as he slides into the champ's new Cadillac. While the car ride is widely known to have taken place—some say to New York—conversation is necessarily speculative. Frazier biographer Mark Kram Jr. writes that the champ was eager to fight Ali and promised to buy him ice cream "after I whip your ass." The drive ended in a collusion between the fighters wherein Frazier told Ali, "We don't wanna be seen too much together." Ali agreed: "Ain't nobody gonna pay to see two buddies."

Played with solid credibility by Cruiserweight Champion James Toney, Joe Frazier was a sharecropper by age six. At sixteen, he moved to Philly to work manual labor, including a meat locker in which he used sides of beef as heavy bags. Meanwhile, Ali denounced his opponent as an "Uncle Tom" for his silence on the war (from which, as a father, Frazier was exempt) as well as his concession that he did not fight for the Black cause but rather to support his wife and five kids. Others jumped on the bandwagon to vilify Frazier's silence on racism. In an October 1972 *Boxing Illustrated* article callously titled "Is Joe Frazier a White Champion in Black Skin?", Bryant Gumbel wrote, "By referring to his opponent as 'Cassius Clay,' Frazier has allied himself... with those who are against Ali. ... [and] to be against Ali is to be against the majority black population." Gumbel's denouncement of Frazier as "a ghetto black in the fullest sense of the term" is a cruel extension of Ali's persistent use of Uncle Tom that prompted Frazier to excoriate the middle-class Louisvillian as having been brainwashed by "those sorry ass Muslims." "Fuck your religion," he added, "*this* is black." Despite NOI aversion to "sport and play," the fighter was accepted back into the fold upon his reinstatement, telling Herbert, "I never left." The NOI had regained its masthead.

Once the contracts were signed, Ali mercilessly taunted his opponent as "a tool of the white establishment" and "too ugly to be champ." (His pejorative rhetoric and bullying behavior reached an apex in the lead-up to his third meeting with Frazier in 1975's "Thrilla in Manilla," not covered within the film's ten-year scope.) Cruel, divisive, and hurtful, Ali declared that "the only people rooting for Frazier are white people in suits, Alabama sheriffs, the Ku Klux Klan, and maybe Nixon." (He was right about the latter, who referred to Ali as "that draft-dodging asshole.")

Millions of Black and White Americans fell into step, mistaking Frazier's unwillingness to discuss race as apathy. Kram Jr. writes, "Joe just didn't understand where Ali was coming from, and Ali did not understand why Joe did not understand." When Joe's children were hassled at school because of Ali's televised rants, Ali ignored Joe's request to let up.

The 1974 main event was a *grosse soirée* to which even showbiz luminaries had difficulty scoring ringside seats. (To skirt a ticket hassle altogether, Frank Sinatra volunteered as a photographer for the March 1971 issue of *Life Magazine*'s coverage of the bout by Norman Mailer, who also gained free rein to roam ringside.) Fifteen rounds unfold in just forty-five seconds—less if one considers the numerous slow-motion shots—as Frazier clinches a unanimous decision. Ali didn't take the belt back as planned and Frazier never bought him ice cream.

The three-year lead-up to the rematch is compressed to sixty seconds that cover Ali's return-to-the-ring-dispatching of Jerry Quarry and a blink-or-you'll-miss-it reenactment of his 1973 defeat of future champion Ken Norton. (Apparently, Ali's *loss* to the same Ken Norton five months prior lies outside Mann's narrative intent.) Although Ali won his 1974 rematch with Frazier, it was not a title bout. He wasn't champion again—yet.

Frazier despised Ali's decidedly non-playful trash talk, recalling years later that it "cut me up inside." Nevertheless, the two remained friends long after their careers ended. In a 1990 appearance with Ali on the *Phil Donahue Show*, Frazier graciously answered the questions put to Ali, though it was plain to the half-witted audience that Ali could no longer speak. Praising his former opponent's skills, Frazier contended that it was Parkinson's, not boxing, that had diminished Ali's motor functions. Upon Ali's death, Dr. Samuel Goldman of the Parkinson's Institute and Clinical Center speculated that "there's a good likelihood that his Parkinson's is a consequence of repetitive head trauma."

As he aged, Frazier grew less forgiving of "the scamboozas who thought nothing of taking about me as if I was some dumb head-scratching nigger." Ali, meanwhile, had grown contrite: "I... called him names I shouldn't have called him. I apologize for that... It was all meant to promote the fight."

Most viewers are unaware of the 1960s political upheaval in the Republic of Congo. In a scene inserted like a sidebar during Malcolm and Ali's meeting in Africa, a Congolese advisor to the country's newly branded dictator, Mobutu Sese Seko (Malick Bowens), leans into the new president's ear: "It is done." After the execution of Prime Minister Patrice Lumumba four years prior, Mobutu's army had completed their coup. In 1971, Mobutu changed the Congo's name to Zaire.

In early 1973, Frazier lost the title to the hulking, ominous George Foreman. Seventeen fights after his reinstatement, Ali was finally given his long-deserved shot to reclaim the crown.

Speaking at a press conference and looking like the devil engulfed in sulfur, Don King (Mykelti Williamson) explains how the upcoming title bout will serve as an active measure toward racial equality. A "reptilian motherfucker," per Mike Tyson, the promoter-cum-swindler once held a fundraiser that raised $15,000 for an all-Black children's hospital and brought in $30,000 for himself. With King's signature 2,500-volt flat-top and a coke nail like a claw, Williamson is comic, repugnant, and transparently duplicitous. King once said, "I transcend earthly bounds... god touches me, and I do something even more stupendous." The scheming bullshitter orates on why the fight will be held in Zaire: "It will fill the souls of the unrequited need of the black proletariat, that is, the discouraged, dispirited, denigrated denizens of the demimonde that is called the ghetto." But really, why Zaire?

Don King came of age running an illegal gambling operation out of his Cleveland basement. He accumulated two murder charges—one for stomping a man to death over $600, buying him four years in the Marion Correctional Institution. To block any other promotional companies from organizing an Ali-Foreman bout, King swooped in with the promise of a five-million-dollar purse for each fighter. However, no reputable domestic venue would let the ex-con stage the event in their state. Not only did King need an overseas venue, he needed the funds to cover the promised purses.

Among King's backers was the American Advisor to Zaire, who helped persuade Mobutu to hold the bout in his home country. Amid the culture wars at home, Michael Ezra writes that King "exploited the idea of blackness for money." The proceeds—ostensibly designated for the improvement of Zaire's ghettos and infrastructure—were instead funneled into Mobutu's regime. With burlesque flourish, a beaming Bundini announces, "There's gonna be a rumble in the jungle," thus bequeathing the most anticipated sporting event of all time its official title—certainly an improvement on King's original, heavy-handed "From the Slave Ship to the Championship."

Ali had noticeably diminished. He slurred. He forgot poems mid-stanza. He'd even started to drool. The great speed of the pre-suspension Cassius of old was gone, and it wasn't just age. Ali's doctor, Ferdie Pachenko, called the upcoming Foreman bout "an act of criminal negligence." Yet as depicted here by Paul Rodriguez, the doctor appears blissfully unconcerned. When Ali's manager, Angelo Dundee (Ron Silver), tells his boy, "I don't want your head to become a target," he has no idea that's precisely how Ali will play it.

Green and yellow hand-painted billboards adorn Zaire's capital city of Kinshasa: "A fight between two blacks in a black nation, organized by blacks and seen by the whole world, that is a victory for Mobutism." Hundreds of naive but impassioned murals in Ali's likeness adorn the sagging fences and crumbling walls the boxer passes as he runs through labyrinthine alleys, leaps over pads of hyacinth, zips past favelas, and bounces up stone stairways trailed by a throng of children who chant, *"Ali boma ye!"* (Lingala for "Ali, kill him!") Reinforcing the film's frequent stretches of hollow action, Roger Ebert singles out this sequence as the epitome of time wasted. "All very well," he wrote in the *Chicago Sun-Times*. "But he runs and runs and runs, long after any possible point has been made—and runs some more."

The film suggests that Ali and Foreman (played by professional heavyweight Charles Shufford) never met. But the former had already marshaled his verbal warfare, partly by telling locals that his opponent was Belgian, Zaire's former colonizers. On the home front, the *New York Times* reported Ali as having told his opponent, "I'll beat your Christian ass, you white, flag-waving (expletive deleted)." He also warned Foreman's fans and followers: "When you get to Africa, Mobutu's people are gonna put you in a pot, cook you, and eat you," a curiously suspect take on the motherland. Foreman, now the 25-1 favorite, had his game plan: "beat on every angle of Ali's cowering and self-protective meat."

Woven into the surrounding, prefab exoticism is Ali's courtship of Veronica Porché. Is this a vague reference to Ali's chronic infidelities? If it is, it's the only one. His affair and marriage (never legally recognized) to the sixteen-year-old Wanda Bolton while he was still married to Belinda are passed over entirely. In this way, his relentless catting remains concealed. So too does his penchant for younger, often underage women, exemplified by the casting of the thirty-five-year-old Michael Michele as the eighteen-year-old Porché.

King reserved a quarter of Kinshasa's Stade Tata Raphaël's 80,000 seats for American VIPs. To his great expense, fewer than fifty opted to shell out the exorbitant ticket price—hotel, airfare, and vaccinations not included. Instead, the crowd consisted almost entirely of locals in the nosebleeds at twenty bucks a head. Despite the thousands of empty seats wrapped around the front rows, the film packs the stadium to capacity.

Readers should be spared a blow-by-blow account of the abridged, eight-round, thirty-three-minute barnburner as recreated here. So should viewers: with the original fight (along with the others discussed) available on YouTube, there's little excuse for forgery. Notable, however, was Ali's perplexing turn in technique. In the opening round, he moves to the ropes to let Foreman have at him, confirming Dundee's concerns of allowing his head "to become a target." As filmed above the waists, Smith and Shufford do their best to mimic the genuine article. Ceding foot movement to punishment, Ali fends Foreman's blows with his elbows and arms, tiring out the younger fighter with a strategy he famously dubbed the "rope-a-dope."

(For a thoroughly expository account of the fight, viewers should turn to Leon Gast's documentary *When We Were Kings*. Filmed mainly in Kinshasa during the fight and its build-up, its completion was shelved for over two decades. Clinching the Oscar for Best Documentary upon its 1996 release, the fighters attended the award ceremony together, where Foreman helped Ali onto the stage.)

A barrage of straight punches to Foreman's face culminates in a wizzing right that puts him down for good. As Smith stands alone in the ring, the heavens open up to hammer rain down on the victor: Black freedom fighter. 4-1 underdog. The wrath of Allah made flesh. So what if the rain started a half hour *after* the fight? In the service of melodrama, Mann knows precisely how and when his viewers want their boxing films to end.

Ali won eleven of his fourteen fights following the Rumble and continued to rely on his capacity to absorb blows to tire opponents. In 1981, he lost his final bout in a dull, 15-round decision. Although he maintained, "Only god knows about my brain," even he was aware of his decline. Asked in his final post-fight interview if his skills "might have gone," he replied, "They have gone. Not '*may* have gone.' They have gone."

Elijah's death in 1975 mollified the Black and White public's wariness of Ali. Meanwhile, the fighter expressed contrition for things he'd said earlier in his career: "White people wouldn't be here if god didn't mean them to be." At last, the fighter praised the country that had come to embrace him for his anti-war stance, his roundabout approach to combating racism, and speech that had grown slow and halting. In 1976, the NOI was renamed the American Muslim Mission. Helmed by Elija's son Wallace, the sect was revamped and rehabilitated to reject Black nationalism and accept White members before its disbandment in 1985. After Elija's death, Ali converted to Sunni Islam, an inclusive Islamic teaching practiced by roughly ninety percent of contemporary Muslims.

The cherry-picked, revisionist history surrounding the Ali mythos began in earnest during the denouement of his career in the late seventies. It's worth noting that the seeds of adoration were sown not only by Ali's boxing record or activism but also by what might be called the Ali "brand." Still one of the most famous faces on the planet, the fighter shilled candy, boxing equipment, and shoe polish. He even teamed up with Superman to battle an alien invasion in a 1978 DC comic book. "Superman," Ali tells the Man of Steel in the final panel, "WE are the greatest!" More than a fighter, activist, and brand, Ali came to symbolize America as much as the red-caped White boy from Krypton.

As discussed in the cases of Regina King's *One Night in Miami* and Gast's *When We Were Kings*, other films have turned their historical lens on Ali. Among the most curious is Jimmy Jacobs's 1970 documentary *a.k.a. Cassius Clay*. Made during Ali's suspension, the film puts the fighter's media cachet on par with his boxing notoriety. In 1977, Columbia Pictures released *The Greatest*, a biopic account of Ali written by the fighter and once-blacklisted Ring Lardner Jr. Directed by Tom Gries and based on Ali's 1975 memoir *The Greatest: My Own Story*, the film stars Ali and Bundini as themselves, along with an imperious James Earl Jones as Malcolm X. Made when Ali was reevaluating his separatist ideology, the film's core message is how one Black man rose to fame in a society that hated him for his skin color.

As noted more than once, *Ali*'s exacting, expository narrative begs clarification. Still, the film sets a near-perfect outline for a history lesson in its examination of the man, fighter, agitator, and activist who claimed to have "done handcuffed lightning and thrown thunder in jail." Mann poises the viewer for a deeper delve into both Ali and the host of friends, enemies, and hangers-on that revolved around his radiance like the moons of Jupiter—the most massive of planets named for the god of storms, wind, and of course, thunder and lighting.

16
ROCKY

Directed by John G. Avildson
United Artists, 1976

A portrait of Christ presides over the ring at the Resurrection Athletic Club in a sober reminder that His flock lies not with the penitents in church but with the shills and moneychangers in the stands clenching crumpled bills. As the Savior dips the host like nourishment to the slugger dubbed "The Italian Stallion," Sylvester Stallone's bare-bones narrative launches guerrilla filmmaking to the nascent dominion of the blockbuster.

Rocky had about the same odds of clinching the Oscar for Best Picture as Stallone, the film's writer and titular hero, had of getting his script into the hands of the formidable producers Irwin Winkler and Robert Chartoff. With a handful of uncredited roles (including a subway thug in Woody Allen's 1971 *Bananas*), bit television parts, and one starring role in Martin Davidson and Stephen F. Verona's *The Lords of Flatbush* (1974), Stallone was on the fast track to central casting as a perennial Italian greaser. With a bankbook that showed $106.00, the twenty-nine-year-old Hell's Kitchen native penned his script in a spiral-bound Mead notebook over a four-day frenzy in November of 1975.

Despite a lack of prominent connections, Stallone always kept a folded copy in his pocket on the off-chance of passing it on to an industry-heavy. In a backhanded stroke of luck, he presented it to two agents who'd just turned him down for a role. Unimpressed with Stallone's audition, they nevertheless bought the script on the spot for $2,500 before turning a quick profit and selling it to Winkler and Chartoff for $6,000.

Struck by the script's urban realism and naturalist dialogue, Winkler and Chartoff, who would go on to produce *Raging Bull* five years later, also knew it would be a tough sell. A stouthearted bruiser, a familial drama, a love story, and a title fight that doesn't enter the narrative until halfway through the film, it was a gamble they were willing to take. As they began to consider marketable names, including James Caan, Ryan O'Neil, and Burt Reynolds, Stallone threw down his gauntlet: only he could play this guy "who's never gotten a break." Lacking clout, connections, or bargaining power, Stallone remained intransigent. This was *his* story, the only difference being the switching out of his plight as a struggling actor for that of a boxer. Winkler and Chartoff agreed that no recognizable Hollywood draw would bring the same veracity to the story but countered with a few conditions of their own: Stallone would not be paid for his acting work on the film *or* the script. Instead, he'd earn a small percentage of the box office intake.

As to the budget, the producers also remained cautious. Who would want to see a drama about a bunch of foundering sad sacks in the first place? The answer, it turned out, was everybody, and the crushing lines of hopeful viewers extended the film's run for months. A critical success, all but one of the film's five leads were nominated for Academy Awards, while Stallone took in $2.5 million for what turned out to be the year's highest-grossing film. With humility belied by his tireless efforts to see his project come to fruition, Stallone told Johnny Carson during an appearance on *The Tonight Show* in 1976, "If I had known it was going to be this difficult, I never would have made it." Humble for sure, but in light of his astronomic payday, it's hard to believe that Hollywood's newest megastar regretted his efforts.

With a budget set for 1.1 million, filming had to be fast, cheap, and on the down low. The on-site shooting was completed in less than a week—usually after dark to elude the local teamsters looking for a cut. If one accepts the "city-as-character" concept, it's never sunny in *Rocky*'s Philadelphia. Streetlamps illuminate a gang of street-corner crooners. Pallid neon flickers nebulously. The rumble from the el punctuates conversation like thunder in a haunted house.

On the more sophisticated end of technology, Garret Brown's Steadicam made its third outing following its first uses in Hal Ashby's *Bound for Glory* and John Schlesinger's *Marathon Man* (also from 1976). Initially operated solely by its inventor, the device—as discussed in Chapter 13—assures smooth tracking shots even when used on rough, irregular surfaces like the sidewalks in the pre-gentrified neighborhood of Fishtown, where it slinks around tenebrous street corners and ascends stairs with impartial fluidity.

A militaristic squad of horns accompanies a screen-filling title card of which Stallone remarked, "I've never seen such large credits for such a little movie." Subsequent credits loom like sidebars over the action itself—in this case, Rocky's walk home from the fight. Such placement of text was common to the decade's spike in aggressive urban realism in throwing the viewer directly into the story without a moment wasted. (This soon became standard, and a precursor to today's interminable cold openings.) But *Rocky* eschews the violence inherent to seventies urban peril by immediately affirming the lead character's mental stability. He may not be bright, but nor can he be counted among his contemporary sleuths and trigger-happy vigilantes. Despite the persistent presence of loafers, gamblers, and second-rate hoods, *Rocky* establishes itself as a flip side to films wherein deliverance from implicit threat comes by way of misguided violence. As the relatively new MPAA ratings system, established in 1968, kept its eagle eye on the new decade's rise in violent grindhouse cinema and its attendant revolving door of psychos, *Rocky* swaps tough justice and existential jitters for a swipe at civility.

Roger Ebert wrote that *Rocky* "doesn't try to surprise us with an original plot... with twists and complications; it wants to involve us on an elemental, and sometimes savage, level." With forthright chronology, the "elemental" manifests in an immediacy of narrative, a staunch commitment to the present, and an unexplained past that assures the viewer remains in the moment.

This refusal to divulge a past is perhaps best exemplified in Rocky's dreary one-bedroom apartment where his pet turtles, Cuff and Link, are the first to hear about the evening's victory at the Resurrection Club: sixty dollars "less fifteen locker room and cornerman, five-dollar locker and towel and seven percent tax." $35.80 richer, Rocky shakes fish flakes into a goldfish bowl and gives Moby Dick the news, after whom there's no one left to tell. This gentle and innate protection of animals was a prominent selling point to Winkler and Chartoff in its application of the seventies "new sensitive man" upon the picture-perfect tough guy. (While Moby has passed, Cuff and Link turned fifty in 2021.)

The apartment probably contains more Catholic iconography than all other boxing films combined, including *Raging Bull* in all its *imitatio Christi* (though *Rocky* is not without aspirations to redemption through blood spilled).

An artless crucifix keeps vigil over the single bed, and a cheap print of Caravaggio's *The Calling of St Matthew* appears to depict the same Christ who presided over Rocky's basement brawl entering a drinking den and pointing at the boozy tax collector and soon-to-be-apostle. Like the ring, it's not the sort of place one would expect find Jesus. But in his own words, he was not out "to call the righteous, but sinners to repentance."

On closer inspection, the poster is revealed to be a 1969 novelty print by Beatles poster artist Fabio Traverso titled *The Renaissance Minstrels,* in which the faces of the fab four are superimposed over the drunken riffraff and Christ is cropped from the image entirely. Of the original painting, Pope Francis observed that "when Christ makes us his disciples, he does not look to our past, but to the future," and for Rocky, the future is all there is. If the Catholic iconography, brass knuckles, and bayonets that ornament the walls are any indication, it's a cinch to count Matthew—who wrote about hell more than all other three apostles combined—among Rocky's progenitors.

On the mantle sits a photo of Rocky's hero and ostensible namesake, Rocky Marciano. Among the greatest heavyweights of all time, "The Brockton Blockbuster" held a perfect record of forty-nine wins and zero losses before he was killed in a plane crash the day before his forty-sixth birthday in 1969. Although Stallone has insisted that the name Rocky Balboa was based solely on the devout Catholic

Blockbuster, several other fighters and facets jibe with the iconic moniker. Rocky's hard-scrabble beginnings and criminal transgressions are closer to those of Rocky Graziano, a young Brooklyn hood-turned Middleweight Champion whose birth name of Barbarella (Stallone's mother's maiden name) neatly correlates with the Balboa surname. While the moniker "The Italian Stallion" was used by the 1970s-80s heavyweight and actor Lee Canalito, it remains unclear who borrowed from whom as the actors had worked together the previous year. Finally, Stallone, Italian for "stallion," completes the colossal mash-up of names in which ethnicity proves essential. (Stallone is half-Italian Catholic, a quarter French, and a quarter Ukrainian Jew.) When a reporter asks Rocky how he came up with his fighting moniker, the boxer replies that he "made that up one night while [he] was eating dinner."

Like the pre-canonized Matthew, Rocky's also a collector, working the docks as a leg-breaker for the affable, asthmatic loan shark, Gazzo (Joe Spinnell). When Rocky gives a deadbeat another week to pay up instead of breaking his thumb as instructed, it's evident that his heart's not in his work. His leniency is not shared by Gazzo, whose driver calls Rocky a "meat bag"—an insult that proves prophetic to Rocky's future training regimen. As Gazzo's car vanishes down the quay, a cargo barge bobs on the oily water while the first notes of Bill Conti's montage-anthem *Gonna Fly Now* debut not with the familiar, booming brass, but in melancholy piano strains that weave into a hopeless landscape. Like the East River in *Killer's Kiss*, the Delaware wallows blackly like a poison mote.

This predilection for forgiveness bespeaks Rocky's placid nature and implies the eternal male pecking order that defines the boxing film through ill-gained wealth and, when necessary, violence. Gazzo may not have a hand in the fight game, but relations between fighter and hood persist and overlap. Organized crime is nonexistent, and petty crime peripheral, with Gazzo providing an ancillary link to old-school thuggery. There's no Syndicate. No fixes. Just old-fashioned loansharking, and even a felonious capitalist like Gazzo remains a friend and supporter.

When Rocky's locker is handed off to a younger prospect, the gym's truculent proprietor, Mickey Goldmill (Burgess Meredith), fulminates over the prime years the fighter wasted breaking thumbs and fracturing legs. His face looks like an angry pepper as his first line—"*Shut up!*"—resounds through the gym. In an instant, the bird-like, doddering roles on which the actor largely made his name crumble under Mickey's fury.

A thirty-six-year Hollywood veteran, Meredith brought Hollywood legitimacy to the tiny production. With a career that began at the 14th Street Theatre in New York, he studied alongside a young John Garfield and other communist-leaning actors until he was expelled for responding in the negative when asked if he loved The Group Theater more than himself. Blacklisted from 1949 to 1954, the sixty-eight-year-old actor had appeared in over 120 films before signing on for *Rocky*.

Rocky extracts a thirteen-year-old girl from a group of corner troubadours to walk her home and warn her about getting a reputation as (and he doesn't like to say it) a whore. When she tells him to screw off, her point is well taken. After all, who's the real whore here? Rocky won't be redeeming anyone until he tends to himself.

The pet shop across the street from Mickey's Gym is a wholly different kind of weigh station for innocents waiting to be lifted from confinement. Like Rocky or the store's mousy clerk Adrian (Talia Shire), the wide-eyed, blameless animals are resigned to their internment. Through the silver bars of the bird cages, Adrian is established a silent prisoner to her loneliness.

Adrian's docility and plain dress perfectly counter-balance Rocky's expansive need for conversation. Through horn-rimmed glasses, she steals furtive glances at the guy in the leather jacket with his sweatshirt tucked in his sweatpants talking to the caged birds. "Like flying candy," he observes; a chatty Saint Francis preaching to his sparrows.

The would-be fisherman of souls lifts a passed-out drunk off the sidewalk and carries him back into the bar from which he stumbled. Inside, Adrian's brother Paulie (Burt Young) combs what little hair he has in a sliver of broken mirror in the back of the house. He appeals to Rocky to ask his sister on a date. He's also on Rocky to talk to Gazzo about getting him some collecting work. "Breakin' bones don't bother me."

Despite the cigar fixed as if with papier mâché to a protruding lower lip and a stocky carriage that exudes listless pugnacity, Young was a lean boxer during his service in the Marines with a perfect 17-0 record. An inveterate character actor, he was soon typecast playing hoods and heavies. Fresh off his role as a (very literal) bone-breaker in Karel Reisz's *The Gambler*, Young fleshes Paulie into a coil of repressed and seething alienation propelled by a mutual resentment of and perverse codependency on his sister. *"I don't get married because of you!"*

In its unerring commitment to the present, Rocky and Paulie's history is never referenced as it bears no relevance to the story (though it is revealed in *Rocky III* that Paulie protected Rocky from neighborhood bullies when they were kids). While Rocky is trying to pull away from collecting work, Paulie would consider the gig a move up. As to his current job, slinging bloody cow carcasses in a meat locker is antithetical to Rocky and Adrian's devotion to the safeguarding of all creatures. Respectively barbaric and meek, brother and sister make for shadowy compliments to Rocky's own aversion to violence.

As romance develops between Rocky and Adrian, Paulie's rationale for his stagnation crumbles. The autonomy he's long swept under the rug as Adrian's ostensible attendant isn't so cut-and-dry. Maybe it's Adrian who's been caring for *him*. The siblings' small two-bedroom, already a hell mouth of developmental inertia, is further disrupted when Paulie rages in jealousy and resentment at the loss of his sister's virginity: *"You're busted!"* Smashing lamps and furniture, a porcelain statue of Mary, the original virgin, narrowly avoids the business end of his Louisville Slugger.

Adrian recounts how her mother told her that her looks would never get her far. Better to develop her mind. Coming off of the cunning, divisive fatales of previous decades, conventional intelligence never fit traditional feminine wiles. But this was 1976, and second-wave feminism, which lasted roughly from the early 1960s through most of the seventies, was at its zenith. Roe v. Wade was handed down in 1973. The Women's Educational Equity Act, which protected gender discrimination in education, was passed the following year. In 1975, U.S. Military Academies were required to admit women. Ten weeks after *Rocky*'s release, the profoundly sexist Miss America contest was scandalized following a speech containing the first use of the dreaded F-word ("feminism") in the competition's history, uttered by no less than the newly crowned victor, Rebecca Ann King.

The decade saw an unprecedented spate of feminist-leaning films, including Frank Perry's *Diary of a Mad Housewife* (1970), Scorsese's *Alice Doesn't Live Here Anymore* and John Cassavetes's *A Woman Under the Influence* (both from 1974), Bryan Forbes's *The Stepford Wives* (1975), and Ridley Scott's *Alien* (1979). It also kicked off a gruesome deluge of so-called rape-revenge films, most notably, Mier Zarchi's 1978 grindhouse offering *I Spit on Your Grave*. In tacit rejection of conventional beauty, Hollywood renounced the cheesecake glamour of previous decades for female actors like Shire, Carol Cane, Veronica Cartwright, Shelly Duvall, Teri Garr, and Sissy Spacek. If Bette Davis had been relegated to an "eight" by 1930s Hollywood standards, this new crop of female actors demonstrated that beauty truly lies in the eye of the beholder. And in Rocky's eye, Adrian's a perfect ten.

The film tips the halfway mark as Eros' pangs are eclipsed by Thanotos's thundering call, which, like the imperious finger summoning Saint Matthew, beckons the hero to what Stallone himself referred to as a "calling." But this time, the command doesn't come down from the Christian savior but from the god of war himself.

Heavyweight Champion Apollo Creed (Carl Weathers) sits in his shirtsleeves and vest surrounded by his entourage as they scramble to find a challenger for the upcoming Bicentennial title bout on New Year's Day. Just because the scheduled fighter broke his hand doesn't mean the business-minded champ will wait another two hundred years for a payday like this. They need another fighter, fast.

This abrupt deus ex machina that propels *Rocky* to its second act affords any purist more than enough ammo to decry the film as fantasy. (They rarely do; no one's here for the boxing.) With flagrant disregard for the hard-and-fast rules that dictate a fighter must first poise himself as a contender, Apollo and the promoter concoct a sham spectacle that will still bring in the purse they've been counting on: how about giving the shot to a local nobody or, as Apollo gingerly words it, "a struggling boxer?" After all, America is the land of opportunity, and here they are in its first city where, just five years prior, Ali and Frazier took their famous car ride.

Perusing an enormous record book of Philly boxers, Apollo's finger starts to tap on a name. "This is the guy, Rocky Balboa. The Italian Stallion. The *Eye*-talian Stallion." After all, who discovered America: "an Italian, right? What would be better than getting it on with one of its descendants?" The promoter agrees. "It's very American." "No," Apollo corrects him, "It's very smart," so poising the bout not as a celebration of Brotherly Love but as a subtle racialist battleground. When a reporter asks Apollo if "it's significant that [he's] fighting a white man on this most celebrated day of independence," the champ doesn't miss a beat. "Does he find it significant to be fighting a black man?"

In 1976, only four of the thirty top-watched television shows centered around Blacks, with *The Jeffersons*, *What's Happening!!*, *Good Times*, and *Sanford and Son* ranking consecutively at numbers 24 through 27. Excluding *The Jeffersons* who, per the opening theme, had moved on up, Blacks were portrayed as disenfranchised, confined to segregated urban neighborhoods, the projects, and the junk business. While these shows attracted both Black and White audiences, the networks kept the former in their place by doubling down on stereotypes, where even *The Jeffersons'* fish-out-of-water Blackness was played for laughs. On the big screen, Blacks were largely relegated to supporting roles or genre-adherent camp like Gordon Parks's *Shaft* (1971), Jack Hill's *Foxy Brown* (1974), and Bruce D. Clark's boxing film *Hammer* (1972). The latter starred Fred Williamson, who appeared in Robert Altman's *M*A*S*H* as the neurosurgeon "Spearchucker" Jones, a character pivotal in the film's castigation of racism.

"It was lonely being a black actor in the 70s," wrote actor Lenny Henry, best known as an unrecognizable shrunken head in 2004's *Harry Potter and the Prisoner of Azkaban*. Recalling contracts in which "you have to have so many colored actors," the British actor Cleo Sylvestre elaborates: "if you were picked for anything, you'd always be thinking: 'Perhaps they only chose me as the obligatory black.'"

Apollo's conservative clothes and keen business acumen ran contrary to what many 1976 audiences expected of a Black man, let alone a Black boxer. His refined elocution exemplified the public's conception of "Whiteness" more than Rocky's primal vocabulary and mumbled nasal slur— the result of nerve damage at birth. In *Slaves to Fashion: Black Dandyism and the Styling of Black Diasporic Identity*, author Monica L. Miller dates clothing as a signifier of success among Blacks to the seventeenth century, writing, "Sometimes the well-dressed black man coming down the street is asking you to look and think." But unlike Jack Johnson in his fur hats or Ray Robinson's pimped-out suits,

Apollo isn't flashy. It's a lot more lucrative to surround himself with square White guys who can crunch numbers.

Weathers, and in all likelihood, an evasive Stallone, modeled Apollo on then-reigning Champion Muhammad Ali. It's an outlandish stretch for a character who hypes the fight dressed as Uncle Sam and espouses America as "the land of opportunity" when just a year prior, Ali told Alex Haley in *Playboy* that "America's day is over... it gonna burn!" While Apollo publicly promotes his unwavering patriotism, it's impossible to envision Ali dressed in those red, white, and blue trunks and making his entrance on a plywood boat like Washington crossing the Delaware. (In their own Bicentennial bout, George Foreman and Joe Frazier weren't above dressing up as George Washington and Betsy Ross in posters promoting the fight.) As Apollo said, many people would like to see a Black fighter "get it on" with an Italian. But this wasn't 1915, and in a decade dominated by Black champions, allusions to a race war smack of the disingenuous.

Weathers recounts, "I saw Apollo's life as a mirror of certain elements of Ali's life. It had to do with politics; it had to do with race relations; it had to do with war." But the war was over. Jim Crow had been dissolved a decade prior. The Black Power movement had mellowed, and Apollo shows no inclination to antagonize the establishment. Quite the opposite: the only element that *does* align Apollo with Ali was a six-foot-six liquor salesman from Bayonne, New Jersey named Chuck Wepner.

Having amassed 338 stitches over a fourteen-year career (120 the result of a ruinous shellacking at the hands of Sonny Liston), Chuck "The Bayonne Bleeder" Wepner was never a top contender. He was, however, the only one of three White fighters per *Ring* magazine's 1974 top ten heavyweights who Ali had yet to fight. (The Black pin-ups in Rocky's old locker that Mickey gave to a more promising fighter offer a sly hint at the absence of Whites in the game.) Following Ali's Rumble with Foreman in Zaire five months prior, Don King wanted a mixed-race title bout to shield the waning, dazed Ali from top-tier Blacks. The woeful mismatch took place in October 1974, just weeks before Stallone started his script.

Before the fight, Ali had buttons and pennants printed that read "Give the White Guy a Break," a relatively benign dig at the absence of Whites in the division. When he encouraged Wepner to "use the N-word" at press conferences to boost gate sales, the latter refused, recalling years later that "[Ali] respected that... I wouldn't go along with making the fight a race fight." Despite 40-1 betting odds, the third-rater became the fourth fighter in the champ's career to take him the distance. *Almost.* The fight was stopped due to Wepner's excessive bleeding nineteen seconds before the final bell. Stallone's ongoing refusal to credit the Ali-Wepner bout as a catalyst for his script rings cagy at best and duplicitous at worst. In 2003, Wepner sued the actor for $15 million for "promotion of the *Rocky* movies... without consent and compensation." Three years later, the tight-lipped Stallone settled with "a minute percentage" of the original amount.

In an office bigger than Rocky's apartment, the promoter wears a plaid jacket and a smile like a knife wound to give Rocky the news. Seizing on Apollo's platitude that's fast-become the film's most salient maxim ("Do you believe that America is the land of opportunity?"), boxing's most fundamental rules disintegrate to forward a fantasy in which the underdog's struggle looks a lot more American than the champ's swagger—or his bankbook.

Dubbed "The Slaughterhouse Kid" as an up-and-comer, Ali's opponent Joe Frazier tipped Stallone off to his old practice of using sides of beef as heavy bags. (To add insult to his many injuries, Frazier was fired from the Cross Brothers Slaughterhouse for a broken hand upon his return from the 1964 Olympics, where he took home the gold.) Soon, the same "meat bag" who refused to break a debtor's thumb is shattering ribs on frozen carcasses with wraps soaked in bovine sinew and blood. Frazier later recalled that Stallone "used the story about me training by running up the steps of the museum in Philly. But he never paid me for any of my past. I only got paid for a walk-on part." Smokin' Joe had been snubbed again. "*Rocky* is a sad story for me."

Mickey climbs a dark staircase steeped in age and abandoned hopes, just like him. The cat's been in the cradle for a long time. Only days before, the Merciful Father knocking on Rocky's door called the same Prodigal Son a tomato. Now, in a rasp like churning gravel, he wistfully recounts his fifty years in the business. The scar over his left eye took twenty-one stitches; the right needed thirty-four. His nose was busted seventeen times. And that night in September of '23 when Luis Firpo knocked Jack Dempsey out of the ring? Mickey fought that night, too, but no one remembers. "Why?", he growls like a man who missed the last train: "'Cause I didn't have a manager!" Can it be that Mickey sees in Rocky his own last vicarious shot at legitimacy? Maybe, but why should Rocky care? Mickey never did.

Seven minutes later, the trainer descends the stairs. Nothing has changed other than that he and Rocky, Adrian and Paulie, Apollo and Gazzo are seven minutes older, and the fight is seven minutes closer. Rocky catches up with Mickey on the corner. Their conversation, drowned out by the rumble of the overhead train, is not for the viewer's ears, but when it's over, Rocky puts his arm around his new manager.

Rocky moves through Mikey's gym like a grey storm cloud pushing through a rainbow; his sweats a blur amidst the splashy trunks and national colors worn by the other fighters. Amid relentless sets of crunches, Mickey promises Rocky that when they're finished, he's "gonna eat lightning and crap thunder," echoing Ali's claim to have "done hand-cuffed lightning and thrown thunder in jail."

The narrative that follows charts a timeline in which it's literally impossible for Rocky to get into fighting shape. Can he—can *anyone*—ascend from basement bruiser to something approaching a worthy contender within a month? With the fight scheduled for the first of the year, the week that follows Christmas seems like months. The Stallion breaks a half-dozen raw eggs into a dirty glass with a baker's expertise and downs them before his morning roadwork. He performs one-armed push-ups. He tramples rotten vegetables underfoot while jogging through the outdoor Italian Market, cheered on by pedestrians. No extras were used, nor did the crew obtain a permit to film. In a moment of breezy improvisation, Rocky catches an orange tossed by a fruit peddler who, having no idea who Stallone was or what all those cameras were doing there, thought he was doing a kindness to a grungy jogger trying to push through the melee.

In 1915's *Birth of a Nation*, director D.W. Griffith pioneered what he dubbed "parallel editing," employing multiple cuts to build dramatic tension. Latvian filmmaker Sergei Eisenstein earned the title "Father of Montage" for his 1925 film *Strike*, in which ghastly imagery of a slaughterhouse alternates with footage of a workers' strike. Early into his career, director Don Siegel held the now-obsolete title of "montage director" for Warner Bros. Years later, he described that the typical director "casually shoots a few shots that he presumes will be used in the montage and the cutter... make[s] some sort of mishmash out of it." Siegel, who had created the montage sequence for 1942's *Casablanca*, could not have foreseen how the format would become an action film mainstay throughout the following decades.

Unlike the brief training sequences depicted in boxing films of the 1940s and 50s (see Kirk Douglass's droll spring-weight routine in *Champion*), the rallying determination and sheer duration of Rocky's iconic training montages was something new altogether. Countless cuts from action to more action render dialogue pointless amid the agony and sweat inherent to what was to become a hard-and-fast template for numerous films during the following decade, including every *Rocky* sequel. Over the course of two minutes and eighteen seconds, the iconic workout established what has come to be known as the 'long-form montage."

With militaristic marching orders, Bill Conti's bombastic *Gonna Fly Now* pioneered the musical score as an intrinsic element of the nascent action montage. The blare of skippy exultation pushed through a bossy trumpet and voices that swing from empowerment ("Getting strong now/Won't be long") to enervated perseverance ("Working hard now/It's so hard now") landed the track at the top of Billboard's Hot One Hundred list in July of 1977. Setting a prototype for similar motivational jingles, *Gonna Fly Now* is hard to top as it pushes the film beyond the fairy tale realm into something approaching mythology. "I read the script," Conti explained. "I [knew] how it ends. He loses, [but] we want to manipulate the audience to think he can win." But with the championship no longer the end goal, the audience never feels manipulated. Rocky is finally alive. In one of the Stedicam's most beloved usages, Rocky is followed up the steps of the Philadelphia Museum of Art to mark his ascent from the grime of Fishtown to what the actor called a "house of learning."

As a visual artist, Stallone painted a portrait of his character before writing his script, telling *Artnet News* in 2021, "I made a self-portrait with a more defined 'pug face' than I had back then, but to capture his sadness, I switched the brush with a screwdriver and carved the eyes." In what sounds like an act suspiciously akin to boxing, Stallone remarked, "Painting is where I feel close to a bare-naked truth, so much so that I look at the canvas as some sort of an enemy."

Rocky prays alone in his dressing room like Christ at Gethsemane. Victory is unlikely, and at this point, irrelevant. Paired down to its ineffable core, dignity is still Rocky's soul motivator in what's less of a title fight than the strive for self-validation. Only this time, it's not just the bums in Fishtown that are watching.

Rocky enters the ring in a grubby pink robe, the result of the cheap red embroidery used by the crew that bled out in the wash. By contrast, Apollo hops and bops in his Uncle Sam hat, the picture of faux patriotism, financial gain in the guise of "opportunity," and cheap burlesque disguised as the American dream.

A blow-by-blow of the most patently irresponsible bout in cinematic history is time wasted. Every punch lands. Eyes swell and close, and blood jets from Rocky's brow when Mickey relieves the pressure from a swollen hematoma with a single-edge razor. Fifteen-rounds are truncated to six-and-a-half minutes interspersed with card girls who've traded out bikinis for Statue of Liberty ornamentation complete with silver-green body paint; a revolving door of *Goldfinger*'s Margaret Nolans covered in oxidized copper. With a budget that allowed for a scant six hundred extras to fill the stands, the bout is shrewdly filmed from different angles to approximate a sellout crowd.

No savior presides over The Spectrum Arena tonight; His assistance is still best disbursed among the losers and shills back in Fishtown. If Rocky was bestowed his calling that night at The Resurrection Club (and Stallone's comments and the film's persistent Catholic imagery suggest that he was), he's on his own now. Like Saint Matthew's relatively benign martyrdom by assassination, Rocky's embodiment of the *imitato Christi* is considerably less conspicuous than the grisly flagellations of *Raging Bull*. Still, no referee in the history of modern boxing would have let this one go the distance. The past two hours have culminated in a bloodbath wherein the viewer has had their faith tested and come out a zealot. Open cuts, purple eyes swollen like blinders, and enough blood to fill a small pond, the only way this can end is in victory. But for "such a little movie," victory is relative.

At the final bell, Conti's exultant score blasts as the nobody, the tomato, the meat-bag, finishes on his feet. Who cares if he was outpointed? What matters is that he's standing. Held next to all the boxing films that end in the protagonist's victory, Rocky's loss is the more invigorating, and the crowds that poured from theaters bobbing, weaving, and punching the air are a testament to the film's efficacy, even in defeat. How could they know that the fairytale they just watched mirrored Stallone's decidedly non-fictional struggle? Or that another eight installments (and counting) were to follow?

17
ROCKY III

Directed by Sylvester Stallone
United Artists, 1982

In the original *Rocky*, Mickey riffs on Corinthians 6:2 ("Behold, now is the favorable time") when he barks, "Like the bible says, you ain't gonna get a second chance!" Unlike the suits in Hollywood, the trainer had no way of anticipating the industry's growing affinity for sequels that developed concomitantly with the rise of the blockbuster during the mid-1970s. Following the whopping success of Stallone's original Stallion—now filmdom's most beloved boxer—there was every incentive to continue his saga and follow him to further glory. After all, it's not like he took the belt from Apollo in the original: that was Rocky's fight, a chance to beat the inner bum who nearly sacrificed whatever talents he demonstrated in the ring for fast cash in the leg-breaking racket. Few films provided such a near-perfect platform on which to build, and it's hard to imagine a character more malleable to suit his cultural mores than Rocky Balboa.

A summary of *Rocky*'s second installment (which, like the third, was written—and now directed—by Stallone and again produced by Chartoff and Winkler) will bring the reader up to speed. As the 1970s teetered on the cusp of the most insidiously violent and deceptively sexualized decade of twentieth-century cinema, 1979's *Rocky II* sees the titular hero marry Adrian, blow through the Bicentennial bout purse, and tumble to the canvas together with Apollo in the last moments of their rematch to rise somewhere around the nine count and emerge the new Heavyweight Champion—the perfect kiss-off to seventies grit, ambiguity, and existential vagaries.

A synthesized bass sends the woofers throbbing. The screen fades in a thunderclap. A blistering whistle of fireworks and the concussive hum of halogen explode to create a Vegas Strip neon title card featuring a crude replica of the Stallion himself as the convulsive guitar strains of Survivor's power anthem *Eye of the Tiger* sweep the theater like an angry buzzsaw. If the viewer isn't dazzled by the spectacles that unfold throughout the song, they might notice that the film hasn't even reached its opening credit sequence.

Clips emerge in which the Stallion defends his title

in a string of achingly incompetent fight renditions culminating in ludicrous knockouts via clumsy, open handed swipes and uppercuts that knock opponents a full foot off the canvas. Hair stiff with product, Rocky's now-clean-shaven face assumes angular contours to complement his new bodybuilder's frame. Rather than raise his arms in triumph with a face smeared in gore, the untouched victor winks to the crowd or takes dainty bows like a lumpy Lord Fauntleroy.

But while Rocky's felling his string of second-raters, a snarling, ominous figure sneers from the stands. Meet Clubber Lang (Mr. T, in his cinematic debut), the rising contender who grunts out crunches in his one-bedroom garret and runs through Philly's empty barrios and slums like he's looking for trouble. Shoving refs aside and pummeling floored victims, Clubber's tactics exhibit more grounds for penalties and disqualifications than had he brought a gun into the ring.

There's Rocky's face on *People Magazine*. On *Ring Magazine*. On foreign publications from around the world. He's even on *The Muppet Show*. It seems impossible to escape the cult of Rocky as commercial endorsements for cars, credit cards, and watches flash by. In keeping with the new wealth-worshipping standards of the Reagan era, Rocky's a corporate brand. But all these side gigs and their ensuing royalties have gotten in the way of training. He's getting complacent, and as the opening track fades, sportscasters are predicting that a Balboa-Lang match can't be far off.

The credit sequence begins in earnest at a video arcade, that ubiquitous eighties equivalent of the Kinetoscope parlors, now almost a century old. Living in a mansion the size of the White House with Adrienne, Paulie, and Micky, Rocky reads his son fairytales and drives him around the patio grounds in a golf cart outfitted like a surrey with isinglass curtains. Burgess Meredith's grizzled Micky is still his manager and trainer, but pairing his fighter with low-ranked chumps isn't doing his boy any favors. Is it possible that he, too, senses Rocky's indolence?

In the eighteen months between Ronald Reagan's taking office and the release of *Rocky III*, constrictions on 1970's permissiveness within cinema had already begun to take effect. In turn, studios were spurred to seek new means of *selling* sex and violence without *showing* too much sex and violence. While strict oversight of the MPAA ratings codes made this easy regarding wide theatrical releases, the accessibility of R, X, and unrated films made possible by the VHS boom gave unsupervised children access to some of the most sexual and violent content around.

Popular films destined for theatrical distribution were hobbled in their graphic demonstrations of the previous decade's gore that reached its peak in 1980, forcing directors to make repeated cuts to their films to earn an R-rating. The same applied to sex, a perennial subject that enjoyed unprecedented tolerance during the seventies, when such films as Bernardo Bertolucci's X-rated *The Last Tango in Paris* (1972), Nicolas Roeg's *Don't Look Now* (1973), and Louis Malle's *Pretty Baby* (1978) became enmeshed in the intellectual mainstream. By Reagan's second term, onscreen sex had turned mainly to the suggestive. Instead of nudity (namely genitals of both varieties), bare bottoms and the occasional nipple had to suffice until the introduction of the NC-17 rating in 1990.

The last gasp of racy entries to usher in the new decade were by and large tailored to audiences too young to see them in theaters. Bob Clark's *Porky's* (1981), at the time Canada's highest-grossing film, was foremost amid the rise of teen sex-romps accessible though VHS rentals and late-night "Skinimax" cable offerings. While nudity did not disappear from popular cinema altogether, it was curtailed in order to enforce limited depictions of flesh that, as with kisses during the Haye's Code, were subject to arbitrary limits on screen time.

Numerous other so-called erotic entries geared to adult audiences were mitigated from the explicit to the merely suggestive. Tooth by tooth, the new regime was methodically defanging cinema under ever-harsher restrictions imposed by puritanical pressure from groups like Jerry Falwell's Moral Majority, established in 1976. The Reagan administration's campaign to rid the country of material that fell under the vague realm of the offensive led to the implementation of a fifty percent defunding of the National Endowment for the Arts along with censorship and warning labels on music and video media.

If sex, terror, and gore were hobbled, it was open season for gun violence, where the shoot-first, ask-questions-later approach became standard protocol and body count mattered. In December of 1985, Reagan told the *Los Angeles Times* that Stallone's relentlessly violent but markedly bloodless *Rambo: First Blood Part II* of the same year was his favorite film: "Boy, after seeing *Rambo* last night, I know what to do the next time [a hostage crisis] happens."

The action film was evolving, and over-muscled behemoths like Stallone and his bodybuilding counterpart, Arnold Schwarzenegger, had set the new gold standard. Never had Hollywood featured such anatomical specimens, including smaller but no less ripped actors in a trend that has yet to let up. It was the perfect combination of Eros and Thanatos: the stouthearted male whose attendant capacity for ass-kicking stemmed wholly from his "desirable" anatomy.

But desirable to whom? If studios expected females to flood cinemas to moon over sweaty male musculature, what they got were throngs of scrawny adolescent males, most of whom were content to admire and idolize rather than conform to this new set of impossible body standards. As fetishization of the male body became commonplace, the new macho came to meld with the homoerotic.

As the AIDS crisis doubled down on the country's homophobia, popular cinema dabbled in male gender-bending on multiple, often unexpected levels. Sydney Pollack's critically acclaimed *Tootsie* (1982) featured a man who disguises himself as a woman to land an acting role. Variations followed. In 1983, Michael Keaton assumed the tasks of homemaking and child-rearing in Stan Dragoti's *Mr. Mom*. In Leonard Nimoy's *Three Men and a Baby* (1987), three bachelors are saddled with an infant and struggle to perform quotidian maternal tasks like feeding and diaper changes.

Of all genres, the action hero remained the most fetishized, feminized portrayal of masculinity. After all, how better to emphasize the idée fixe of manhood than a shirtless, musclebound super-human swinging a machine gun like a giant dick while somehow managing to skirt the new constrictions? Amid the political sea change that brought new oversight to film content, the screws were kept loose regarding gun violence in an assertive, jingoist interest of pairing Iran-Contra flame whips with big-screen super-soldiers.

Rocky III's inaugural bout comes as a fundraiser that pits Rocky against a six foot-seven wrestler called Thunderlips (a thirty-year-old Hulk Hogan, who took his own swipe at gender-bending in the 1993 flop, *Mr. Nanny*). Recalling *Requiem for a Heavyweight*'s final moments in which a wrestling bill is pasted over a poster of the ex-boxer, the exhibition bout is both the film's most entertaining sequence and an ominous pitch for the World Wrestling Federation (now the World Wrestling Entertainment) as combat sport's newest incarnation. Incorporated in 1980, the organization exploded in earnest under new ownership in 1982, when it introduced the world to performers like Hogan along with a rogues' gallery of giants in lipstick and rouge. Once again, a confounding new image of manhood, replete with steroidal bods, histrionic rants, theatrical choke-slams, and phony piledrivers was imposed on children amid the new cult of body-worship.

Before the 1980s, bodybuilding was largely considered a facet of the gay underground subculture—a theme explored in depth as early as 1951 in the Japanese novel *Forbidden Colors* by Yukio Mishima. In George Butler and Robert Fiore's 1977 docudrama *Pumping Iron*, Schwarzenegger and other bodybuilders set out to correct the misconception. In a scene featuring Schwarzenegger's voiceover as he fires off curls, the Mr. Universe contender describes the transference of libidinal energy to his muscles as "like coming." Pause. "With a woman."

The feminized connotations behind the name Thunderlips need no elaboration. In the tradition of Gorgeous George, the 310-pound wrestler proclaims himself "the ultimate object of desire" and "a mountain of molten lust," an allusion to hot, spewing lava that will also be passed over. The sequence reads as a conversion/perversion of artistic combat made unadulterated theater. Bodies are slammed to the ground, fighters are thrown from the ring, and—unlike today's novelty fights in which MMA fighters pitted against boxers observe the Queensberry rules—it is the boxer who must conform to the wrestler's tactics. When the dust settles, Rocky asks Thunderlips why he was so rough. "That's the name of the game." Nobody likes a boring fight, and as the new emissary of combat sports, Hogan's laconic warning suggests such baroque displays of manufactured pandemonium are what keep the fans coming back.

The phenomenon wasn't just limited to sports or the big screen. Male teens who embraced the metalhead aesthetic bought into a dress code comprised of long feathered hair, conspicuously brash layers of makeup, and tight leather-and-stud clothing—another staple of seventies gay subculture. In a 2005 *Fresh Air* interview, Terry Gross asked Rob Halford of the heavy metal band Judas Priest if the band's fashion expressed the singer's own homosexuality. Were it true, Halford responded, "it was entirely subconscious." (It should be noted that the band was a particular bugbear with Tipper Gore's Parents Music Resource Center for its decidedly heterosexual content.)

In the December 1996 issue of *Esquire*, Stallone told feminist icon Susan Faludi, "Women will show a great deal more of their soul. And I would aspire toward that aspect of the feminine." While he wasn't referring to the brand of action hero he created fourteen years prior, the actor had inadvertently touched upon Rocky's hyper-masculine body as intentionally genre-conforming and unintentionally gender-bending. "To a lot of people," observed Faludi, "you are your body." She had a point, and *Rocky III* (along with Ted Kotcheff's *First Blood* from the same year) was the film in which Stallone commenced his physical transformation into an eighties action hero. The *Backlash* author invoked a passage from Sam Fussell's 1991 memoir *Muscle: Confessions of an Unlikely Bodybuilder*, in which the scholar admits that "gussying up [his] body like that was a principally feminine exercise." Stallone agreed, though his ongoing adherence to bandoliers and grenade launchers indicates that, twenty-seven years after the interview, the actor continues to ensure the survival of the archetype he helped originate. Always follow the money.

The success of the original *Rocky* so endeared the public to the tenacious underdog that the Philadelphia Museum of Art's steps are still mobbed with tourists raising their arms for the camera. In a blatant act of self-aggrandizement, Stallone commissioned a bronze, life-size sculpture of his fictional fighter to be placed on top of the steps to further cement the character's role within local lore. (It was to be thirty-three years before the city unveiled a statue of Joe Frazier—Philly's true Heavyweight Champion.)

The statue is unveiled in the film as the city expresses its gratitude to Rocky in a well-attended display of hyperbolic praise. Like a kid with a new toy, which is more or less what the statue was to the actor, the fighter feigns unworthiness before revealing his plan to retire. He's thirty-four. It's time to give someone else a shot. Then a turbulent heckle full of indignant malice rises above the mob to demand a shot at the champ he thinks is ducking him.

It's hard to underestimate the ubiquity of Mr. T throughout the early-mid 1980s. Born Laurence Tureaud, he was the youngest of twelve children to share a two-room apartment with his parents in the infamous Robert Taylor Projects on Chicago's South Side. Having witnessed countless incidents of murder, rape, and other forms of violence as a child, Tureaud assumed the role of bodyguard to weaker kids liable to fall prey to neighborhood thugs. Disgusted with the treatment disenfranchised Blacks continued to suffer at the hands of Whites, he changed his name to Mr. T when he turned eighteen, telling *Playboy* in 1983 that "I self-ordained myself 'Mr. T' so the first word out of everybody's mouth is Mister."

Following a stint in the army's Military Police Corps, Mr. T worked as bodyguard to heavyweights including Ali and Frazier and luminaries like Michael Jackson, Diana Ross, and Steve McQueen. The tough guy routine was no act. An early proponent of hip-hop bling that weighed up to sixty pounds, Mr. T foreswore his signature gold chains following his clean-up efforts on Hurricane Katrina: "It would be a sin against God for me to wear my gold when so many people lost everything."

After spotting Mr. T on television's short-lived *America's Toughest Bouncers*, Stallone offered him his first acting role as *Rocky III*'s irredeemable villain. Loath to be typecast as the perpetual bad guy, the born-again Christian who made his own feather earrings cashed in on his newfound fame to model himself as kid-friendly, an image he crafted through Saturday morning cartoons, anti-bullying

PSAs, a children's cereal, and numerous appearances on sit-coms geared to the younger set.

The rise of Mr. T and the continued presence of Carl Weather's Apollo speak more to the viewing public's growing penchant for action stars than to race. Unlike the original film, in which the press takes an interest in the interracial pairing of Rocky and Apollo, *Rocky III* eschews all mention of race. Nevertheless, the decade remained shaky when casting Black actors as leads. Like his fellow athlete Jim Brown, Weathers was, almost without exception, relegated to ensemble casts (his 1988 vehicle *Action Jackson*, directed by Craig R. Baxley, was a critical flop).

As Whites were fulfilling the new masculine ideal through time spent at the gym, the most famous Black actors worked in the field of comedy. As the young, decidedly non-buff Eddie Murphy dominated the box office, studios eased him into action roles through team-up buddy films like Walter Hill's *48 Hours* (1982) and Martin Brest's *Beverly Hills Cop* (1984). John Landis's fish-out-of-water comedy *Trading Places* (1983) riffed on the perception that Blacks have no head for money. If this sounds like progress, it should be stressed that, Murphy notwithstanding, Blacks were depressingly scarce among the decade's highest-grossing actors.

The Jeffersons was one of history's longest-running sitcoms and the third top-rated show the year of *Rocky III*'s release while *The Cosby Show*, which premiered in 1985, topped the charts throughout the decade's second half. Unlike the ghetto vibes of seventies shows like *Good Times*, Cosby's sitcom featured an upper-middle-class Brooklyn family espousing heavy-handed lessons steeped in eighties family values. In 1986, *The Oprah Winfrey Show* commenced a twenty-five-year run to become the highest-rated daytime talk show in American television history, making its host the wealthiest Black person of the twentieth century.

Before the masses at the statue's unveiling, Clubber challenges the man he dubs a "paper champion." "Politics, man. This country wants to keep me down! They don't want a man like me because I'm not a puppet!" While Clubber's indignation invokes the same fear Sonny Liston imposed on the public when he took the title from the god-fearing Floyd Patterson in 1962, his words are that of a grizzled Ali, a self-proclaimed victim of the system held down by The Man.

Perhaps most off-putting to audiences were Mr. T's feathered earlobe adornments and Pawnee haircut that speak to a fashion movement that came to represent bad behavior. Just over two years after the The Sex Pistols released their seminal punk album, 1977's *Never Mind the Bollocks, Here's the Sex Pistols*, Nancy Reagan initiated her reductive, demonstrably fruitless "Just Say No" campaign against drugs that raged in PSAs and bumper stickers throughout the eighties. During his 1980 campaign, her husband and soon-to-be-two-term president's classification of marijuana as "probably the most dangerous drug in the United States" spawned a new crop of cinematic gangs bound not by race but by drug use and punk aesthetics. Such transgressions, along with visual stylistic cues—stud collars and all—aligned loud but harmless fashion statements with danger. But unlike those naughty video cassettes or the music Tipper Gore was working to eradicate, it was impossible to slap a warning sticker on a haircut.

Only when Clubber makes sexual advances to Adrian does Rocky accept his challenge. It's the only moment in the film in which Adrian is a plot device. Even more pertinent is her treatment as a sexual being to be fought over like a prize—a victim of jungle law. With this singular exception, Adrian is relegated to an ancillary character, once again struck dumb and keeping the film firmly rooted in the male realm. And why not? In the six years since the original, the franchise had abandoned the theme of personal struggles for the eighties ideal that with money comes sophistication. Nor was *Rocky III*'s target demographic interested in their hero's love life.

The quirky female actors of the seventies again took a back seat to the sexualized woman in all her predatory danger that reached its apex in Adrian Lyne's *Fatal Attraction* (1987). Women's most distinguished roles saw them cast as strippers, stalkers, or classic fatales. Even family-friendly franchises followed suit: James Bond's 1983 outing—among the least sexy in the *007* catalog—was bequeathed the mildly debauched title *Octopussy*. The same year, the third *Star Wars* installment featured Carrie Fisher's scantily clad body collared and chained to an enormous space slug.

In 1983, Vanessa Williams became the first Black contestant to be crowned Miss America. When *Penthouse* magazine published unauthorized photographs of her naked body toward the end of her year-long reign, Williams relinquished her title as the *Philadelphia Inquirer* described her fall from "America's darling to a national disgrace." It was Williams's sexuality, not her color, that led to her downfall.

Mickey confesses to having "hand-picked" Rocky's opponents to keep his fighter safe (*i.e.*, padding his record with easy wins while protecting him from more potent fighters). It's another bit of fantasy: Mickey's in no position to cherry-pick opponents as new contenders rise. As for Clubber, "This guy's a dinosaur!" Mickey growls in reaction to the challenger's ferocity in the face of Rocky's cavalier civility. "And to be civilized," he adds, "is the worst thing that can happen to a fighter."

While Clubber continues to train in solitude, Rocky rents out the ballroom at Philly's Bellevue Stratford hotel to make an exhibition out of his regimen, jumping rope for fans while Paulie hawks Rocky swag. Anything for a buck, but when fight night arrives, things do not go well for the Stallion, who is kayoed as Mickey lays on his deathbed from a heart attack in the dressing room. (His subsequent internment in a Jewish mausoleum is a fitting nod to the man who claimed to have fought the same night that Firpo knocked Dempsey out of the ring in 1923, the same decade in which Jews rose to prominence within the sport.)

The viewer has already seen Apollo serve as a ringside commentator during Rocky's defeat, and he doesn't want to see the sport descend into darkness under the new champ's bad intentions. Recalling Mickey's words regarding Rocky's complacency, Apollo invokes a combination of psychological warfare and determination that Rocky had in spades during their two bouts. "You lost your itch," he tells his ex-opponent in reference to the ineffable trait he calls the "the eye of the tiger."

When the band Queen denied Stallone the use of their best-selling 1980 single *Another One Bites the Dust* for the film's theme song, the actor commissioned Survivor to record what would become a runaway smash. With lyrics like "So many times it happens too fast/You change your passion for glory," *Eye of the Tiger* covered the film's principle theme while tying for *Billboard Hot 100*'s longest running top-ten single of the decade. (It was also used by Newt Gingrich, Mitt Romney, and Mike Huckabee in their presidential rallies until they were sued by Survivor's founding member.) Yet, for all its deadly mystique, the tiger image remains unconvincing when recalling Rocky's perpetual look of bewilderment throughout the first two films. In any case, eyes and tigers take a backseat to another round of Conti's *Gonna Fly Now*, because it's time for Rocky to get his "itch" back.

Rocky sprints across seashores in a the three-and-a-half-minute montage where he fires off a series of weight-training exercises inherent to the bodybuilder's regimen but deleterious to a fighter's. In *The Arc of Boxing: The Rise and Decline of the Sweet Science*, Mike Silver uses a promotional photo for the film featuring Stallone with arms flexed in the traditional strong man pose to illustrate the decline of lithe, pliant bodies conducive to a boxer's movement and speed. According to the author, *Rocky III* post-dates the last wave of great heavyweights as a new generation of fighters began incorporating heavy lifting into their routines. "A boxer," wrote Max Schmeling in his 1977 autobiography, "should have long, flexible muscles" for which weightlifting is an impediment. To Silver, bodybuilding, eighties fitness fads, and Hollywood's new obsession with size contributed to what the author considers boxing's downfall in the century's final decades.

As discussed in Chapter 16, *Rocky* can be credited with standardizing the montage format for the new decade. While textbook examples of the montage were featured every week from 1983 to 1987 on the small screen in the Mr. T vehicle, *The A-Team*, its appearance almost forty years later in 2018's *Creed III* (the ninth *Rocky* film) amounts to little more than franchise branding. The same can be said for *Rocky III*. In the years since Rocky drank eggs and ran the museum steps, the drama inherent to the original training sequence can never be repeated.

Rocky and Apollo's *Iron John* bonding ranks as a high

watermark in a decade replete with homoeroticism in film wherein the top honor falls to Tony Scott's *Top Gun* (1986). Described in the *New Yorker* by Pauline Keal as "a shiny homoerotic commercial," the film boasts lines like, "I'd like to bust your butt." Other examples include Andrei Konchalovsky's *Tango and Cash* (1989) in which Stallone and Kurt Russell, filmed naked from behind, have the following exchange: "Aw, c'mon, how come yours is bigger than mine?" "Genetics, peewee." Rowdy Herrington's *Road House*, also from 1989, features a pretty villain who snarls, "I used to fuck guys like you in prison."

Conti's score reaches a pitch with highs that would make a dog wince before soaring higher still. At the same time, the camera spills its adoration on Stallone and Weathers's musculature via close-ups meant to capture every throb and sinew. Calves, biceps, and pecs glisten as the new besties splash in the surf and embrace in a freeze-frame punctuated by the ding of a bell. Showtime.

In overlapping the boxing and action genres, the only acceptable conclusion is a definitive knockout. But unlike its predecessors' smashed jelly jar faces, *Rocky III*'s finale is utterly bloodless. Shortly after Clubber wake up on the canvas, Mr. T began to marshal his newfound fame and claim his place as a children's role model, never to play the villain again. As for the hero, Philadelphia's white knight is safely reinstalled.

Not a film to be watched on the basis of merit, *Rocky III* nevertheless serves as a perfect time capsule and cultural indicator in its anticipation of a decade's struggle to define masculinity under the specter of an increasingly conservative and capitalist regime. Amid threats of nuclear warfare, film and television continued to bring national anxieties to the cultural fore (including Rocky's micro-cold war in the series' next installment, where he takes on the dreaded Russian, Ivan Drago). As to the present film, and in what sounds like a message pointedly directed to its viewers, Mikhail Gorbachev's 1994 assertion that "America must be the teacher of democracy, not the advertiser of the consumer society" came a little too late.

18
FAT CITY

Directed by John Huston
Columbia Pictures, 1972

If *Fat City* isn't the best boxing film (and a preponderance of serious fans of the sweet science would say that it is), it's far and away the most credible. With no contenders, no champions, and no happy endings, the film brims with false idealism and bum luck.

An aerial shot hovers over a rectangular swath of concrete sprawl surrounded by farmland before an abrupt cut reveals a sign at the city limits: Stockton, CA—Pop—112,000. Bubbly, seventies sit-com typeface hovers over migrants and rummies—mostly Black and Latino—who chat and loiter, steel nips from paper sacks, and squint into the sun as though checking to see if it's still there. Tenements, official city buildings, and flophouses are razed, giving city blocks the appearance of a mouth with half its lower teeth knocked out. Other buildings slump like mastodons awaiting the same extinction. Amid the rubble, decay, and a million dead and dying hopes, two boxers at the Lido Gym push blindly against fate despite the awareness that their futures hold no hope in the ring. Probably because fate is a meaningless construct around here—a copout used to justify the various missteps and misfortunes the residents of *Fat City* bring upon themselves.

Careers end without ever taking off. Half-assed comebacks are thwarted by booze and women, and a million circumstances lead men to believe their hard-luck dye was cast long ago. In a haze of lost opportunity and self-delusion, fresh young hopefuls, punch-drunk canvasbacks, and itinerant journeymen plod and paw toward the glory and money despite the epiphany that comes from knowing, "with terrible lucidity, that the sport was for madmen."

Based on Leonard Gardner's terse 1969 novel, even the title—Stockton's one-time nickname and tongue-in-cheek slang for prosperity—mocks its denizens like the credits' carefree typeface. The author, a Stockton native, trained at the Lido in his teens, where he amassed seven bouts as an amateur welterweight. "Surrounded by the sloughs, rivers, and fertile fields of the San Joaquin River delta," Stockton is represented in equal parts Latino, Mexican, Black, and White. Without a hill in sight, it's prime territory for the day laborers who travel by bus to work the fields picking underripe peaches as hard as baseballs and onions so fragrant they'll permeate your clothes. It depends on the season. Although the author describes the city as "a hot boxing town," Stockton never produced a champion. In fact, he adds, "there was nobody remotely like a champion."

In a flurry of wrecking balls and bulldozers, the destruction of old Stockton paved the way for a proliferation of commerce and shopping malls that came to fruition in the nineties. After the economic meltdown of 2007, it was the second-largest American city to file for bankruptcy protection. "Everyone called it Skid Row," recalls Gardner as though speaking of a fabled Mayan civilization or the lost continent of Atlantis.

John Huston was a fierce-swinging former California Amateur Lightweight Champion who blasted into filmmaking with his 1941 adaptation of Dashiell Hammett's *The Maltese Falcon*. Having started as a screenwriter, his script for Raul Walsh's *High Sierra* (1941) commenced a directing career that began by establishing Bogart as one of Hollywood's highest-paid actors. After working together on 1948's *The Treasure of the Sierra Madre* and *Key Largo*, their collaboration on 1952's *The African Queen* garnered Huston the Oscar for Best Director and Best Screenwriter while Bogart took home the statuette for Best Actor.

During the first decade of his forty-six-year career, Huston worked with such Warner staples as Lauren Bacall, Bette Davis, John Garfield, and Edward G. Robinson. In 1947, he helped the fiercely anti-HUAC Bogart lead a protest mission dubbed "Hollywood Fights Back," wherein a slew of heavies, including Bacall, Garfield, Robinson, Ira Gershwin, Burgess Meredith, and Frank Sinatra flew to Washington, D.C. to confront the Committee. Although Huston was staunchly anti-blacklist, he believed such aggressive tactics did more harm than good. "I disapproved of what was being done to the Ten, but I also disapproved of their response."

In his 1980 autobiography, *An Open Book*, Huston wrote, "I admire directors ...whose every picture is in some way connected with their private lives, but that's never been my approach... I like to draw on sources other than myself." (Like most of his films, *Fat City* reveals nothing of the adventurer that prompted author Ian Freer to dub Huston "cinema's Ernest Hemingway.") Thirty-four of his thirty-seven films are adaptations, though Huston, who usually penned his own scripts, deferred to Gardner when adapting *Fat City* for the screen.

A half-century after the book's release and its subsequent glowing reception (*Fat City* vied with Kurt Vonnegut's *Slaughterhouse-Five* for the 1970 National Book Award), the eighty-nine-year-old Gardner remains guarded about why he never wrote another novel. Upon *Fat City*'s 2015 re-release, David Lida of the *Paris Review* asked Gardner if it bothered him that he hadn't written more. "I'm sensitive to that stuff," the author replied. "I resent it...it makes me uncomfortable." After all, he was a working writer who pulled in a steady salary scripting for television, despite never owning one.

Following his adaptations of *Moby Dick* (1956) and *The Bible: In the Beginning* (1966), Huston decided that it didn't take a lot of money to make a good picture. "The smaller the film, the better the movie," the director asserted as he shifted from adaptations of pulp classics and grandiose epics to intimate retellings of books, including Carson McCullers's *Reflections in a Golden Eye* (1967), Flannery O'Connor's *Wiseblood* (1979), Malcolm Lowry's *Under the Volcano* (1984), and *Fat City*. At once confined and liberated by the razor-focus of his chosen source material, Huston devised a direct means of communication with audiences not through expensive sets or multiple edits but by placing his actors—and so the viewer—into the drama without flash or flourish. No mean feat when working with the likes of Brando, Richard Burton, Bette Davis, Albert Finney, Errol Flynn, and Elizabeth Taylor.

In its scrupulous avoidance of glamor, prosperity, and even life's fleeting moments of contentment, *Fat City* is a work of distilled Realism. Born of a rejection of nineteenth-century Romanticism in all its inflated drama and idealism, Realism saw authors and painters turn to everyday, often sordid subject matter through portrayals of laundresses, drinkers, prostitutes, and other inelegant figures. While previous boxing films frequently applied Romantic trappings to their Pollyanna denouements (and still do), Stockton's residents make their homes in drinking dens, squalid garrets, or crushed under the physical exertion of farming with no motivation or opportunity to improve their lot. Call it Realism or call it reality, it amounts to the same.

"You pan from one object to another," wrote Huston, equating the filmgoing experience with the simple act of looking around. Similarly, Realism's primary goal was the unidealized presentation of objects and people as they appear to the human eye. "We are forever cutting in real life," continued the director. "Notice how you involuntarily blink. *That's a cut.*" Like that same blink or that same cut, *Fat City* lets its cast drift under the same punishing sun and stars as the rest of the city's denizens, all of whom comprise a piece of the time capsule that preserves the lost world Gardner remembers so well.

Despite their shared history as ring amateurs, Huston and Gardner were bound by more than their boxing pasts. Gardner's fascination with the "rough and tough" crowd from the long-closed Lido and the winos slumped over bars echoed Huston's own philosophy. "Personally," wrote the director, "I admire the down-and-outers who have the heroism to take it on the chin in life as well as in the ring." *Fat City* takes two such down-and-outers who represent both sides of the same slug coin: "One," wrote Roger Ebert in his glowing, contemporaneous review, "with a lifetime of emptiness ahead of him, one with an empty life already behind."

Despite Huston's "admiration" of life's losers and

bums, there's nothing to envy in the ⸝
of characters seamlessly woven into
Excepting *The Set-up* as a singularly faithfu. ⸏
the sport, both writer and director were unimpressea ⸏
classic boxing films. "They were all the same," Gardner says
dismissively. "It's a fixed fight, and he won't take a dive... I
thought there needed to be a boxing film done another way
[and Huston] was all for it." With less than six minutes of
boxing, *Fat City* speaks to the business at its lowest levels: an
homage to its appeal among anyone who gave it a shot only
to discover it's a losing proposition. Not everyone gets to be
champion. Some don't even get to fight at all, and when they
do, it usually means a long drive, a hundred bucks minus
expenses, and a maybe broken rib for good measure.

At its core, *Fat City* is an honest portrayal of men's
reluctance and ultimate failure to maintain relationships
with each other and with women—at least at the same
time. The divide is pronounced, and while drinking and
screwing are tempting, a man also has to make a living—a
responsibility into which women do not factor in *Fat City*.
Clingy and needy, frightened and meek, contemptuous and
aggressive, the film constantly reminds viewers that such
qualities apply equally to men.

Amid this impossible balancing act between the sexes,
unexpected catastrophe can strike at any time. Sometimes
there's a new baby on the way. Sometimes a guy has to
keep himself in booze and stand the drinks for a change.
Sometimes he'll even try for that comeback no one will

remember in two months. Still, it beats farming with the migrants, who are lucky to bring in $150 a week. But again, a man has to provide, if only for himself, even when it means picking fruit off the ground to fill those endless burlap sacks. Like the film's principle characters, Gardner did his own time working the fields, and it wasn't for research.

Billy Tully (Stacy Keach) wakes up in the Hotel Coma. The hotel's actual name, it was so dissipated at the time of shooting that the crew rallied to postpone its demolition until the scene was completed. Yellow rays seep through the blinds in bright strips where an unread copy of *The Ring* lays on the mattress and an empty fifth stands on the night table. Billy lights a cigarette and glances over at the spent bottle, the embodiment of Gardner's doomed inquest: "And was this where he was going to grow old? Would it all end in a room like this?"

With half a heart, Billy peppers the heavy bag at the local Y, where the only other occupant is a kid working the speed bag. As the young man builds a rhythmic tattoo, Billy moves to an easy shadowbox to get a better look.

Eighteen-year-old Ernie Munger (Jeff Bridges) just comes here to mess around. He's never fought. He's not even an amateur. What about Billy? Is he a pro? He was, but "I'm all out of shape." There's no shame in Billy's words, nor is there any pride—going to seed is just a matter of course and not uncommon to fighters with nothing on their roster. Besides, he can get back in the game any time.

Meanwhile, he tells Ernie to introduce himself to

his trainer Ruben at the Lido. As Ernie heads outs, he turns to Billy and tells him he saw him fight once. ("Did I win?" "No.")

Is Billy's casual effort to initiate something like mentorship the closest he'll get to reliving his faded glory days? Are those days even glorious now that they're gone? Were they ever? Selective memory and revisionist history can soothe a battered ego, but Ernie could be Billy's discovery—maybe even his friend. Billy's not so far gone as to understand that doing the kid a good turn, with no expectation of payback, is good sportsmanship, good karma, and a bit of good living for a change.

After a day of training at the Lido with Ruben (Nicholas Colasanto, who would play Tommy Como eight years later in *Raging Bull*), Ernie emerges "bruised, fatigued, and elated" in the knowledge and security that he's joined the ranks of the ineffable fraternal order Gardner dubs "the company of men." Meanwhile, Ruben laments that Billy "married some broad, and she undid all the good I did him." Of course, that can happen to anyone—even Ernie.

Billy is parked on his stool at the Old Peerless Inn and meets the raucous Oma (Susan Tyrell). Fueled by alcohol like a generator burning black smoke, her voice rises careless and indignant at any perceived provocation while her taciturn Black boyfriend Earl (1960s Welterweight Champion Curtis Cokes) looks on with resigned tolerance.

Gardner describes old Stockton's bars as filled with "some of the most god-awful women," along with other rowdy sots and wet brains that alternately caused trouble or sat staring into their empty glass. Like the barflies of T.C. Boyle, Charles Bukowski, and Jean Rhys, drinkers' founder in the stench of stale beer and conversations are forgotten as fast as they unfold while the world outside remains wholly unaware of their absence.

Oma's incessant rants, in which she laments the persecution she endures for her interracial coupling with Earl, presently sitting in jail for a minor infraction, is another of the film's primary themes that stress Stockton as a racial and ethnic melting pot. (Still, Billy always knows when he's the only White guy on the farm-bound bus that leaves at dawn.) When he asks Oma why Earl was sent to jail, she responds with drunken indignation at the treatment of Blacks. "They won't leave you alone in this world," she cries, inserting herself into Earl's predicament. "You don't know what you have to take when you're interracial."

Ruben sits up in bed while his wife drifts off next to him. He's thinking about his fighters and the puny purses they're bringing in. But it's all he can secure for the guys he trains. "I got nothing against coloreds," he muses on his several Black trainees, but "Anglos don't want to see two colored guys fight. They want a white guy." Speaking of which, Ruben just met a White kid today who shows some promise. His name is Ernie Munger. Maybe this kid "could turn into a good-lookin' white heavyweight," Ruben tells his wife, now fast asleep.

Ernie should be resting up the night before his first

fight. Instead, he's knee-deep in mud, splashing around lake-size puddles to get his car unstuck. His sweetheart Faye leans over from the passenger seat for a snuggle when it finally gets moving. Most of the night was spent in the back of the car. Now the lovers, no longer virgins, move over the flooded road as if fleeing a crime scene. Ernie might have broken the golden abstinence rule, but what he does with his dick—especially at eighteen—the night before a fight is his business. Besides, writes Gardner, "To appear in the ring tomorrow without ever having won this other battle seemed presumptuous and dangerous." How can a boy truly integrate into the company of men without fully becoming one first?

Faye asks if she was good, setting off a panic in Ernie that causes his mind to spin from swagger to self-doubt. How did she know what to do in the first place? Ernie might have sealed the deal, but does he measure up to Faye's past experiences? And just how experienced is she? Once again, the Madonna-whore complex rears its head as the rain assumes a *Brontë-esque* pathetic fallacy in which inclement weather serves as a harbinger of things to come. For Ernie, this makes a once-in-a-lifetime rite of passage considerably less auspicious. Look into those dark puddles long enough and the deluge, along with coming unprotected inside Faye, spell impending dread. He won't get much sleep tonight.

In 1962, Huston probed the manifold nature of human neuroses in *Freud: The Secret Passion*, wherein the psychoanalyst undergoes self-analysis. The director, who called

Freud a "messiah" with an "almost biblical detachment," deftly adapts this "detachment" to opposite poles in which the "close-legged" Faye and the promiscuous Oma are presented as little more than passive receptacles. To the men of *Fat City*, this detachment is born of fear: commitment, pregnancy, and the possibility of winding up alone. With unfounded suspicion, Ernie projects Faye's experience in one realm on his own lack of experience in the ring.

For Oma, the years have rendered the sex act so mundane that true intimacy is impossible. "I've never been ashamed of the act of love." If drinking impedes her physical desires, she can always seek stimulation in conflict. "Struggle," writes Gardner, "is dramatic," and Oma is forever creating her own.

If Billy or Ernie were asked what they're seeking, neither would have an answer. Since Ernie learned that Faye is pregnant, his compass has been stuck between union and self-agency. Billy tells himself that he pines for his wife, and sometimes he does, but his play for Oma demonstrates that he'll settle for anyone. But Oma's not anyone. Fueled by liquid courage and Tyrell's own volatile temperament, she's the only loser in town with the guts to express her convictions and ensure that everyone's listening.

Ruben drives four young fighters to an amateur bout in the city. As they wrap their hands in the dressing room, one of them pipes up, "You want to know what makes a good fighter? Believing in yourself! The will to win! You wanna kick ass, you kick ass!" Ernie's not so sure. But it sounds good spoken out loud. Believe you're the best, and maybe you are. The kid's put down in the first. Ernie holds his own until the blood that pours from his nose prompts the ref to call a technical knockout. His first fight, his first loss.

As long as Billy's picking onions and shaking fruit off trees at $7.23 an hour (in 2023 money), his future as a washed-up bum is sealed. Farming is survival for survival's sake that makes life a walking death, and so he returns to the Lido for his comeback.

Oma's vocal contempt for males is belied by the fact that she's never without one. At this very moment, she's at the bar with Billy denouncing every man as a lout, and White men as "the vermin of the Earth." There's not much Billy can say, but Oma's not finished. "Who do you think killed the American Indian?" Implicit in her tirade is the lack of earning potential for Black fighters as mused upon by Ruben. Her sympathies lie with Earl. More importantly, it foreshadows a tough Middle American Indian who rides the 2,100 miles north from his native Zapotec territory of Oaxaca on a Greyhound to meet Billy in the ring.

Soon, a fight poster, "Billy Tully vs. Arcadio Lucero," is taped to the hotel window where a man in a cheap fitted suit with a cardboard suitcase checks in. Lucero (former California Light Heavyweight Champion Sixto Rodriguez) lies on the single bed with a perennially swollen nostril that gives his nose the appearance of having been folded to one side. Lifting the toilet seat, a staggered stream of blood clouds the water—a souvenir of a recent blow to the kidney. With over two hundred fights and his best days behind him,

Lucero "went where there was work." It's not his first time in Stockton.

"Journeyman," derived from the French *journée*, or "day," denotes a worker who's paid by the day and frequently moves from job to job. For boxers, travel is necessary (recall Ruben's drive—five hours each way—with his car full of amateurs, all of whom lost). In his book *Journeymen: The Other Side of the Boxing Business, A New Perspective on the Noble Art*, Mark Turley spoke with several such fighters, many of whom hold surprisingly positive attitudes. "The way I look at it is I'm losing but I'm not," said the English ex-super middleweight James Child. "The money I'm earning is... helping me get to my goals, so I'm winning in my way." While Child retired with a record of eighteen losses and one win, losers still get paid, and his single fluke victory caused many a bookie to lose his shirt.

Keach and Bridges are spared the exacting scrutiny by fight fans due to their low-level status as boxers within the story. Gardner was satisfied with their lackluster skills: "They didn't look like champs, but they weren't playing champs."

For Billy, and in all likelihood, the diminishing Lucero, the fight's outcome is ultimately meaningless. Nothing lasts forever, and some things are all the more doomed for the dim flicker of hope they do offer. When Ruben hands Billy his net purse of a hundred dollars, those plans to keep off the sauce and stay in training suddenly look less enticing. Billy holds up the bills and shakes them at Ruben. "Is that all my blood's worth?" Ruben doesn't have to remind him that, if he doesn't keep in shape, it is.

Billy comes to collect his clothes at Oma's and the door opens to reveal the freshly sprung Earl, who congratulates Billy on his victory and hands him a box with his things. The door frame under which they stand becomes the line that separates their inherent bond as men from Earl's virtual possession of Oma. She's his responsibility, and he doesn't need help from anyone else. A man will always do a good turn for another if he can (Billy sent Ernie to the Lido, Ruben gave Billy his shot at a comeback, and Earl held onto Billy's clothes instead of throwing them away), but he also needs to know when it's time to disappear. Nothing personal.

A finale, in which the city exudes its restless monotony with more nihilistic gloom than *The Set-up*'s hammer-smashed hand, comes in a chance encounter between Billy (drunk and out of training) and Ernie (sober on the heels of a decision win).

"Don't let anyone knock marriage, kid," a drunken Billy once told Ernie in rueful regret at his own failed union. "You don't appreciate it 'til it's gone." But ever since Ernie went pro, he's been having a hard time maintaining a career while savoring the joys of fatherhood. He may be off to a decent start like Billy before him, but how long can that last? Life's not going the way he planned since joining up with the company of men.

Billy's wisdom can't mean much to a guy for whom manhood commenced with a sham baptism in the mud.

Billy looks past the viewer and pleads with Ernie to stay a little longer. "Before you get rolling," he slurs with finality, "life makes a beeline to the drain."

It's a conversation that Ernie will soon forget. There's still time before he discovers it for himself.

19
GIRLFIGHT

Directed by Karyn Kusama
Screen Gems, 2000

Karyn Kusama started training at Gleason's Gym in Brooklyn in 1992 when she was twenty-two. Five years later, she wrote the script for her debut film *Girlfight* at the suggestion of director John Sayles, who agreed to finance the film's million-dollar budget in conjunction with The Independent Film Channel. Asked at the time of the film's release if she was a boxer, Kusama replied, "I was. I'm not now." Maybe not, but her first-hand experience at one of the world's most renowned boxing gyms (Gleason's opened in 1937) brings an honesty to *Girlfight* rarely seen outside of documentaries. Like a living organism, *Girlfight*'s fictional gym hums and throbs with the thud of heavy bags, swishing ropes, reverberating whaps from speed bags, and shoes that shuffle, pivot, and grind rosin into the ring.

The manifold reasons as to why an individual takes up boxing are pertinent to every fighter's story. *Girlfight* goes further by pressing the viewer with what, in 2000, was a more compelling question: why a girl?

First-time actor Michelle Rodriguez scowls at the fourth wall with pupils that bore into the screen with such menace that the camera should be commended for mustering the courage for the stare-down. A consummate badass best known for her roles in the *Fast and Furious* franchise and television's *Lost*, Rodriguez never looked tougher than her first five seconds on camera. With her bad-girl cred sealed in the opening shot, it's a safe bet that she won't need a gun, a hotrod, or Vin Diesel for backup.

Diana Guzman (Rodriquez) is a Latina high school student in Red Hook. She's also a troublemaker, and one more infraction will get her expelled. Not that she cares. With no head—or background—for the uptown subtleties of *Mean Girls*-style bullying, Diana is primal, aggressive, and unabashedly violent. Loitering in the girls' room like a coiled sidewinder, she escalates a verbal quarrel between two girls before pummeling one of them to the floor. It all happens so fast that the viewer is quick to forget how the fight started. Diana's even quicker.

Diana lives with her father, Sandro (Paul Calderon), and her placid, artistic younger brother Tiny (Ray Santiago), in a project apartment where the mystery of their mother's suicide hangs like a ghost over the family dinner table. While Sandro finds a modicum of peace playing cards around the smoky table with a clowder of uncool cats and reprobates, the quiet hostility he exudes toward his children is mitigated by eyes that flit in concern for their welfare. Another call from Diana's principal might exacerbate his frustrations, but her brother's delicate mien and scrawny frame remain his most significant source of unease.

Sandro sends Tiny to boxing lessons at an unnamed, Gleason's-style neighborhood gym to prepare his son for the company of men. But Tiny's gentle nature betrays no trace of his sister's seething rage. He's not a coward, but he's not a fighter, so when Diana shows up at the gym to see him sucker-punched by a bigger kid who fights dirty, she waits for them to step out of the ring. Still in his headgear, the bully flails backward with a single blow from her bare fist. She's ready for more. He isn't.

The gym's head trainer Hector (Jaime Tirelli, named for Kusama's trainer and Gleason staple Hector Roca) almost witnessed what could be his new star pupil in action. Slamming girls around school corridors is one thing, but this informal smackdown indicates an absence of fear, pain, and most importantly, men. Diana hasn't even signed up yet, but as her enthusiasm to join the gym is sparked, so too is the age-old consternation—on-screen and off—surrounding the female proclivity to physical violence.

Women's crossover into what many consider the inherent, atavistic territory of men (recall Jack London's "old red blood of Adam") has long hampered their progress in combat sports to something beyond cheap amusement, throwaway undercards, and gimmicky catfights. Unwritten but sacrosanct laws that define females as the nurturing embodiment of Eros are confounded and dismantled when said nurturer engages in such a blunt expression of the death instinct. Unsurprisingly, these so-called transgressions from traditional, "hard-wired" femininity are born largely of the male expectation to gender conformity. Only during the past twenty years has this attitude started to abate as the practice gains wider acceptance as an essential facet—and money-maker—within the game. If the overarching tenet is that primates are naturally aggressive, this necessarily extends to females.

In her slim volume *On Boxing*, Joyce Carol Oates asserts that boxing "is a purely masculine activity and inhabits a purely masculine world." The female boxer, she continues, "is parody; she is cartoon, she is monstrous." But a lot's changed since the book's 1987 publication, starting with the establishment of the Women's International Boxing Federation, the first women's sanctioning body, two years later. (Today, there are two women's sanctioning bodies, not including the four dominant bodies, which also approve women's bouts.) By the 2020s, the popularity and frequency of women's fights have made enormous strides in deconstructing outmoded attitudes toward gender roles. On October 15, 2022, the first-ever all-female boxing card—featuring eleven bouts and twenty-two fighters—made history in London. But like anything that calls for social change, nothing happens overnight. Sometimes it takes 2,500 years.

Author and English literature professor Allison Dean dates imagery of women fighters to Etruscan bronze statuettes from around 330 B.C.E. depicting females in combat with men. From there, chronology grows muddled, the result of a centuries-long efforts to erase women's boxing from record. Of course, such fights did occur—mainly to the delight of men. One illuminating example is the Englishman William Hickey's gleeful account of a mid-eighteenth-century fight between "Two she-devils... engaged in a scratching and boxing match, their faces entirely covered with blood, bosoms bare, and the cloths torn from their bodies."

While the following paragraphs provide a cursory timeline and select highlights, a thorough history of women's boxing falls well outside the scope of this book. Those seeking a more completist narrative should consult L.A. Jennings's 2014 book, *She's a Knockout! A History of Women in Fighting Sports*.

The first recorded female bout took place in England in 1722. Although the reigning cultural draws in Regency England were more of the Jane Austin variety, the self-proclaimed "European Championess" Elizabeth Wilkinson Stokes and other female bruisers provoked a more prurient curiosity in spectators. Stokes's most famous bout occurred in 1728, when she accepted a challenge from a mule driver named Ann Field: "as the famous... ass-woman dares me to fight her for the 10 pounds, I do assure her I will not fail meeting her for the said sum." The *London Journal* reported that the epic dustup unfolded "to the no small satisfaction of the spectators."

Although most female prizefights were conducted out of the larger public eye, attendees delighted in these hair-pulling, flesh-clawing spectacles (the Queensberry rules would not be established for another century and a half). Yet in an age steeped in nationalism and eugenics due to a rapid rise in immigrant birthrates, the responsibility of men to maintain a degree of physical prowess occasionally extended to women in the effort to strengthen the "white stock." Despite the pretext of female self-defense as protection from the foreign influx, the majority of "mashers" were, unsurprisingly, spouses and other domestics.

By the mid-nineteenth century, women's boxing was relegated to one of many newfangled fitness fads, spurring men to poke fun at their make-believe emasculation at the hands of their wives—often by way of newspaper comics depicting cowed husbands beaten black and blue. As Victorian standards dictated frailty, ineffectuality, and even hysteria as uniquely female traits, boxing again fell firmly into the male realm. Women's bouts didn't disappear but were consigned to evermore clandestine affairs among the lower classes—usually as a means of score-settling.

In 1769, the *Chicago Tribune* described one such fight as "exciting" and arousing "disgust and pity" in its spectators. Nevertheless, only a fraction of names and recorded bouts of the day survive. In his 2012 article "Disappearance: How

Shifting Gendered Boundaries Motivated the Removal of Eighteenth Century Boxing Champion Elizabeth Wilkinson from Historical Memory," Christopher Thrasher writes that the fighter's disappearance from historical record coincided with a century "when her narrative no longer supported newly dominated notions of gender hierarchy." Of course, such "notions" have always existed, though their formal manifestation has repeatedly waxed and waned.

"There is little evidence," writes Jennings, "of boxing matches with female fighters occurring in the United States prior to the mid-nineteenth century." While the release of Edison's 1901 production *The Gordon Sisters Boxing* saw women's boxing regain traction, the arrival of Dempsey's million-dollar gates and roaring twenties gender norms once again saw female fighters demoted to objects of mass derision.

Despite numerous court battles throughout the twentieth century, states were slow to grant women professional licenses. Fitness fads, on the other hand, began to gain traction. In 1904, the *New York Times* touted the benefits of non-competitive women's boxing, of which the practitioners were dubbed "new girls" or "boxing girls." More like powderpuff sparring than genuine fighting, new girls served the two-fold purpose of maintaining their figures for the benefit of their menfolk and spawning sporty, sexy, if not altogether practical athletic fashion.

The rise in women's self-defense that accompanied second-wave feminism during the 1960s and '70s was a valuable means of garnering protective measures against male-on-female violence, with group classes providing solidarity that fostered physical empowerment and protection over fitness. At the height of this cultural uprising in 1974, New York State Athletic Commission chairman Edward Dooley issued a dire warning that female boxing would "erode the sport's image as the 'manly art of self-defense.'"

According to a 2010 study by Jocelyn A. Hollanter, female college students who took self-defense classes reported a sense of collective support and suffered proportionally fewer sexual assaults than their non-self-defense counterparts. Two years before the #MeToo movement gained traction in 2017, the trend saw another surge, attributed to threats from homophobic opponents of the LGBTQIA community and xenophobic attacks on Muslim women. As of the 2020s, students of boxing and other forms of self-defense continue to increase under a growing plague of xenophobia, white supremacy, and increasing threats to reproductive rights.

The issuing of boxing licenses to women was stunted for decades due to its licensure on a state-by-state basis, and despite a formalized sanctioning body, the legality of professional women's boxing was not recognized on the national level until the USA Boxing Commission lifted the ban in 1993.

The breakthrough match that made fans pay attention in earnest is widely regarded as a 1996 undercard to a title rematch between Mike Tyson and Frank Bruno.

So upstaged were the headliners by the preceding slugfest between Chrissy "The Coal Miner's Daughter" Martin and Deidra "Dangerous" Gogarty that the commentators' patronizing tones fast turned to ungrudging praise, inclusivity, and even calls for equal pay for women boxers.

The year after *Girlfight*'s release, boxing writer and sports historian Bert Sugar was unequivocally pejorative in anticipation of the 2001 non-title bout billed "Ali v Frazier IV." Featuring the former heavyweights' daughters Laila "She Bee Stingin" Ali and Jacqui "Sister Smoke" Frazier, Sugar wrote, "Maybe they're fighting because they love the accessories... After all, they're wearing gloves, fighting for a purse and a belt, and wearing satin shorts." He also expressed concern that the bout would demean the Ali-Frazier legacy. The artful spectacle had the crowd in Verona, NY on their feet, prompting an unsmiling Laila Ali to snarl, "Our critics can now go eat crow." Sugar, who said the bout "will either make women's boxing or completely destroy it," kept mum.

In a sport where discussion of male sexuality is rare to non-existent, the newly crowned Olympic champion Nicola Adams was the first openly lesbian boxer to fight in the Olympics. (Held in London in 2012, the games were the first in modern history to feature women's boxing.) Currently a top-ranked UFC fighter, Amanda Nunes became the first openly lesbian champion. Old stereotypes die hard, and Rodriguez recalls that, upon being cast, her brother told her, "You're gonna look like some butch up there." He was wrong: when it comes to the networks, promotion, and the viewing public, the opposite is true: strong is sexy.

In *Ultimate Fighting and Embodiment: Violence, Gender, and Mixed Martial Arts*, Professor Dale Spencer of Carleton University writes, "Tennis and MMA have been able to hyper-sexualize the women who participate in those sports, especially when they already have a certain physical appeal going for them." Objectively speaking, the current top-ranked female boxers are notably attractive—a trait that holds considerably less weight among male athletes. Spencer elucidates how the media "promote those women [to] maintain a level of popularity that is roughly equivalent to the male side of the sport." And numbers don't lie. As of 2022, the UFC holds over a hundred female fighters and has featured sixteen women-headlined pay-per-view fights. Despite this spike in viewership, Spencer stresses that women's combat sports continue to elicit a "level of fetishization [that] speaks to what [men] expect when it comes to the ring," so relegating women "to novelty-entertainment." While being allowed to fight has been one bugbear in the uphill battle female combat sports participants have endured, the real challenge is to be taken seriously.

Of course, the hyper-sexualized strong girl isn't confined to sports. By way of example, consider Wonder Woman's introduction in 1941 as both children's superhero and vehicle for her creator's bondage kink. Eighty years later, the same heroine can be seen on the big screen played by a former Miss Israel pageant winner, again proving that real or fictional, tough girls are a lot more palatable when portrayed by babes.

In 1897, the *San Francisco Chronicle* praised boxer Cecile Richards in equal parts for her beauty and her skill, hinting that women's boxing would become more popular if more fighters looked like she did. "Poverty of the imagination," writes Sarah Deming in her essay *The Real Million Dollar Baby*, "keeps sportswriters fixated on women boxers' physical appearances or history of sexual abuse, as though these things had any currency in the ring at all." This is especially pertinent considering the infrequency with which past trauma, especially that of a sexual nature, is mined among male participants.

Despite previous chapters' numerous invocations of Freudian theory, the oft-contended psychoanalyst's limp insights into feminine psychology range from staunch incuriosity to prudish misogyny. In asserting that "feminine masochism" (*e.g.*, stepping under the ropes to get punched) denotes a past trauma, Freud offers just one of many examples of his penchant for jamming square pegs into round holes. (To the psychoanalyst's credit, the rare but resounding references to Diana's mother expose a daughter bruised and broken by the past.)

A 2014 article published by the University of Minnesota Tucker Center for Girls & Women in Sport concluded that "forty percent of all sports participants are female, yet women's sports receive only four percent of all sport media coverage." Depending on the source, this number has either climbed to five percent or plummeted drastically. "Female athletes," the article continues, "are much more likely than male athletes to be portrayed in sexually provocative poses." In her 2001 critique in *The Brooklyn Rail* titled "No Winners Here: The Flawed Feminism of Girlfight," Anju Reejhsinghani speculates as to "whether a less attractive actress, or one portraying a lesbian boxer ... would have attracted the same attention." Perhaps not, but nor is *Girlfight* an explicitly feminist film. Yes, the boxer is female, but her wish to fight not for money or a title but for respect is a theme common to countless boxing films featuring males with similar soul-searching aspirations. *Girlfight*'s protagonist may be a woman, but she's also an individual, not a microcosm of women's boxing.

Moving like a missile toward Hector's office, Diana opens the door without knocking and drops a wrinkled tenner (his weekly rate) on the desk. As he struggles to evade Diana's desire to box ("It's just that girls are built *different* than boys"), an old-timer suggests she stick to aerobics. Her eyes dart at him just long enough for him to close his mouth, and with the Hamilton sitting on Hector's desk, he has no good excuse. As for Diana, she has a new trainer.

Of course, girls *are* built different than boys. In her book *Without Apology: Girls, Women, and the Desire to Fight*, Leah Hagler writes that, while not necessarily better suited to boxing, women have greater endurance than men. They also have superior balance and greater flexibility while men can carry more oxygen and have larger, leaner muscle mass.

Most distressing is the lack of research into brain injury in women. Robert Stern of Boston University's Chronic Traumatic Encephalopathy Center admits to having "no idea at all about whether there are sex-based differences in CTE... because we haven't seen any women's brains that have shown signs of it after athletic exposure." As a result of this paucity of subjects, Stern admits that "only two women have ever, anywhere, been diagnosed with the disease."

In accordance with such biological differences, the World Boxing Commission changed women's bouts from twelve three-minute rounds (the maximum length permitted for males) to ten two-minute rounds under the banner of "science, not sexism." Unlike their male counterparts, female fighters must also test for testosterone levels prior to fighting, including a mouth-smear to confirm the XX chromosome. Though no longer barred from fighting when menstruating, women are still required to take a pregnancy test before stepping under the ropes.

Like anyone who grew up fighting on instinct, Diana's initial combos flail with scrappy slaps and mechanical rock 'n' socks. The alpha-tomboy who never jumped rope skips for a beat before it winds and tangles around her calves. But she's a fast learner.

Rodriguez trained at Gleason's for four and a half months, sparing the viewer the onus of comparison between an actor and a practiced boxer. After all, she's not playing a professional. Like Diana, Rodriguez was also a fast learner—so fast that, within just two months, offers started coming in from the vultures that hung around the gym poaching for talent. As one of 350 hopefuls in an open casting call, the twenty-one-year-old Rodriguez was not, according to Kusama, the "experienced, professional, Latina actress who could still play eighteen [years old]." Yet her lack of experience brings further authenticity to a film in which a professional actor might have smoothed the edges required to play a character who, Kusama continues, "demands a sort of unschooled sensibility."

Rodriguez was nothing if not unschooled, and when it was her turn to read, she started with the stage directions. Never having seen a script, she attributes her selection to her "pessimistic little PMS attitude." She was so unpolished that Kusama considered replacing her until Sayles and the producers at IFC Films convinced her to give the fledgling actor a little time to acclimate. "Other producers," speculates Kusama, "would have said, 'Huge risk, find a star.'" But after a couple of days, Rodriguez "was able to ask questions and start talking about what she felt was real for the character." Her efforts earned her the Independent Spirit Award for Best Debut Performance and Cannes' Award of the Youth, and the film tied for the Grand Jury's top prize at Sundance. Along with "the instincts of a natural actor," Rodriguez was wholly unafraid to take as many punches as training—and filming—required. "As a boxer," continues Kusama, "she was fearless in an almost frightening way."

In his autobiography *Undisputed Truth*, Mike Tyson writes, "If I hadn't boxed, I'd be breaking the law. That's my nature." The statement is both an unapologetic admission of the human proclivity to violence and a solid case for the hopeless entwinement of nurture vs. nature. In furthering the age-old debate, Cohen recounts one of her trainers telling her, "If you're a well-adjusted, basically happy person, you don't box." While Tyson refers to crime and Cohen to sports, the violence at their core is not mutually exclusive. Diana's no thug, but punching girls in the head, paired with a lack of adult role models and an unstable household, makes for an easy slide into a post-high school life of crime. As to those happy, well-adjusted people who don't box (and in a final reference to Freudian theory), whatever keeps them grounded might come at the cost of repressed aggression on the brink of overload.

When it comes to fighting, gender doesn't discriminate. Born into poverty in Flynt, Michigan and systematically raped as a child from age five, contemporary boxing sensation Clarissa Shields echoes Tyson's self-appraisal: "If I hadn't found boxing, who knows where I'd be at, with the anger inside of me?" The psychological benefits of training, even without the intention of going professional, are one way of keeping the demons at bay. Hector's investment in his protege grows as Diana hones her skills. She's instinctive. She's fast. But is she ready to step into the ring? What kind of battle does she hope to wage? And how far is she willing to take it?

The fervor and heartache at Hector's gym aren't exclusively externalized through boxing. In a 2000 interview with Bette Gordon in *BOMB* magazine, Kusama stressed the importance of colors to denote mood within the film. With this in mind, it follows that the gym's red walls are no accident. In a 2014 BBC article titled "How the Colour Red Warps the Mind," David Robson correlates the color's association with emotions including anger, power, courage, and love "with a strong link to sexuality and increased appetites." Robson even cites a 2014 study by the University of Durham that determined that boxers who wear red are five percent more likely to win bouts than their opponents in blue.

Diana's become more comfortable fighting in the ring, where the stated rules and driving pace alleviate the frivolity and ambiguity of the high school scraps that, not so long ago, served as outlet for her rage. Meanwhile, the spark of passion, sex, and maybe something like love arrives in the form of Diana's fellow trainee Adrian (Santiago Douglas). Having sized each other up, they're soon stealing kisses wherever and whenever they can.

Following a knock-down kitchen brawl with her father, Diana overpowers him and tightens her chokehold on this principal source of her anger and isolation. When Sandro pleads with her to stop, she reminds him that her mother also begged. Her actions won't bring any immediate healing to the home, but the anger that brings her demons to the surface exposes an unspoken truth that, in the long run, just might repair their broken relationship.

Having defeated an iron-chinned southpaw in her first amateur bout, Diana's ready to move forward when calamity strikes and her scheduled opponent abruptly pulls out to turn professional. (Incidentally, a second-time fighter like Diana taking it up with a boxer ready to turn pro doesn't sound like much of a match.) With no available female opponent, she's paired with Adrian, who opposes the bout for reasons that need no explanation. Among the film's subtle feminist messages isn't Diana's willingness to fight a male, but her need to fight at all. Adrian's trainer begs the commission to cancel the fight. A loss to a girl would kill all chances of his boy's dream of going pro. But when fight night arrives, a woman looks over the program and speaks aloud to no one in particular: "It doesn't look like a misprint to me." Enter the announcer, who blares, "History in the making... New York's first inter-gender amateur bout!"

The first? Maybe, but there's always the possibility that such bouts had taken place in New York and other states, though if they did, they were never reported. These are the amateurs, where fighters who don't move on to the professional circuit are forgotten. Perhaps some rough clarity can be found in months spent pouring through shelves of record books, but a prolonged Google search for "inter-gender boxing" generally turns up fetish videos featuring scantily clad women in boxing gloves punching men in the face. Entertainment at its finest.

In her book *Men, Women, and Chainsaws: Gender in the Modern Horror Film*, Carol J. Clover explains how the classic horror film "puts... the female body on the line if only to put the male psyche on the line." If female-on-male-violence shakes the masculine order when the female protagonist (aka "the final girl") ultimately kills the (inevitably male) slasher, *Girlfight*'s inter-gender violence is even more loaded as guns and machetes are swapped out for hand-to-hand combat. A marauding psycho's death at the hands of a woman is an old formulaic feat of ingenuity, but the notion of a male's physical domination at the hands of a female peer is nothing short of mortifying. As Kusama recalls, the beating Diana gives her father evoked the loudest applause from test audiences both male and female.

If *Girlfight* can be said to have an overarching feminist bent, it manifests in this co-ed bout that's best viewed as good drama intentionally devoid of message, though Kusama describes her own experience sparring with a man as "ridiculously romantic... that someone's trying to communicate with me in this really psycho environment."

When Diana drops Adrian in the first round, he rises. But in a game that's fifty percent psychology, it's already clear who the winner is, even though Diana is considerably less experienced than Adrian (recall his manager's eagerness to see his boy turn pro). When the final bell sounds, the lovers remain tangled in a clinch indistinguishable from an embrace as Diana is declared the winner. (For what it's worth, she was the fighter in blue.)

Reejhsinghani takes issue with Kusama's shoehorning this inter-gender bout into the film under the pretense of a lack of female competition, noting that women's fighting wasn't as rare in 2000 as *Girlfight* suggests. In other words,

Hector wouldn't have any trouble finding a female replacement instead of pairing his fighter with a male. "Had Kusama set the movie in Peoria, or Sacramento, or Seattle," Reejhsinghani writes, "[Diana's] isolation might have been far more believable... If there were female boxers anywhere, they'd be in New York." Aside from her observations on Rodriguez's beauty, Reejhsinghani's critique is more a reality check than a full-on rebuttal of the film's subtle feminist bent—by design or by accident, real or perceived.

Diana may have overcome her social maladjustment, but her heart has grown vulnerable while honing her body and taming her temper. That's the gamble when anger and isolation are traded out for self-compassion, confidence, and love. But is love the only means by which to validate a happy ending?

Kusama's assertion that Diana will *not* wind up with Adrian allows for what she calls "illusory closure." That life is forever riddled with ambivalence is the only closure the film offers, which is no closure at all. To audiences that cling to the assumption that Diana and Adrian's affections will continue beyond the end credits, Kusama rolls her eyes: "God, you've watched too many Julia Roberts movies." There's no room here for assumed, invented, or contrived conclusions. Diana's still a work in progress.

Although *Girlfight*'s lack of resolution is a rarity among recent boxing films, Diana's willingness to face life's constant uncertainties is a necessary element when contending with their infinite vicissitudes both in and out of the ring.

20
TYSON

Directed by James Toback
Sony Pictures Classics
2008

A good documentary can make even the dullest subject enthralling, and there's nothing dull about Mike Tyson. James Toback's deeply introspective examination of the fighter makes a fitting coda to a string of films that began 111 years earlier when *The Corbett-Fitzsimmons Fight* was projected to an audience dazzled by new technology and screaming for blood. *Tyson* also stands as a cautionary tale wherein absolute power—in the form of money that comes with impossible fame—corrupts absolutely. And to the young Tyson, if it wasn't absolute, it might as well not exist.

In 2007, Toback called Tyson about a documentary

they'd discussed making two years prior on the heels of the fighter's retirement. They'd known each other for twenty years—Mike even appeared playing himself in Toback's 1999 film *Black and White*. In 2009, the director told *Sports Illustrated* about a walk he and the then-nineteen-year-old fighter took twenty-three years prior in which they discussed "madness." He didn't elaborate.

Filmed when Tyson was forty-one, he was just off a daylong stint in Sheriff Joe Arpaio's Tent City jail in Arizona for possession of cocaine. A week later, he was back in California working the twelve steps and bringing milk and cookies to support meetings in an outpatient program at L.A.'s ultra-exclusive Wonderland Treatment Center. There was no coke, no marijuana, and no sex, but his cocktail was formidable: two anti-depressants, one mood stabilizer, and two mood regulators for bipolar disorder. Sober, maybe, but cloudy, and seriously jonesing for the real stuff.

Toback's edits devote just five minutes (the last five) to Tyson's addictions. Still, the subtle thread of recovery that runs through the film is discernible in the ex-fighter's thoughtful demeanor when he discusses his multiple and manifold traumas. Despite his ongoing dependence on drugs, sex, and booze, this recovery thread may not be *quite* as pervasive as Tyson recalls: "I was basically doing an addict documentary." Six weeks later, he was back on Cialis, poking every prostitute in a ten-mile radius, and snorting up the finest snow Los Angeles County had to offer.

While Toback approached the documentary format with neutrality in his effort to show rather than tell, the film goes a step further in that he and Tyson entered the project with no plans or agenda. Despite an apparent desire to absolve a man who is one of his heroes, Toback judiciously lets his subject speak for himself. If viewers walk away with more questions than answers, it's because Tyson doesn't have them, nor has he fully grasped how he managed to transcend the game to become an instantly recognizable cultural icon even among people who'd never seen a fight. Toback eschews expositions and explanations because he's not looking for them. The very process of Tyson's cogitation *is* the explanation.

Toback culled five old-school psychoanalytic prompts to "stimulate [Tyson's] unconscious." The prompts would launch each day's session, where, following roughly forty-five minutes of silence, his subject would begin to speak. Dozens of hours from the five-day shoot were then edited to a seamless ninety minutes. "The idea," said Toback, "was never to make a documentary in the conventional sense. The analogy I use is a self-portrait."

Day one. Toback told Tyson to describe his first memories, setting the springboard for a day of steady musings and long silences that offer a window to a mind twisted with strained pathways in hopeless disarray at the time of filming due to immeasurable self-loathing, excruciating rage, and a desperate swipe at self-forgiveness.

There's no room here for a remotely cohesive exposition

on Tyson's life: his childhood, family, reform schools and correctional institutes, shifting management, convoluted negotiations, waxing and waning finances, frantic mood swings, rehab stints, and countless out-of-the-ring exploits can fill volumes. Likewise, the film's running time necessitates omitting numerous biographical bullet points, and whatever content Toback left on the cutting room floor forever remains a mystery. But Mike's merry-go-round of strained relationships and trouble with the law was never the film's point. The issue was simply to let the man speak.

Tyson's narrative blueprint is marked by four major episodes in a life that ascended from impossible poverty to inconceivable wealth almost overnight. Each episode could comprise its own book. Two of them already do. The other two, falling as they do into the sewer of tabloid scandal, consumed forests of newsprint in their day.

As the film's only source, Tyson is, by definition, an unreliable narrator. Yet so disarming are his struggles to communicate that the viewer's trust is secure. Although he condemns much of his past behavior, he holds no shame around the depression, anxiety, and addiction that's followed him since his mother added gin to his bottle to put him to sleep when he was a baby.

November 22, 1986. With a professional record of 27-0—including five first-round knockouts in under a minute—Tyson pummels the aging Trevor Berbick (who beat Ali in the latter's final bout), and the fight is stopped in the second. At twenty, Mike Tyson had just become history's youngest Heavyweight Champion. Multiple views of the slaughter are set inside subscreens that advance, recede, and overlap while Tyson speaks over the action. "The first question we ask is who am I? Madness. Chaos."

In a pressed, light blue Armani shirt, Tyson tries to vocalize whatever demon he's chasing inside his head. Resurfacing, he musters words and muscles vocabulary to articulate the fiend he's finally managed to corner. Despite his frequent pauses ("Now I'm gonna cry," he interrupts himself when his voice starts to break), his mild speech impediment turns words like "despicable" into staid, solemn music.

Non-fight fans who associate Mike Tyson with ear-biting, explosive press meetings, and scary headlines will find his gentle demeanor incongruous with their expectations. However, he quickly puts them at ease as he interrupts himself mid-sentence more than once: "I deal with a huge inferiority complex."

By all accounts, Toback did not. In the late sixties, the twenty-eight-year-old journalist conducted a series of interviews with Jim Brown for an assignment in which he was to portray the athlete/activist as "a malicious monkey hungry to devour white bananas." Instead, he befriended the running back and dropped the job to write *Jim: The Author's Self-Centered Memoir of the Great Jim Brown.*

According to a 1971 *New York Times* article by Calvin C. Hernton, the circumstances behind the short volume extend beyond the simple fact that "Brown is a great athlete and a great man." Instead, Hernton argued, Toback's impetus stemmed from the fact that "[Brown] is also a black man around whom exists an aura of mammoth sexuality" and that "associating with Brown constitutes a sort of proving ground for Toback's sexuality." Toback didn't deny it and even said it would help him "learn of and perhaps acquire some of [Brown's] sexual powers." Thirty years after the consummate (White) tough-guy Harvey Keitel was emasculated by Brown's "mammoth sexuality" in the director's 1978 debut, *Fingers*, Toback's fetishization of his present subject still feels familiar. In the same way those flabby, pasty-white Victorians were unmanned in the presence of muscled Blacks like Jack Johnson, the flabby, pasty-white Toback trembles in idolatry under his senseless theory of boosting his sex appeal through osmosis. (Recall his description of *Tyson* as a "self-portrait.")

Toback discusses Tyson as an archeologist would speak of a priceless African fetish. Grave but dazzled, he describes Tyson's body. "Add to that the face." He speaks slowly. "...Add to that the voice..." Overcome by his subject's thousands of sexual encounters, Toback's removal of himself—and his ego—from the film is a blessing to the viewer.

In twisted surveillance on the streets of Beverly Hills, the director tried to gauge if women wanted to watch a film about his chosen subject—a convicted rapist. "Come to my editing room," he told the women who said they did not. If, after five minutes, the woman wanted to leave, he'd send her off with a hundred dollars. If she decided to stay, she could finish the film without being paid. According to the director, all thirty-five women who agreed to what he pruriently calls his "proposal" stayed to the end. What else did Toback show them in his "editing room?"

In October of 2017, thirty-seven women accused Toback of unwanted sexual advances. Considering the litany of public lawsuits against Tyson for sexual misconduct—some spurious, some valid—one might assume that the boxer and director are cut from the same cloth. Yet their vastly different backgrounds (one a Black, dirt-poor Brooklynite; the other a Jewish, well-to-do Manhattanite) and willingness to discuss past infractions disprove any affiliation in the sexual realm.

Michael Gerard Tyson was raised among pimps, sex workers, and murderers in the impoverished Bedford–Stuyvesant neighborhood of Brooklyn. At age ten, his mother and two siblings moved to the dreaded Brownsville projects. "We went from being poor to being serious poor to being fucked-up poor." He did not meet his father, a player he claims, "had a reputation as the baddest hustler and pimp in Brooklyn," until his late twenties. In a 1998 *Playboy* interview, the cantankerous thirty-two-year-old told Mark Kram he did not know Purcell Tyson's occupation. In a lie of Baroque proportions, he also told Kram that he'd tried drugs but "it wasn't my thing. I never got hooked."

Short, chubby, with a high voice and lisp, the other kids—thieves, murderers, addicts—called young Mike "Little fairy boy." Tyson officially entered the gangsta fold when some local gang members asked him to help maintain the pigeon coops they kept on local rooftops. "You don't fuck with pigeon guys," Tyson wrote of a rival flyer thrown off a roof for messing with someone else's birds. Likening pigeons to boxing, he explains that birds from the same flock know and recognize one another and are even capable of love. "But when I feed them, they'll kill each other for the food."

Tyson stopped going to school in the second grade. Life was an unending string of break-ins, muggings, and theft. He also made a pigeon sanctuary in an abandoned coop on a rooftop near his home. When a bigger, older neighborhood punk tore the head off one of his birds, Tyson went on the offensive for the first time in his life and knocked the kid out cold. From then on, the twelve-year-old, two-hundred-pound thug took all comers. Word spread. Challengers started coming in from rival neighborhoods. When Tyson was through with them, they wished they hadn't.

With thirty-eight arrests by age thirteen, life was a revolving door of special-ed schools that ultimately landed Tyson in a lock-down facility where he was diagnosed with "hyperactivity" and "manic depression." "They skipped the Ritalin and went straight to the big T," he writes of the Thorazine he was fed. Soporific, mellowing, and mentally crippling, the noxious antipsychotic didn't stop Tyson's ferocious attacks on inmates, guards, and counselors.

When an ex-boxer and counselor named Bobby Stewart promised to teach the thirteen-year-old Tyson to box on the condition that he behave himself, Tyson kept out of trouble. Sensing potential, Stewart determined a path to assure the young man would not return to the streets: tough love and focused discipline from the guy who could make it happen. At fourteen, Tyson was sent to Catskill, NY to study under the mentorship of legendary boxing trainer Cus D'Amato.

Cus D'Amato. Curses and adoration. The marriage of the sacred and profane held within a singular moniker. Cus, a philosophical titan whose theories on the use of fear to one's advantage could fill a dozen self-help books, told his new charge that "fear is the greatest obstacle to learning. But fear is your best friend. Fear is like fire. If you learn to control it, you let it work for you." For Tyson, the fear of stepping under the ropes was mainline to his aggression. "I'm scared," he says, recalling those long walks to the ring, but his confidence grows the closer he gets. "Once I get in, I'm a god." After watching his new charge spar just three rounds, Cus made his pronouncement: "That's the Heavyweight Champion of the world."

Tyson consumed every aspect of boxing's history and technique, a prerequisite he believes is necessary for any great fighter. Under Cus, the new student developed curiosities that extended beyond the ring to historical colossuses like Alexander the Great, Hannibal, Machiavelli, and Shaka Zulu. Biographies of Jack Johnson, Jack Dempsey, and Errol Flynn instilled the notion that great men are defined by their sexual conquests. With astounding retention and a well-worn dictionary, Tyson devoured the writings of Nietzsche, Mao, Sun Tzu, Che Guevara, and Tolstoy. But perhaps his veneration of the *X-Men* villain Apocalypse, whose solipsist logic ("I'm not malevolent. I just am") best conveys the image he wished to cultivate as an up-and-comer.

Despite a childhood surrounded by promiscuity and prostitution, Tyson was a late bloomer. Shy and inept around girls, he took comfort in that most of his heroes abstained in order to save their stamina for the ring. Still, out there in the Catskills, it was "jerk off and train. Jerk off and train." His stamina was just fine, and soon, his sparring partners stopped showing up. If girls remained intimidating, there wasn't a man on the planet that Mike—who'd just scored the fastest knockout in amateur history—was afraid of.

Cus sent the eighteen-year-old into his first professional fight with the words, "Be afraid of your opponent but don't be afraid to hurt him... throw punches with bad intentions... you are a scourge from god." It took a minute and forty-seven seconds for the scourge to batter his opponent to submission. Twenty months later, he was Champion.

Silent and snarling, Tyson cultivated a persona wholly antithetical to Ali's. He wasn't political. He wasn't clever. His boasts were not meant to amuse or entertain. And he wasn't pretty (he always believed he was ugly). He stepped under the ropes in black trunks and no socks and no pleasantries. If an opponent stared or pretended that they weren't afraid, Tyson would smack a kiss or flash his pubic hair. Squaring off during the instructions, he looked at them "as if they were food," winning the fight before the first bell sounded. "I keep my eyes on my opponent. I keep my eyes on him. I keep my eyes on him." Then the inevitable moment when his opponent "looks down for that one-tenth of a second" and "I already know I broke his spirit."

The unimaginable fame that came with the belt saw the floodgates of Tyson's sexual life burst open like a dam that held the culmination of eighties excess at bay. The $1.5 million purse was also nice, though within fourteen months he'd be pulling $20 million a fight. Cus, who had died the previous year, never got to see his charge become Champion, leaving Tyson both unmoored and free to indulge the id without reprisal from the one person he respected. A fixture in the public eye through television interviews and celebrity appearances, the belt came to mean less and less. "Just the money and the pussy." These are not fond memories. "A lot of pussy."

Movie stars, supermodels, moony-eyed starfuckers, and high-end sex workers swarmed him like flies. He dove in headlong, though he frequently returned to Brownsville for action, where his incredulous pimp friends told him not to "be fucking these hoes and nasty bitches." But big or small, skinny or fat, pretty or ugly, Tyson admits that his "only criteria was breathing." (Sometimes he just needed a break from that $40,000 Dom Pérignon to sip on some three-dollar jug wine.) With a revolving bevy of women in every bedroom of his mansion, Tyson's life came less to resemble that of an athlete than a symbolic reenactment of *Caligula*, only with better booze, a lot of cars, and a *lot* of coke.

In 1988, Tyson saw the twenty-four-year-old actress Robin Givens, a star on the teen sitcom *Head of the Class*, in a low-budget TV movie. They became an item and Mike proposed when Robin announced she was pregnant just a month into their relationship. "I was too young to be married," he admits, "Then, of course, I started being a pig and had my extracurricular activities on the side and me not being, um, the most cautious and most—using the most skullduggery of tricks, I got caught most of the time." Such passages provide insight into a mind's grinding, churning cogs as it carefully pairs thoughts with words.

Tyson should have sensed something fishy when Robin brought her mother, sister, and publicist on their first date. A transparent team of gold-diggers, Givens and her mother ("I do come as a package," the actress told Barbara Walters) pursued Mike's money from the outset. With no prenup, Robin's first order of business was the purchase of a five-million-dollar mansion in New Jersey for her mother.

Next on their agenda was a play for Tyson's career. Having squeezed out his Catskill management team, they turned to two high-profile players: Don King and Donald Trump, the latter having wangled his way into the fight biz in 1987 to boost his Atlantic City casino. Already peripheral figures in Tyson's world, they were happy to join the feeding frenzy and help take control of the golden goose.

The next order of business for the mother-daughter team was to commit Tyson to a rehab or mental facility and gain complete control of his finances. When they hired a shrink to prescribe the lithium that made him docile, the doctor handed Mike the script. "Don't take this shit," Tyson recalls the doctor telling him. "I wouldn't." But Tyson wasn't very good at following orders—especially doctors.'

Tyson had the WBA belt, and now it was time to unify the title by fighting International Boxing Federation champ Michael Spinks. One side of the split-screen homes in on pre-fight footage of a terrified Spinks staring at the abyss like a lamb to the slaughter. Conversely, Tyson laments the so-called fans who called him an animal, "but then they pay five hundred dollars to see it." In the third-fastest knockout in boxing history, he dropped Spinks in a minute and a half. Not a bad day's work for $22 million—roughly $245,000 a second.

In September 1988, Tyson appeared with Givens on 20/20 for a now-infamous interview with Barbara Walters. Tyson doesn't spend much time recounting the episode here, but his residual anger is palpable. Despite a brow as serene as a marble carving of Alexander, his elocution still manages to render epithets like "wretched swine" into unadulterated profanity.

In meek silence, Tyson sat behind his wife as she relentlessly humiliated him on national television and told Walters that he was "not physically abusive, but mentally abusive." Hers, she said, was a life of constant fear. "He shakes. He pushes. He swings. Sometimes I think he's trying to scare me." She even revealed his recent diagnosis as a "manic-depressive" while the cowed fighter nodded in deference through a lithium haze. (As noted, he didn't always listen to doctors.) "I know they expected me to go crazy on television." He looks down at the floor. "I can't believe I sat there and didn't say anything."

The divorce was bitter and contentious. With several last-ditch accusations for which neither daughter nor mother would go on record, Robin's new favorite phrase was, "You can't quote me!" As new facts about the "wretched swine" emerged, including her false claim of having attended Harvard Medical School, her credibility lay in shambles. Robin was the villain, especially among the Black community. In the March 1990 issue of *Ebony*, Laura B. Randolph called her "the most hated woman in America." Despite the $10 million settlement of which replete records still exist, Givens told the press that she "didn't receive one dime."

Tyson stays measured when recalling the marriage that ended twenty years earlier. "We were kids." A long pause as he shakes his head at that which can never be undone. "Just kids."

1990. Tyson was undefeated, out of shape, and partying like a pro when he flew to Tokyo to fight the 42-1 underdog Buster Douglas for an easy payday. With those odds, even the reporters stayed home to save money on plane fare. But Tyson was not "mentally prepared"—a thin euphemism for intoxication that he uses more than once. The only exercise he managed to squeeze in (literally) before the bout was a willing array of randy Japanese hotel maids.

In one of the biggest upsets in boxing history, Tyson was put down for the first time in his career. Unfazed, he plowed through four new opponents on his way back to the title when a new brand of catastrophe struck.

July 19, 1991. Tyson was in Indianapolis shooting a rap video at the 1991 Black Expo, surrounded by a coterie of star-struck Miss Black America hopefuls. At around two a.m., he invited Desiree Washington—the eighteen-year-old Miss Black Rhode Island—to his room at the Canterbury Hotel, where they had sex. Three days later, Washington checked into the E.R. and reported that Tyson had raped her. He was arrested the next day.

Washington claims that she came to Tyson's room under the assumption that they were going out to a restaurant or club. By her own admission, she excused herself to remove her panty shield in the bathroom, later testifying that she had the opportunity to leave the hotel room several times but chose not to. With no condom, intercourse was concluded when Tyson pulled out before ejaculation.

It was late when Washington asked him to drive her back to her hotel. According to Tyson, he told her that she was welcome to stay but that he was too tired to drive. She got angry. He called her a "bitch." Virginia Foster, the chauffeur who drove her back, described Washington as visibly shaken. Foster also noted that, when she escorted Mike to his room upon his arrival in Indianapolis, he started to kiss her and opened his fly. Her claim was never presented to the jury.

The trial lasted from January 26 to February 10, 1992. Deputy prosecutor Greg Garrison (who replaced Mike Pence as the host of Indianapolis's conservative talk radio program *The Mike Pence Show* in 2000) announced that "Tyson picked the wrong place to commit a crime. Indiana is different from Palm Beach or D.C. or L.A."

Tyson was a boorish, arrogant defendant who answered one of the jury's queries by telling them, "I just wanted to fuck her." Big mistake, especially in front of hard-line Judge Patricia Gifford.

The examining doctor who deemed two minor lacerations "consistent with forced or very hard intercourse" conceded that though he'd seen similar wounds in non-rape cases, they were "incredibly unlikely to happen in consensual sex." A photo of Washington's bloody underwear loomed luridly on a giant screen, a tactic of the prosecution that Tyson believes sealed his fate as evidence of forced penetration, even though Washington was menstruating.

King hired celebrity lawyer Alan Dershowitz to file what was to be a fruitless appeal citing the exclusion of several exculpatory witnesses, namely a handful of pageant hopefuls with varying or contradictory accounts of the incident as told to them by Washington. Three additional defense witnesses who claimed to have seen Tyson and Washington kissing in the limo were also prevented from testifying.

Washington's glowing credentials included class president, honor-role student, and volunteer work with the mentally handicapped. Tyson had a different reputation, though that didn't stop numerous so-called Black leaders (Jesse Jackson, Al Sharpton, and of course, King) from holding rallies proclaiming Tyson's innocence. Other members of Tyson's inner circle weren't so sure: "The reason he doesn't show any remorse is that he doesn't feel like he was guilty of the crime he was convicted of," Pete Hamill told Charlie Rose in 1994. "Now I find that very unlikely."

On March 26, 1992, Tyson was handed a six-year sentence of which he served just under three. Starting with an interview on ABC-TV, Washington went public, claiming she'd been offered $1 million to drop the suit in a last-ditch attempt by King to save his moneymaker. A full two years into his sentence, Tyson was offered a speedy release if he apologized to Washington. He declined. "I couldn't confess to that shit if I didn't do it. I would have been a bigger prisoner in my mind."

Of course, Tyson was no choirboy. Having spoken at length concerning past behavior in his relations with women, several other contestants described him as having been very free with his hands during the Expo. In his autobiography, Tyson describes a 2006 episode in which he attacked seven prostitutes in his hotel suite. Blinded by

Hennessy, coke, and a morphine drip in his arm, he claims to have thought that they would rob him but managed to throw them out before doing any real damage. In his grouchy *Playboy* interview with Kram three years after his release, he said, "A lot of young women don't know what they're getting themselves into. Then they find, Hey, I'm above my head in this shit." In a 2009 appearance on the *Oprah Winfrey Show*, he told the host that he "truly wanted to sock [Givens]." In a moment of daytime television morbidity, the audience roared with laughter.

The 2022 Hulu mini-series, *Mike* takes a different tack by addressing the episode from the accuser's point of view. "The more we dug into Desiree's story," co-writer Samantha Corbin-Miller told the *Los Angeles Times*, "it became abundantly clear that this episode [of the series] was hers," adding that thus far, the story had primarily "been told through the eyes of Mike." She's not wrong. "I felt caught between the impulse to sympathize with a person's lived experience," wrote Albert Samantha in his *Buzzfeed* review of the miniseries, "and the urge to hold a wrongdoer fully accountable for their sins."

In the same way, Tyson's account, as presented in Toback's film, supports A.O. Scott's caveat that *Tyson* "is not an entirely trustworthy movie, but it does feel profoundly honest." Despite his fetishization of his subject, the director gingerly leaves it to the viewer to exonerate, condemn, or accept the black hole of ambiguity.

Tyson describes his time at the Plainfield Correctional

Facility as "dehumanizing." A witness to prisoners who died from toxic homemade hootch, raped female guards, and smeared shit on the walls, he wrote, "I lost my faith in God." After a bumpy start, Tyson was a model prisoner who preferred the isolation of the hole where he could train undisturbed in his preparation to take back the title after his release. Unlike the three years Ali lost during his draft-dodging suspension, Tyson had no sparring partners and no boxing facilities.

In jail, Tyson developed a profound kinship with Edmond Dantè, the falsely imprisoned hero of Alexandre Dumas's 1846 epic *The Count of Monte Cristo*, which he repeatedly read while inside. (Is there an irony in that Dantè's travails were set in motion through a forged, bogus signature—familiar territory to anyone who'd ever dealt with King?) Visitors included Maya Angelou, Florence Henderson, Spike Lee, and Tupac Shakur. John Kennedy Jr. was another caller who, in 1998, paid Tyson a second visit when the fighter was briefly imprisoned for assaulting two motorists in a driving altercation. "From that visit," John-John told *People Magazine*, "I had total respect for him."

Like many imprisoned Blacks before him, Tyson adopted the Muslim faith, which had grown considerably less radical since Elijah Mohammed's tenure. Initially unable to grasp "the spiritual side of Islam," he "used Islam to subsidize my time and it helped me greatly. ...That was my first encounter with true love and forgiveness." Today,

Tyson is a moderate Muslim whose curiosity extends to every faith and spiritual interest—even astrology.

Footage of Tyson's release reveals a sober, smiling figure in a Muslim taqiyah. At a chiseled 214 pounds, he'd left permanent dents in the cement floor of his cell from his incessant shadowboxing. Surrounded by an enormous entourage headed by King, Tyson went directly to the local mosque, where he prayed alongside Muhammed Ali.

The tone grows somber as Tyson stands on a deserted Malibu beach under a crepuscular orange sky. When Toback asked if Tyson had ever read Oscar Wilde's *The Ballad of Reading Gaol*, the ex-fighter admitted he had not. Written while Wilde was incarcerated for "gross indecency," Tyson memorized it overnight and recites it in a voiceover. As Tyson had just retired from boxing, one line embodies the question on everyone's mind: "For none can tell to what red Hell/His sightless soul may stray."

Tyson left jail with $20 million in the bank and serious debt. He had blown through his money like Monopoly bills and was naive and gullible in his dealings with King. Only days before his release from prison, he signed a contract with the promoter's company that gave King exclusive rights to promote all his future fights. Tyson quickly came to distrust King, who he maintains "would kill his mother for a dollar." Alone with his thoughts, his brain again simmers with the effort to articulate his feelings before he shakes himself free of resentment. "He doesn't know how to love anybody."

With four-years-probation, Tyson fell back into his old habits when he got out. Coke—always his drug of choice—was boring without hookers, and that worked both ways. His vile temper returned as he was slammed with countless spurious lawsuits by venal gold diggers and runty ambulance chasers seeking eight figures in compensation for minor or fabricated infractions. None were worth the media frenzy, and Tyson settled out of court.

The ferocious warrior was back—in and out of the ring. Arrogant, cocky, drunk, coked-up, smoking the kindest herb his drug tzar pals could supply, and screwing himself silly, the public could only wait for the next scandal while fans celebrated his return to the sport. *Sports Illustrated*'s Richard Hoffer credited the fighter with boosting boxing's return to the limelight following the lackluster years during his absence. Though Tyson scorned public sentiment almost as much as himself ("I just can't imagine anybody being jealous of my life"), he obliged their vicarious bloodlust.

Tyson's depression could no longer be ignored. His anxiety caused his hair to fall out in patches. He was prescribed Zoloft, but King confiscated the pills in the weeks before a fight to make him "belligerent." He was better off stoned: In 2000, he smoked a joint before his bout against Andrew Golota and scored a TKO in the second. Golota suffered a broken cheekbone, a concussion, and a neck injury. The fight was retroactively deemed a no-contest when Tyson tested positive for marijuana. He'd forgotten his whizzer, a rubber penis filled with clean urine. According to Tyson, the weed "didn't affect me. It affected Golota."

King signed Tyson to fight Evander "The Real Deal" Holyfield, only to see the bout shelved when Tyson went to jail. A hymn-singing Christian with New Testament verse embroidered on his purple robe, Holyfield fought dirty. When he took the title from Buster Douglas shortly after the latter felled Tyson in Japan, King unwisely wrote him off as an easy win to poise Tyson for a unified title.

While Tyson's last four fights generated relatively weak pay-per-view sales, his meeting with Holyfield smashed all previous records. Trump paid $12.5 million—the largest site fee in history—to host the bout at his MGM Grand Garden Arena in Vegas, and a third of the $54.95 pay-per-view orders came from viewers who had never purchased a televised fight.

In the sixth round, Holyfield leaned in with a head butt that opened a cut above Tyson's eye. With four-and-a-half inches on an opponent, an accidental head-butt is unusual but not impossible. But then came another. And another. Despite Tyson's complaints, referee Mitch Halpern deemed them accidents. By the eleventh, Tyson was on the ropes with a head covered in goose eggs. The fight was stopped.

The rematch took place seven months later. It's both tempting and not entirely inappropriate to bandy the taboo of cannibalism when discussing the infamous Bite Fight—even though Tyson, as it were, never swallowed.

Nevertheless, his history of outlandish, cannibalistic threats was worrisome. "I don't want to sound like a Neanderthal man," he wrote in his 2017 book *Iron Ambition: My Life with Cus D'Amato* of an early opponent, "but I wanted to get my hands on him and chew him up." Five years after the Bite Fight, he said of his opponent Lennox Lewis, "I want to eat his children."

Bereft of his Zoloft before the rematch, Tyson was especially cantankerous. Mistrustful of King and unable to channel his aggression like he'd been taught under Cus, he told reporters, "I'm kind of angry at certain people, but it keeps you sharp and witty by being revengeful and bitter."

June 28, 1997. Holyfield's head-butts were even more egregious, and Tyson was more revengeful and bitter. When he answered the third bell without his mouthpiece, it was quickly returned to him. Did he have some plan in mind? Late in the round, the fighters fell into a clinch when Tyson rolled his head over Holyfield's shoulder and took an inch-long piece of cartilage from the top of his right ear. Mills Lane docked him two points for what should have been an immediate disqualification. Thirty-four seconds before the bell, Tyson again went on the oral offense, now laying into the left. Inexplicably, Lane let the round play out before Tyson was disqualified.

"A guy can't do his best when he's real scared," Tyson said after the bout. Fifteen years later, Holyfield echoed the observation: "People don't bite because they're mean. People bite because they're scared." Demented with the fear

Cus equated with fire ("If you learn to control it, you let it work for you... Let it go out of control, and it can hurt you"), Tyson had metaphorically burnt down the ring, which was immediately rushed by hotel security, doctors, and the Vegas police. Commentator Steve Albert screamed. "Mike Tyson has apparently lost his reason!"

The Grand went on lockdown. Looters mobbed black-jack tables and snatched over $200,000 in chips. Every gambler at every sports betting station at every casino in town was losing their mind. Sixteen of the fifty people said to have been injured in the stampede went to the hospital. Chaos reigned. Back in the ring, Holyfield took a knee in prayer while Tyson remained unmanageable and almost slugged two LAPD cops. When he got home, he drank some booze, smoked a joint, and went to bed.

Despite the remorse Tyson has expressed for his past actions, he is more accepting of the Bite Fight as a primal enactment wherein the rules were eclipsed by rage, blind instinct, and fear. Invoking the time when Cus compared him to a cat— "The best killing machines on the planet"—he describes how they toy with their prey to the point of dis-memberment and ultimate consumption. (Having owned a menagerie of tigers, Tyson took an interest.) As far as the press, the public, and a handful of *New Yorker* cartoons were concerned, the boxer had joined the ranks of Polyphemus, Saturn, and Jeffrey Dahmer.

Another author venerated by Cus was the Russian Fyodor Dostoyevsky, whose 1872 novel *The Possessed* features a self-proclaimed nihilist named Stavrogin who bites a governor's ear at a ball. "I neither know nor feel good and evil," he gravely states, "... I have lost any sense of it." In the same way that Stavrogin's bite was a composite attack on Russian bourgeois ideology, Tyson ravaged the cultural zeitgeist of money, gossip, fame, and double-dealing that consumed his private and professional life. "I have to be the savage," he said in a contemporaneous interview, "to put in place the bourgeoisie and erudites who think I'm scum, who think I'm trash." Maybe, but his regression to the primordial black soup of the id wasn't part of the plan. "I went insane... I didn't care about fighting no more by the Queensberry rules. He butted me with his head intentionally to hurt me, so I wanted to hurt him."

"Bite of the Century." "Fighter of the Ear." "Pay Per Chew," and twenty-five years later, "Tyson Bites": ear-shaped gummies from Tyson's cannabis farm. The tabloids and late-night hosts had a field day. Tyson was handed a two-year suspension and fined three million dollars. In a whirlwind of addiction, he underwent a series of psychological evaluations at Massachusetts General Hospital in Boston where he was diagnosed with "depression, anger, low self-esteem, irritability, and lack of impulse control." Quite the list, though the doctors deemed him mentally fit to return to the ring.

On January 22, 2012, a scuffle broke out at a press meeting with Tyson's upcoming opponent Lennox Lewis. When a reporter yelled, "Put him in a straitjacket!" Tyson blasted him with a tirade that would make Apocalypse tremble: "Put your mother in a straitjacket! ...I'll fuck you in your ass, you punk-ass white boy!" There were no pauses. "...I'll eat your asshole alive, you bitch! ...I'll fuck you till you love me, faggot!" His image remained cemented.

Tyson was at his second heaviest fighting weight since his last bout almost a year ago, and it showed. He told the press that he was only fighting because he was broke. With a brain still swimming from the bricks of coke he'd hoovered on a recent European tour, he looked lost and hopeless inside the ring until Lewis put him down in the eighth. The same day, his second wife Monica served him divorce papers.

"I look in the mirror every day, and I know I'm not Clark Gable," Tyson said of the iconic tattoo inked on the left side of his face. In 2003, he asked a tattoo artist to cover his face with hearts. The tattooist refused and instead designed the Maori warrior pattern that has become inextricably linked to the Tyson image. "I just hated myself then," he told the *Guardian*'s Donald McRae in 2014. "I literally wanted to deface myself." "But" he said on *The Rosie Show* two years earlier, "that's what people do when they're high."

On June 11, 2005, Tyson's failure to answer the bell for the sixth round against Kevin McBride marked the end of a career for the man who ranks at number sixteen on *Ring Magazine*'s hardest punchers of all time—just below Sonny Liston, a fighter Tyson called "orgasmic." "I don't got the fighting guts anymore." He retired at thirty-nine.

Granted a brief leave from a different rehab center (he'd finished his stint at Wonderland), Tyson was again coked to the gills when he attended the premiere of *Tyson* at Cannes. He celebrated even harder when it snagged Best Non-Fiction Film at such festivals as The New York Film Critics Circle Award and The National Society of Film Critics Awards. Tyson hadn't even seen the film before the Cannes screening. When it was over, he told Toback, "It's like a Greek tragedy, only I'm the subject."

Grossly out of shape with a nose covered in powder, Tyson tried, with some success, to reinvent himself as an actor. His appearance in Todd Phillips's 2009 *The Hangover* and its 2011 sequel made his face recognizable to a new generation of kids, and by the time *The Hangover Part II* hit the theaters, Tyson was sober. His one-person show, *Undisputed Truth*, ran for two weeks at the MGM Grand in Vegas in 2012. Lucid, clearheaded, and less tortured than he was for the *Tyson* interviews, the raconteur regales with tales of Givens, Washington, biting, and the White Bitch he calls cocaine. Struck by the performance, Spike Lee took the show on the road where, ironically, the opening venue was in Indianapolis.

On October 22, 2017, the *L.A. Times* reported that Toback had joined the ranks of sexual predators that continue to run through the film industry like a cancer. Just seventeen days earlier, the *New York Times* broke the story of the allegations against producer Harvey Weinstein. By the end of the month, the #MeToo hashtag was in full force.

According to the *L.A. Times*, over four hundred women alleged that Toback had rubbed his groin on their legs to ejaculation, instructed them to masturbate, and invited them to his home (or maybe his "editing room") with the promise of acting gigs. Greeting them with his pecker out, he often told them that "he couldn't properly function unless he jerked off several times a day." Of course, there were never any acting gigs to begin with.

Toback denied everything, maintaining that he never met his accusers or, if he had, "it was for five minutes, and I have no recollection." It didn't matter: the statute of limitations had expired on every accusation. He wasn't charged or convicted, nor has he worked since.

Demons don't go away. It's something that Tyson has long accepted. With his deep respect for life's mystery and the concurrent urge to make sense of it, it's no hyperbole to credit the growing use of medical cannabis and psychedelics with saving his life. If weed and psilocybin don't fit everyone's definition of sober, at least they keep the inner Apocalypse—the one unleashed by Hennessy and the White Bitch—at bay.

Following a brief relapse in 2013, Tyson told reporters that his alcoholism might kill him. He was sober six days and when he stopped the press conference to interrupt his confession: "God, this is some interesting stuff."

Recovery from a childhood of unspeakable horrors. Recovery from the humiliations of ownership under sanctioned criminals. Recovery from a roller-coaster of chemically induced rage and innate self-hatred. Recovery from psychological ailments that don't discriminate regarding race or income. Recovery from addiction. All are lifelong processes. For Tyson, it might take a little longer. But he's not worried about what comes next. "If life is great," he told William Shatner in 2020, "death has gotta be glorious."

SOURCES

INTRODUCTION

Barthes, Roland. "The World of Wrestling." *Mythologies*. Les Lettres nouvelles. 1957. Published in English by Farrar, Straus and Giroux, 1972.

Bellows, George. *"An Artist with 'Red Blood'."* *Current Literature* 53, September, 1912.

Bennetts, Leslie. "Do the Arts Inspire Violence in Real Life?" *The New York Times*, April 25, 1981.

Benson, Michael. "RICHES: The numbers behind Floyd Mayweather vs Conor McGregor." *Talksport: The world's biggest sports radio station*, September 21, 2022.

Bodner, Adam. *When Boxing Was a Jewish Sport*. New York: Excelsior Editions, 1997.

Cohen, Leah Hager. *Without Apology: Girls, Women, and the Desire to Fight*. New York: Random House, 2005.

Egan, Pierce. *Boxiana*. Brookline, Massachusetts: Adamant Media Corporation, 2006. First published 1830 by George Virtue.

Ezra, Michael, "Post-Primes and Career Arcs," in *The Bittersweet Science*, edited by Carlo Rotella and Michael Ezra. Chicago: University of Chicago Press, 2017.

Goldman, Ivan G. "*The Ring* is Counted Out: Boxing's Duplicity Devours an Honest Magazine." *Columbia Journalism Review*, January-February, 2012.

Gorn, Elliot J. *The Manly Art: Bare-Knuckle Prizefighting in America*. Ithaca, New York: Cornell University Press, 1986.

Hannigan, Dave. *Drama in the Bahamas: Muhammad Ali's Last Fight*. New York: Sports Publishing, 2016.

Hawley, Samuel J. *The Fight That Started the Movies: The World Heavyweight Championship, the Birth of Cinema and the First Feature Film*. Tucson, Arizona: Conquistador Press, 2016.

Hinson, Hal. "In Defense of Violence," in *Flesh and Blood: The National Society of Film Critics on Sex, Violence, and Censorship*, edited by Peter Keough. San Francisco: Mercury House, 1995.

Levi, Gilbert. ""Nevada's Shame and Disgrace," *New Haven Register*, March 9, 1897.

Littlefield, Bill. "View from Ringside" *Only A Game*. National Public Radio. Boston, Massachusetts: WBUR, March 5, 2004.

Moore, Louis. *I Fight for a Living: Boxing and the Battle for Black Manhood, 1880-1915*. Chicago: University of Illinois Press. 2017.

Moser, Gary Lee, "Non Toxic-Avengers: Boxing's Quarter Century of Acceptable Losses," in *The Bittersweet Science*, edited by Carlo Rotella and Michael Ezra. Chicago: University of Chicago Press, 2017.

Nam, Sean. "Boxing is a Joke!: An Interview with J Russell Peltz." *Hannibal Boxing Media* 25, November 2019.

Oates, Joyce Carol. *On Boxing*. Garden City, New York: Dolphin/Doubleday, 1987.

Runstedtler, Theresa. *Jack Johnson, Rebel Sojourner: Boxing in the Shadow of the Global Color Line*. Berkeley, CA: University of California Press, 2013.

Schmeling, Max. *Max Schmeling, An Autobiography*. Translated by George Von der Lippe. Chicago: Bonus Books, 1998. First published 1977 by Verlag Ullstein.

Scott, A.O., "Guys, Kiss Mom and Come Out Fighting," *New York Times*, December 9, 2010.

Sam Sheridan, "What Boxing is For," in *The Bittersweet Science,* edited by Carlo Rotella and Michael Ezra. Chicago: University of Chicago Press, 2017.

Silver, Mike. *The Arc of Boxing: The Rise and Decline of the Sweet Science.* Jefferson, North Carolina, McFarland & Company, Inc., 2008.

Thang H. Hong, Johnathan Gabe, Pankaj Sharma, and Michael E. J. Lean, "Life Expectancy of "White and Non-White Elite Heavyweight Boxers," *National Library of Medicine Quarterly 66,* December 3, 2019.

Tyson, Mike with Larry Sloman. *Undisputed Truth*. New York: Blue Rider Press. 2013.

Virgil. *The Aeneid*. Translated by A.S. Kline. CreateSpace Independent Publishing Platform, 2014.

Warshow, Robert: *Immediate Experience. Movies, Comics, Theatre and Other Aspects of Popular Culture.* Garden City, New York: Doubleday, 1962.

CHAPTER 1 THE SET-UP

Biesen, Sheri Chinen, "Censoring and Selling Film Noir." *Between: Journal of the Italian Association for the Theory and Comparative History of Literature*, vol 5 no 9. January-February, 2012.

Burr, Ty. "The Actor Who Knew Too Much." *Dartmouth Alumni Magazine*, July-August, 2012.

Castle, Alison. *The Stanley Kubrick Archives*. Cologne, Germany: Taschen, 2016.

Flaskerud, Jacquelyn H. "Neurasthenia: Here and There, Now and Then." *Issues in Mental Health Nursing,* 62, no. 1. July 9, 2009.

Hingham, Charles. *Howard Hughes: The Secret Life*. New York: St. Martin's Press, 2004.

Miller, Wade. *Devil on Two Sticks*. New York: Signet, 1950.

March, Joseph Moncure. *The Set-up*. New York: Pascal Covici, 1928.

Mitchell, Kevin. *Jacobs Beach: The Mob, the Garden and the Golden Age of Boxing*. Boston, Massachusetts: Hamilcar Publications, 2019.

Muller, Eddie. *Dark City: The Lost World of Film Noir*. New York: St. Martin's Griffin, 2019.

Newland, Christina. "Cinema Pugilistica: A Century of Boxing on Film." *The Criterion Collection*. July 22, 2022.

Scorsese, Martin and Robert Wise. "Commentary." *The Set-up*. DVD. Directed by Robert Wise. Culver City, California: Turner Home Entertainment, 2004.

Smith, Imogen Sara. *Lonely Places: Film Noir Beyond the City*. Jefferson, North Carolina: McFarland & Company, 2011.

Stanley, Fred. "Hollywood Crime and Romance; Hollywood Round-Up." *New York Times*, November, 1944.

CHAPTER 2 KID GALAHAD

Abreu, Rafael. "What is the Hays Code — Hollywood Production Code Explained." *studiobinder*, May 2, 2021.

Chilton, Martin. "'I was a Legendary Terror': Bette Davis's one-woman war on Hollywood." *The Telegraph*, October 4, 2019.

Farrell, Charles, "Why I Fixed Fights." in *The Bittersweet Science,* edited by Carlo Rotella and Michael Ezra. Chicago: University of Chicago Press, 2017.

Kanfer, Stefan. *Tough Without a Gun: The Life and Extraordinary Afterlife of Humphrey Bogart*. New York: Knopf, 2012.

Latzer, Barry. "Do Hard Times Spark More Crime?" *Los Angeles Times*, January 24, 2014.

Longworth, Karina. Episode 9. "Six Degrees of Joan Crawford: Bette Davis and What Ever Happened to Baby Jane?" Produced by Karina Longworth. *You Must Remember This,* September 6, 2016. Podcast.

Nugent, Frank S. "THE SCREEN; 'Kid Galahad,' a Crisp Prize-Ring Film, Comes to the Strand and, With It, a New Star, Wayne Morris." *The New York Times*, May 27, 1937.

Patterson, Michael Robert. "Bert DeWayne Morris, Jr. – Lieutenant Commander, United States Navy." *Arlington National Cemetery*, January 18, 2023.

Wallace. Francis. "Kid Galahad." *Saturday Evening Post*, serialized, April 11-May 16, 1936.

Wilson, James Q. "Crime and the Great Recession." *The New Yorker*, April 17, 2017.

CHAPTER 3 CHAMPION

Allan, Nathan. "Censoring the Movies — What was the Hays Code." *Medium*, Nov 23, 2020.

Andrews, Nigel. "Kirk Douglas, Hollywood actor, 1916—2020." *Financial Times*, February 5 2020.

Clark, Jay A. *Becoming Edvard Munch: Influence, Anxiety, and Myth*. Chicago: Art Institute of Chicago, 2009.

Crowther, Bosley. "Kirk Douglas Plays the Hero in 'Champion,' Film of Ring Lardner's Fight Story." *New York Times*, April 11, 1949.

Doherty, Thomas. *Show Trial: Hollywood, HUAC, and the Birth of the Blacklist*. New York: Columbia University Press, 2018.

Douglas, Kirk. *I Am Spartacus!: Making a Film, Breaking the Blacklist*. New York: Open Road Media, 2012.

Lardner, Ring. "Champion." *Metropolitan Magazine*, October, 1916.

Meroney, John and Sean Coons. "How Kirk Douglas Overstated His Role in Breaking the Hollywood Blacklist." *The Atlantic*, 5 July, 2012.

Mitchell, Kevin. *Jacobs Beach: The Mob, the Garden and the Golden Age of Boxing*. Boston: Hamilcar Publications, 2019.

Mondello, Bob. "Remembering Hollywood's Hays Code, 40 Years On," *All Things Considered.* National Public Radio. Boston: Massachusetts: WBUR, August 8, 2008.

Quirk, Lawrence J. *Fasten Your Seat Belts: The Passionate Life of Bette Davis.* New York" William Morrow and Company, Inc., 1990.

Schulman, Michael. "Fatty Arbuckle and the Birth of the Celebrity Scandal." *The New Yorker*, October 4, 2021.

Thomas F. Bradyhollywood. "Producers Feud; Hughes and Kramer in Court Fight Over Fight Films—Warners on Star Hunt." *New York Times*, March 27, 1949.

Walsh, Savanna. "Natalie Wood Was Raped by Kirk Douglas, Her Sister Alleges in a New Book." *Vanity Fair*, November 12, 2021.

CHAPTER 4 GENTLEMAN JIM

Brody, Richard. "DVD of the Week: Gentleman Jim." *The New Yorker,* July 21, 2011.

Elwell, Mina. "The Untold Truth Of Errol Flynn." *Grunge,* July 19, 2022.

Fields, Armond. *James J. Corbett: A Biography of the Heavyweight Champion and Popular Theater Headline.* Jefferson, North Carolina: McFarland & Company, Inc., 2001.

Flynn, Errol. *My Wicked, Wicked Ways.* New York: G.P. Putman's Sons, 1959.

Gorn, Elliot J. *The Manly Art: Bare-Knuckle Prizefighting in America.* Ithaca, New York: Cornell University Press, 1986.

Gregory, Sam. "The End of Bare Knuckle Boxing." *The Sweet Science,* November 3, 2004.

Hartson, William. "Did actor Errol Flynn compete in the Olympic Games?" *Express*, July 29, 2017.

Hawley, Samuel J. *The Fight That Started the Movies: The World Heavyweight Championship, the Birth of Cinema and the First Feature Film.* Tucson: Arizona: Conquistador Press, 2016.

Higham, Charles. *Errol Flynn: The Untold Story*. New York: Doubleday, 1980.

Klein, Christopher. *Strong Boy: The Life and Times of John L. Sullivan, America's First Sports Hero*. Guilford, Connecticut: Lyons Press, 2013.

Landingham, Andrea Van. *Hollywood Horrors: Murders, Scandals, and Cover-Ups from Tinseltown*. Guilford, Connecticut: Lyons Press, 2021.

Longworth, Karina. Episode 36. "Star Wars Episode X: Errol Flynn." Produced by Karina Longworth. *You Must Remember This,* March 10, 2015. Podcast.

Murphy, Edward F. "The Ups and the Downs of the World of Boxing." *New York Times*, October 9, 1977.

Myler, Patrick. *Gentleman Jim Corbett: The Truth Behind A Boxing Legend*. London: Robson Books, Ltd, 1998.

O'Sullivan, Rory. "Joseph Parker Motivated by Challenge of Meehan." *Boxingscene*, August 12, 2015.

Plimpton, George. *Shadowbox: An Amateur in the Ring*. New York: Putnam, 1977.

"The Shamrock Slugger! He could love as well as fight!" *Lubbock Avalanche Journal*. November 29, 1942.

Sherwood, James. "Errol Flynn: The Swordsman." *The Rake*, October 2015.

Wayne, Jane Ellen. *The Golden Girls of MGM: Greta Garbo, Joan Crawford, Lana Turner, Judy Garland, Ava Gardner, Grace Kelly and Others*. New York: Carroll & Graf Publishers, 2004.

CHAPTER 5 THE GREAT WHITE HOPE

Beston, Paul. *The Boxing Kings. When Americans Heavyweights Ruled the Ring*. Lanham, Maryland: Rowman & Littlefield Publishers, 2017.

Breckenridge, Hunter. "Nov. 26, 1914: Langford vs Wills II." *The Fight City*, November 26, 2022.

Callaghan, Morley. *The Loved and the Lost.* Toronto, Canada: Macmillan, 1951.

Canby, Vincent. "'Great White Hope' Brought to Screen." *New York Times*, October 12, 1970.

Christie, Matt. "On This Day: Jack Johnson dominates Tommy Burns to win the world heavyweight title." *Boxing News*, December 26, 2018.

Freud, Sigmund. *Totem and Taboo.* Translated by Abraham Brill and James Strchey. Boston, Massachusetts: Beacon Press, 1913.

Jackson, Ronald L. *Scripting the Black Masculine Body: Identity, Discourse, and Racial Politics in Popular Media.* New York: State University of New York of University Press, 2006.

Johnson, Jack. *In the Ring and Out.* London: Proteus, 1977.

Lawson, Carol. "Howard Sackler, 52, Playwright who Won Pulitzer Prize, Dead." *New York Times*, October 15, 1982.

Lubbock Avalanche Journal. "The Shamrock Slugger! He could love as well as fight!" November 29, 1942.

Moore, Louis. *I Fight for a Living: Boxing and the Battle for Black Manhood, 1880-1915.* Chicago: University of Illinois Press. 2017.

New York Times, the. "Pugilists as Race Champions." May 12, 1910.

Nilsson, Jeff. "A Black Champion's Biggest Fight." *The Saturday Evening Post*, July 2, 2020.

Reyes, Lorenzo. "NFL's national anthem policy: Players on field must stand, show 'respect'." *USA Today*, May 23, 2018.

Roberts, Randy. *Papa Jack: Jack Johnson and The Era Of White Hopes.* New York: Free Press, 1985.

Runstedtler, Theresa. *Jack Johnson, Rebel Sojourner: Boxing in the Shadow of the Global Color Line.* Berkeley, CA: University of California Press, 2013.

Sackler, Howard. *The Great White Hope: A Play*. New York: The Dial Press, 1968.

Turley, Mark. *Journeymen: The Other Side of the Boxing Business, a New Perspective on the Noble*. West Sussex, England: Pitch Publishing, 2015.

Unforgivable Blackness: The Rise and Fall of Jack Johnson. Directed by Ken Burns. Arlington, Virginia: PBS Home Video. 2005.

United Press International. "Race riots in dozen cities follow Johnson fight victory." July 5, 1910.

Ward, Geoffrey C. *Unforgivable Blackness: The Rise and Fall of Jack Johnson*. New York: Knoph, 2004.

Weiner, Bill. "The Long, Colorful History of the Mann Act." *All Things Considered*, NPR. March 11, 2008.

Wooster Daily News. "Black Man is Victor in Battle." July 5, 1910.

CHAPTER 6 CINDERELLA MAN

Beston, Paul. *The Boxing Kings. When Americans Heavyweights Ruled The Ring*. Lanham, Maryland: Rowman & Littlefield Publishers, 2017.

British Movietone. "Max Baer Reveals His Opinion of Braddock's Chances." Posted January 8, 2016.

Garrison, Laura Turner. "How the Neighborhoods of Manhattan Got Their Names." *Mental Floss*, October 7, 2012.

Hague, Jim. *Braddock: The Rise of The Cinderella Man*. New York: Chamberlain Bros., 2005.

Heinz, W.C. *The Professional*. New York: Harper & Brothers, 1958.

Jarrett, John. *Max Baer: Clown Prince of Boxing*. Sussex, England: Pitch Publishing, 2017.

Leisses, Kyle. "Russell Crowe is Riches-to-Rags-to-Riches in Cinderella Man; The Truth About Rocky." *Medium.com*, March 20, 2018.

Mitchell, Kevin. *Jacobs Beach: The Mob, the Garden and the Golden Age of Boxing*. Boston: Hamilcar Publications, 2019.

Schaap, Jeremy. *Cinderella Man: James J. Braddock, Max Baer, And The Greatest Upset In Boxing History*. New York: Houghton Mifflin, 2005.

Smith, Red. "A Champion for his Time." *New York Times*, Dec. 1, 1974.

Sussman, Jeffrey. *Max Baer and Barney Ross: Jewish Heroes of Boxing*. Lanham, Maryland: Rowman & Littlefield Publishers, 2016.

Turley, Johnathan. "Give the Dead Their Due." *Washington Post*, September 17, 2006.

CHAPTER 7 THE PRIZEFIGHTER AND THE LADY

Aycock, Coleen and David W. Wallace. *The Magnificent Max Baer: The Life of the Heavyweight Champion and Film Star*. Jefferson, North Carolina: McFarland & Company, Inc. 2018.

The Boston Globe. Williams, Joe. November 22, 1933.

Cameron, Kate. *New York Daily News, the*. Sunday, April 8, 1934.

Elliot, John. "Nazis Ban Film Starring Baer." *New York Herald Tribune*, March 30, 1934.

Gallico, Paul. *Pity the Poor Giant: Farewell to Sport*. New York: Knopf, 1938.

Hall, Mordant, "Ace of Aces." *New York Times*, November 11, 1933.

Heller, Peter. *In This Corner: 42 World Champions Tell Their Stories*. Boston: Da Capo Press, 1994.

Jarrett, John. *Max Baer: Clown Prince of Boxing*. Sussex, England: Pitch Publishing, 2017.

Leider, Emily W. *Myrna Loy: The Only Good Girl in Hollywood*. Berkeley, California: University of California Press, 2011.

Mayer, Alicia. "W.S. Van Dyke – The Trusted Director, Star Maker, Party Host, and Patriot, with One of Hollywood's Saddest Endings." *Hollywoodessays.com*, December 24, 2012.

Mullally, Frederic. *Primo: The Story of 'Man Mountain' Carnera*. London: Robson Books Ltd., 1991.

Reading Times. Advertisement. November 16, 1933.

Schaap, Jeremy. *Cinderella Man: James J. Braddock, Max Baer, And The Greatest Upset In Boxing History*. New York: Houghton Mifflin, 2005.

Sussman, Jeffrey. *Max Baer and Barney Ross: Jewish Heroes of Boxing*. Lanham, Maryland: Rowman & Littlefield Publishers, 2016.

Thompson, David. "MGM Musicals: All Singing, All Dancing." *The Guardian*, November 10, 2011.

CHAPTER 8 THE HARDER THEY FALL

Acevedo, Carlos. "The Duke of the West Side: Owney 'The Killer' Madden." *Hannibal Boxing*, August 7, 2019.

Doherty, Thomas. *Show Trial: Hollywood, HUAC, and the Birth of the Blacklist*. New York: Columbia University Press, 2018.

Farrell, James T. *Twenty Five Bucks*. Garden City, N.Y.: Sun Dial Press, 1945.

Jones, Ken. "Boxing: Carnera's family sheds new light on tale of sad exploitation." *The Independent*, March 20, 2003.

Kanfer, Stefan. *Tough Without a Gun: The Life and Extraordinary Afterlife of Humphrey Bogart*. New York: Knopf, 2011.

Longworth, Karina. Episode 86. "Kirk Douglas, Dalton Trumbo, and Otto Preminger (Breaking the Blacklist, Part 2)." Produced by Karina Longworth. *You Must Remember This*, June 20, 2016. Podcast.

Mitchell, Kevin. *Jacobs Beach: The Mob, the Garden and the Golden Age of Boxing*. Boston: Hamilcar Publications, 2019.

Mullally, Frederic. *Primo: The Story of 'Man Mountain' Carnera*. London: Robson Books Ltd., 1991.

Muller, Eddie. *Dark City: The Lost World of Film Noir*. New York: St. Martin's Griffin, 2019.

Mcguigan, Barry. "Brilliant Schulberg Budd was more than a contender." *Mirror*, August 8, 2009.

Page, Joseph S. *Primo Carnera: The Life and Career of the Heavyweight Boxing Champion*. Jefferson, North Carolina: McFarland & Company, Inc. 2018.

Plimpton, George. *Shadowbox: An Amateur in the Ring*. New York: Putnam, 1977.

Schaap, Jeremy. Cinderella Man: James J. Braddock, Max Baer, and the Greatest Upset In Boxing History. New York: Houghton Mifflin, 2005.

Schulberg, Budd. *The Harder They Fall*. New York: Random House, 1947.

CHAPTER 9 REQUIEM FOR A HEAVYWEIGHT

Barthes, Roland. "The World of Wrestling." *Mythologies*. New York: Hill and Wang, 1972.

Benedict, Chris. "The Twilight Rounds: Rod Serling explores the dark side of boxing – Round one." *The Grueling Truth*, April 3, 2020.

Delblanco, Andrew. "Night Terrors." *The New York Review of Books,* November 19, 2020.

Gallico, Paul. *Pity the Poor Giant: Farewell to Sport*. New York: Knopf, 1938.

Hughes, James. "Requiem for Rod Serling." *Grantland*, November 19, 2014.

Jackson, Ron. "Deaths and Damage in the Ring." *Supersport.com,* June 9, 2022.

LC Performance. "Interview. Conversation With Rod Serling." Library of Congress video archives.

Nelson, Ralph, dir. *Playhouse 90*. Season 1, episode 2, "Requiem for a Heavyweight." Aired October 11. 1956 on CBS.

Quinn, Anthony. *The Original Sin*. Boston-Toronto: Little, Brown and Company, 1972.

Stone, Paul. "Boxers and Brain Injuries – A Scary Study." *Neurological Rehabilitation Institute at Brookhaven Hospital*, January 14, 2103.

CHAPTER 10 MONKEY ON MY BACK

Bodner, Allen. *When Boxing Was a Jewish Sport*. Westport, Connecticut: Praeger, 1997.

Century, Douglass. *Barney Ross*. New York: Schocken Books, 2006.

De Quincey, Thomas. *Confessions of an English Opium-Eater*. New York: Penguin Classics. 2003. First published September-October, 1821 in *London Magazine*.

The Dick Cavett Show. Season 1991, episode 44, "Ray Arcel." Aired May 31, 1991, on CNBC.

Ross, Barney and Martin Abramson. *No Man Stands Alone: The True Story of Barney Ross*. Philadelphia and New York: J.B. Lippincott, 1957.

Shaller, Lori and Judith Rosenbaum. "Jewish Radicalism and the Red Scare: Introductory Essay." *Jewish Women's Archive*.

Silver, Mike. *Stars in the Ring: Jewish Champions in the Golden Age of Boxing: A Photographic History*. New York: Lyons Press, 2016.

Sugar, Bert Randolph. "Punching Through." Review of *Barney Ross*, by Douglass Century. *New York Times*, February 19, 2006.

CHAPTER 11 BODY AND SOUL

Chaw, Walter. "James Wong Howe's Way with Light." *The Criterion Collection*, September 9, 2022.

Crowther, Bosley. "'Body and Soul,' Exciting Story of Prizefighting, Starring John Garfield." *New York Times*, November 10, 1947.

Doherty, Thomas. *Show Trial: Hollywood, HUAC, and the Birth of the Blacklist*. New York: Columbia University Press, 2018.

Garfield, Julie. "Memories of a Real 'Witch Hunt'." *New York Times*, July 5, 2017.

Hinkson, Jake. "At the Center of the Storm: He Ran All the Way and the Hollywood Blacklist." Noir City Sentinel, November-December, 2009.

Longworth, Karina. Episode 76: "The Blacklist Part 6. He Ran All the Way: John Garfield." Produced by Karina Longworth. *You Must Remember This,* March 14, 2016. Podcast.

Malle, Louis, director. *My Dinner with Andre.* New Yorker Films, 1981.

Martin Scorsese Presents: Body and Soul. Abraham Polonsky, dir. Artisan, VHS, 1990.

Menkin, H.L. *A Menkin Chrestomathy.* New York: Knopf, 1949.

Nott, Robert. *He Ran All the Way: The Life of John Garfield.* New York: Limelight Editions, 2003.

Smith, Mona Z. *Becoming Something: The Story of Canada Lee.* London: Faber & Faber, 2004.

Stanislovski, Konstantin. *An Actor's Work: A Student's Diary.* Translated by Jean Benedetti. New York: Routledge, 2008.

Swindell, Larry. *Body and Soul: The Story of John Garfield.* New York: William Morrow, 1975.

CHAPTER 12 KID MONK BARONI

Anderson, Dave. "For Hagler, It's Old Hat." *New York Times,* March 16, 1987.

Assael, Shaun. *The Murder of Sonny Liston: Las Vegas, Heroin, and Heavyweights.* New York: Blue Rider Press, 2016.

Barthes, Roland. "The World of Wrestling." *Mythologies.* New York: Hill and Wang, 1972.

Cabot, Bruce, Leonard Nimoy and Richard Rober. "Commentary." *Kid Monk Baroni* DVD. Directed by Howard D. Schuster. Los Angeles, CA: Image Entertainment, 2007.

Cave, Nick. *The Sick Bag Song.* New York: Houghton Mifflin Harcourt, 2016.

Conboy, William. "Catholic Athleticism: Faith in the Boxing Ring." *Catholic365*, July, 23, 2022.

Drennan, David. "The Fighting Father: How a Priest Became a Professional Boxer to Save his Local Gym." *The Guardian*, August 25, 2016.

Koehlinger, Amy. "Why boxing was the most Catholic sport for almost 100 years." *America: The Jesuit Review*, March 8, 2019.

Kram. Mark. Jr. *Smokin' Joe: The Life of Joe Frazier*. New York: Ecco, 2021.

LaMotta, Jake. *Raging Bull: My Story*. Hoboken, New Jersey:Prentice-hall, Inc., 1970.

O'Neill, Helen. "Shadowboxing." *Los Angeles Times*, July 26, 1998.

Schmeling, Max. *Max Schmeling, An Autobiography*. Translated by George Von der Lippe. Chicago: Bonus Books, 1998. First published 1977 by Verlag Ullstein.

Sussman, Jeffrey. *Rocky Graziano: Fists, Fame, and Fortune*. Lanham, Maryland: Rowman & Littlefield Publishers, 2018.

Tyson, Mike with Larry Sloman. *Undisputed Truth*. New York: Blue Rider Press. 2013.

Wass, Janne. "Bela Lugosi Meets a Brooklyn Gorilla." *scifist 2.0: A Sci-Fi Movie History in Reviews,* November 11, 2020.

CHAPTER 13 KILLER'S KISS

Alberge, Dalya. "Stanley Kubrick and Kirk Douglas Wanted Doctor Zhivago Movie Rights." *The Guardian*, Nov 9, 2020.

Barnes, Mike. "Irene Kane, Star of Kubrick's 'Killer's Kiss,' Dies." *Hollywood Reporter,* November 3, 2013.

Chase, Chris. "Present at the Creation with Kubrick." *Los Angeles Times,* 14 March, 1999.

Delblanco, Andrew "Kubrick's Human Comedy." *The New York Review of Books*, May 13, 2021. Vol. LXVII, Number 8.

Lubo, Arthur. "Before Stanley Kubrick wrote scripts, he took photos." *Boston Globe*, May 1, 2018.

Ondaatje, Michael. *The Conversations: Walter Murch and the Art of Editing Film*. New York: Knopf, 2002.

Phillips, Gene D. "Killer's Kiss" in *The Stanley Kubrick Archives*, edited by Alison Castle. Cologne, Germany: Taschen Press, 2016.

Rosen, Miss. "Stanley Kubrick's Early Years as a Photographer at Look Magazine." *Shoot.com*, August 7, 2018.

Udel, James C. "Garrett Brown's Steadicam Breakthrough Continues to Grow 50 Years Later." *Variety*, March 29, 2019.

Walker, Alexander, Ulrich Ruchti and Sybil Taylor. *Stanley Kubrick, Director: A Visual Analysis*. New York: W.W. Norton & Company, 1999.

CHAPTER 14 RAGING BULL

Acevado, Carlos. "Dark Corner: Jake LaMotta, Survivor." *The Fight City*, July 10. 2022.

Arnold, Carolyn, Nicholas Christelis and Alex Holmes. "Depression and chronic pain." *The Medical Journal of Australia*. October 29, 2013.

Chodash, Alden. "The Darker Road Of Raging Bull." *The Fight City*, January 7, 2023.

Ebert, Roger. *Scorsese*. Chicago: University of Chicago Press, 2008.

Erikson, Erik. *Childhood and Society*. New York: W. W. Norton & Co, 1950.

Flaherty, Joe. "Interview: Jake LaMotta." *Penthouse*, May, 1982.

Flaherty, Joe. "The Woeful Life of Jake LaMotta." *Deadspin.com*, September 20, 2017.

Freeman, Lew. *Fighting for Life: The Story of Jake Lamotta*. Indianapolis, Indiana: Blue River Press, 2018.

Freud, Sigmund. "The Most Prevalent Form of Degradation in Erotic Life." *Jahrbuch für Psychoanalytische und Psychopathologische Forschungen*, 1912.

Gibson, Paul. "How Sugar Ray Robinson made Jake La Motta his bloody Valentine in 1951." *The Guardian*, February 8, 2016.

Gilby, Ryan. "Blood, Sweat and Tears." *The Guardian*: July 31, 2007.

Glennie, Jay. "The making of a heavyweight: Scorsese and De Niro behind the scenes of Raging Bull – in pictures." *The Guardian*, March 11, 2021.

Goldstein, Richard. "Jake LaMotta, 'Raging Bull' in and Out of the Ring, Dies at 95." *New York Times*, Sept. 20, 2017.

Hamill, Pete. *Why Sinatra Matters*. New York: Little, Brown and Company, 1998.

Hauser, Thomas and Vickki La Motta. *The Vikki La Motta Story: Jake, Raging Bull, Playboy, Sinatra and the Mob*. London: JR Books, 2006.

Haygood, Wil. *Sweet Thunder: The Life and Times of Sugar Ray Robinson*. New York: Knopf, 2009.

Horney, Karen. *The Neurotic Personality of our Time*. New York: Norton, 1937.

Kael, Pauline. "Raging Bull: Religious Pulp, or the Incredible Hulk." *New Yorker*, December, 1980.

Koehlinger, Amy. "Why boxing was the most Catholic sport for almost 100 years." *America: The Jesuit Review*. March 8, 2022.

Kriegel, Mark. "Tyson Fury: 'If I can defeat depression, I can defeat anything.'" *ESPN*, September 10, 2019.

La Motta, Jake. *Raging Bull: My Story*. Hoboken, New Jersey: Prentice-hall, Inc. 1970.

Mitchell, Kevin. "Jake La Motta was not a Great Champion but one of the Toughest, A Boxing Beast." *The Guardian*, September 21, 2016.

Mitchell, Kevin. *Jacobs Beach: The Mob, the Garden and the Golden Age of Boxing*. Boston: Hamilcar Publications, 2019.

Schickel, Richard. "Brutal Attraction: The Making of Raging Bull." *Vanity Fair,* February 2, 2010.

Scorsese, Martin. "Commentary." *Raging Bull: Collector's Set*. DVD. Directed by Martin Scorsese. Beverly Hills, CA: MGM, 2005.

Sugar, Bert Randolph. *The Great Fights: A Pictorial History of Boxing's Greatest Bouts*. Abingdon, England: Routledge Press, 1981.

Sussman, Jeffrey. *Boxing and the Mob: The Notorious History of the Sweet Science*. Lanham, Maryland: Rowman & Littlefield Publishers, 2019.

Valley, Jean. "Raging Beauty." *Playboy*. November, 1981.

CHAPTER 15 ALI

Adams, Neil and Dennis O'Neil. *Superman vs. Muhammed Ali*. New York: DC Comics, 1978.

Ali, Muhammed and Richard Durham. *The Greatest: My Own Story*. New York: Random House, 1975.

Ali, Muhammed and Hana Yasmeen Ali. *The Soul of a Butterfly: Reflections on Life's Journey*. New York: Simon & Schuster, 2004.

Ali & Cavett: The Tale of the Tapes. Directed by Robert S. Bader. New York: HBO, 2018.

Assael, Shaun. *The Murder of Sonny Liston: Las Vegas, Heroin, and Heavyweights*. New York: Blue Rider Press, 2016.

Cavett, Dick. *Brief Encounters: Conversations, Magic Moments, and Assorted Highjinx*. New York: Henry Holt and Company, 2014.

Ebert, Roger. *Ali. Chicago Sun-Times*. December 25, 2001

Eig, Jonathan. *Ali: A Life*. New York: Mariner Books, 2017.

Ezra, Michael. *Muhammad Ali: The Making of an Icon*. Philadelphia, Pennsylvania: Temple University Press, 2009.

SOURCES

Flaherty, Joe. "Post-Primes and Career Arcs," in *At the Fights: American Writers on Boxing: A Library of America Special Publication,* edited by George Kimball and John Schulian. New York: Library of America, 2011.

Gries, Tom, director. *The Greatest.* Columbia Pictures, 1977.

Gumbel, Bryant C. "Is Joe Frazier a White Champion in a Black Skin?" *Boxing Illustrated.* October, 1972.

Haley, Alex. "The Playboy Interview: Muhammed Ali." *Playboy,* October, 1965.

Haley, Alex. "The Playboy Interview: Muhammad Ali." *Playboy* November, 1975.

Kindred, Dave. *Sound and Fury: Two Powerful Lives, One Fateful Friendship.* New York: Free Press, 2006.

King, Regina, director. *One Night in Miami.* Amazon Studios, 2020.

Kram Jr, Mark. *Smokin' Joe: The Life of Joe Frazier.* New York: Ecco, 2019.

Liebling, A.J. "Poet and Pedagogue." *The New Yorker,* February 23, 1962.

Mailer, Norman. "Norman Mailer on The Fight." *Life Magazine.* March, 1971.

Mann, Michael. "Commentary." *Ali* DVD. Directed by Michael Mann. Culver City, CA: Sony Pictures Home Entertainment, 2002.

Mitchell, Kevin. *Jacobs Beach: The Mob, the Garden and the Golden Age of Boxing.* Boston: Hamilcar Publications, 2019.

Montville, Leigh. *Sting Like a Bee: Muhammad Ali vs. the United States of America, 1966-1971.* New York, Doubleday, 2017.

Moore, Louis. *I Fight for a Living: Boxing and the Battle for Black Manhood, 1880-1915.* Chicago: University of Illinois Press. 2017.

Patterson, Floyd. "In Defense of Muhammed Ali." *Esquire,* August, 1966.

The Phil Donahue Show. Season 24, "Ali, Frazier, Norton & Holmes." Directed by Benjamin Caron, featuring Muhammed Ali, Joe Frazier, Ken Norton & Larry Holmes. Aired 1990 on Multimedia Entertainment.

Roberts, Randy and Johnny Smith. *Blood Brothers: The Fatal Friendship Between Muhammad Ali and Malcolm X*. New York: Basic Books, 2016.

Roberts, Randy and Johnny Smith. "Why Muhammad Ali Rejected Martin Luther King's Approach to Civil Rights." *Raw Story*. February 22, 2016.

Sneddon, Rob. *The Phantom Punch: The Story Behind Boxing's Most Controversial Bout*. Lanham, Maryland: Down East Books, 2015.

"Spike Lee Protests Ali Decision." *The Guardian*, March 9, 2000.

Scorsese, Martin. "Commentary." *Raging Bull: Collector's Set*. DVD. Directed by Martin Scorsese. Beverly Hills, CA: MGM, 2005.

Tedeschi, Bob. "Muhammed Ali and Parkinson's Disease: Was Boxing to Blame?" *Stat*. June 4, 2016.

"Was boxing to blame for Parkinson's disease in Muhammad Ali?" *PBS News Hour,* June 5, 2015.

When We Were Kings. Directed by Leon Gast. London: PolyGram Filmed Entertainment, 1996.

CHAPTER 16 ROCKY

Bogdanovich Peter. "Don Siegel, '*Who the Devil Made It.*' (New York: Alfred A. Knopf, 1997)

Briden, Charlie. "Fanfare for a Fighter: The History and Evolution of the Rocky Theme." *Rogerebert.com*, December 18, 2018.

Butler, Brin-Jonathan. Episode 4. "'Rocky' with guest Steven Benedict." Produced by Ring Magazine. *No Happy Endings*. September 27, 2020. Podcast.

SOURCES

British Movietone. "Sylvester Stallone - Friday Night with Jonathan Ross (FULL INTERVIEW)." Online video clip youtube, January 8, 2016.

Ebert, Roger. "Review: Rocky." *Chicago Sun-Times*, January 1, 1976.

Gardner, Sam. "Chuck Wepner Calls the Day he Lost to Muhammad Ali the Greatest Day of his Life." *Fox Sports,* June 4, 2016.

Gergen, Joe. "Rocky's Brother-in-Law Knows the Ropes : Burt Young Tries Boxing in Real Life as Co-Manager of a Challenger." *Los Angeles Times*, February 17, 1985.

Gloversmith, Michael. "William Faulkner and "Parallel Editing." *White City Cinema*, January 16, 2010.

Haley, Alex. "The Playboy Interview: Muhammad Ali." *Playboy*, November, 1975.

Henry, Lenny. "It was Lonely being a Black actor in the 70s. It's Even Lonelier Now Behind the Camera." *The Guardian*. November 6, 2018.

Kram Jr, Mark. *Smokin' Joe: The Life of Joe Frazier*. New York: Ecco, 2019.

Lipsitz, Jordanna. "Remembering Rocky on its 40th Anniversary." *Vanity Fair.* November 20, 2016.

Mifflin, Margot. *Looking for Miss America: A Pageant's 100-Year Quest to Define Womanhood*. Berkeley, California: Counterpoint, 2020.

"Mikhail Gorbachev (1931–2022)." *Biography.com*, Jan 22, 2016

Miller, Monica L. *Slaves to Fashion: Black Dandyism and the Styling of Black Diasporic Identity*. Durham, North Carolina: Duke University Press Books, 2009.

The Phil Donahue Show. Season 24, "Ali, Frazier, Norton & Holmes." Directed by Benjamin Caron, featuring Muhammed Ali, Joe Frazier, Ken Norton & Larry Holmes. Aired 1990 on Multimedia Entertainment.

"Pope Francis reflects on the calling of St. Matthew." *Catholic World News*, April 13, 2016.

Smith, Wendy. *Real Life Drama: The Group Theater and America: 1931-1940*. New York: Alfred A. Knopf, 1990.

Stallone, Sylvester, John G. Avildson, Garrett Brown, Carl Weathers, Talia Shire, Burt Young. "Commentary." *Rocky: 2-Disc Collector's Set*. DVD. Directed by John G. Avildson. Beverly Hills, CA: MGM Video, 2006.

Timmesch, Nick. "Muhammad Ali: The Dream." *Time*, March 22, 1963.

The Tonight Show Starring Johnny Carson. Episode 3570. Directed by Robert Quinn, featuring Sylvester Stallone.' Aired December 16, 1976. NBC.

Udel, James C. "Garrett Brown's Steadicam Breakthrough Continues to Grow 50 Years Later." *Variety*, March 29, 2019.

Yerebakan, Osman Can. "Sylvester Stallone on Why He Painted 'Rocky' Before He Wrote the Movie, and Why It Took Him So Long to Come Out as an Artist." Artnet News, December 21, 2021.

CHAPTER 17 ROCKY III

Armstrong, Jenice. "Long past that Miss A scandal, Vanessa Williams is happy she—and pageant—are back in Atlantic City." *Philadelphia Inquirer*, February 11, 2014.

Eig, Jonathan. *Ali: A Life*. New York: Mariner Books, 2017.

Faludi, Susan. "The Masculine Mystique." *Esquire*, December 1, 1996.

Fussell, Samuel Wilson. *Muscle: Confessions of an Unlikely Bodybuilder*. New York: Poseiden Press, 1991.

George Butler and Robert Fiore, directors. *Pumping Iron*. White Mountain Films, 1977.

Gross, Terri. "Rob Halford." *Fresh Air*. National Public Radio, Philadelphia: Pennsylvania: WHYY, June 21, 2005.

Kreps, Daniel. "Mike Huckabee Settles Eye of the Tiger Lawsuit for $25,000." *Rolling Stone*, June 28, 2016.

Los Angeles Times. "Reagan Gets Idea From 'Rambo' for Next Time." July 1, 1985.Mapes, Jeff. "Marijuana legalization: The Rise of a Drug from Outlaw Status to Retail Shelves." *The Oregonian*, November 9, 2014.

McGrath, Michael. "Nancy Reagan and the Negative Impact of the 'Just Say No' Anti-Drug Campaign." *The Guardian*, March 8, 2016.

Mifflin, Margot. *Looking for Miss America: A Pageant's 100-Year Quest to Define Womanhood.* Berkeley, California: Counterpoint, 2020.

Mitgang, Herbert. "Groups Aim to Counter Book Bans." *New York Times,* September 7, 1982.

Newman, Kim. "Vile VHS: Unspooling the History of the 'Video Nasty' Controversy." *British Film Institute,* May 29, 2021.

Greer, Colin. "Interview with Mikhail Gorbachev." *Parade Magazine, January 23, 1994.*

Pennington, Jesse. "The Lost Meaning of 'Top Gun'." *Salon,* May 28, 2022.

Playboy. "Hanging out with Mr. T." September, 1983.

Schmeling, Max. *Max Schmeling, An Autobiography.* Translated by George Von der Lippe. Chicago: Bonus Books, 1998. First published 1977 by Verlag Ullstein.

Schonfeld, Zach. "Parental Advisory Forever: An Oral History of the PMRC's War on Dirty Lyrics." *Newsweek*, September 19, 2015.

Silver, Mike. *The Arc of Boxing: The Rise and Decline of the Sweet Science.* Jefferson, North Carolina, McFarland & Company, Inc., 2008.

Simon, Scott. "Canada's 'Porky' Film Success." *Weekend Edition.* NPR. May 1, 2004.

Simpson, Oli. "Mr T 'stopped wearing gold after Katrina." *Digital Spy,* September 29, 2009.

The TV Ratings Guide. "1975-76 Ratings History." 1991.

CHAPTER 18 FAT CITY

Ebert, Roger. "Fat City." *Chicago Sun-Times*, January 1, 1972.

Freer, Ian. *Movie Makers: 50 Iconic Directors from Chaplin to the Coen Brothers*. London: Quercus, 2009.

Gardner, Leonard. *Fat City*. New York: Farrar, Straus and Giroux, 1969.

Huston, John. *An Open Book*. New York: Knopf, 1980.

Jackson, Bruce. "Huston, John." Sense of Cinema, July 2019.

Lida, David. "*Fat City*, Fifty Years Later: An Interview with Leonard Gardner." *The Paris Review*, February 6, 2019.

Maltin, Leonard, ed. *(1995)*. *Leonard Maltin's 1996 Movie & Video Guide*. New York: Signet, 1995.

Schoemer, Karen. "In California, Finding 'Fat City' with the Man Who Wrote it." *New York Times*. May 30, 2017.

Turley, Mark. *Journeymen: The Other Side of the Boxing Business, A New Perspective on the Noble Art*. West Sussex, United Kingdom: Pitch Publishing, 2015.

CHAPTER 19 GIRLFIGHT

Clover, Carol J. *Men, Women, and Chainsaws: Gender in the Modern Horror Film*. Princeton, New Jersey: Princeton University Press, 1993.

Cohen, Leah Hager. *Without Apology: Girls, Women, and the Desire to Fight*. New York: Random House, 2005.

Dean, Allison. *Seconds Out: Women and Fighting*. Toronto: Coach House Books, 2021.

Deming, Sarah, "The Real Million Dollar Baby" in *The Bittersweet Science,* edited by Carlo Rotella and Michael Ezra, Chicago: University of Chicago Press, 2017.

Freud, Sigmund. *The Standard Edition of the Complete Works of Sigmund Freud, vol. XIX, 1923-1925. The Ego and the Id & Other Works*. Translated by James Strachey. London: Hogarth Press, 1953–1974.

Gordon, Bette. "Karyn Kusama." *Bomb*, Oct 1, 2000.

Halliday, Ayun. "The Truth Behind Jane Austen's Fight Club: Female Prize Fights Were a Thing During the 18th Century." *Open Culture*, February 23, 2018.

Hollander, Jocelyn A. "Why Do Women Take Self-Defense Classes?" Department of History & Classics at the University of Alberta, vol 16 number 4, April (2010).

Jenning, L.A. *She's a Knockout! A History of Women in Fighting Sports.*

Washington, DC: Rowman & Littlefield Publishers, 2014.

McAlpine, Kat. "How Does CTE Impact Women?" *Boston University Chobanian & Avedisian School of Medicine*, July 11, 2019.

"And Now it's the Boxing Girl; Six-Ounce Gloves the Thing, and She Knows All About Feints, Clinches, and Side-Stepping -- Woman's Latest Fad and Its Advantages." *New York Times, the* August 29, 1904.

Oates, Joyce Carol. *On Boxing.* Garden City, New York: Dolphin/ Doubleday, 1987.

Reejhsinghani, Anju. "No Winners Here: The Flawed Feminism of *Girlfight*." *The Brooklyn Rail*, December, 2000-January, 2001.

Robson, David. "How the Colour Red Warps the Mind." *BBC*, August 31, 2014.

Spencer, Dale C. *Ultimate Fighting and Embodiment: Violence, Gender and Mixed Martial Arts.* Oxfordshire, UK: Routledge, 2013.

Sugar, Bert Randolph. *Bert Sugar on Boxing: The Best of the Sport's Most Notable Writer.* Washington, DC: Lyon's Press, 2003.

Sulaiman, Mauricio. "Science Not Sexism." *wbcboxing.com*, April 17, 2019.

Sylvester, Sherri. "'Girlfight"s Michelle Rodriguez: She pulls no punches." CNN, September 29, 2000.

Thrasher, Christopher. "Disappearance: How Shifting Gendered
Boundaries Motivated the Removal of Eighteenth Century
Boxing Champion Elizabeth Wilkinson from Historical
Memory." Past Imperfect, Department of History & Classics at
the University of Alberta, vol. 12 (2018).

Tonawanda, Jackie. "The Woman Boxer Who Paved the Way."
Unorthodox, Oct 16, 2020.

CHAPTER 20 TYSON

The Charlie Rose Show. Season 24, episode 25, "Author Pete Hamill
Examines the Clinton Administration, His Conversations
with Mike Tyson, and his Memoir 'A Drinking Life."
Produced and edited by Charlie Rose, aired January 27,
1994, on PBS.

Chasmar, Jessica. "Mike Tyson Reveals He's a 'Vicious' Alcoholic 'On
the Verge of Dying'." *Washington Times*, August 25, 2013.

Dostoevsky, Fyodor. *Demons*. Translated by Richard Pevear and Larissa
Volokhonsky. New York: Everyman's Library, 2000. First
published in 1871–72 in The Russian Messenger.

Espinoza, Joshua. "Mike Tyson Recalls How His Fellow Inmates
Reacted When 2Pac Visited Him in Prison." *Complex*,
June 11, 2022.

Gao, Max. "She was Pilloried for Accusing Mike Tyson of Rape. A
New TV Show Tells Her Side of the Story." *Los Angeles Times*,
Sept. 15, 2022.

Heller, Peter. *Bad Intentions: The Mike Tyson Story*. New York: Dutton
Adult, 1989.

Hernton, Calvin C. "Great on the Gridiron, in the Movies and in
Life." *New York Times*, May 16, 1971.

Hoffer, Richard. "Out of the Darkness After Three Years in Prison and
an Hour at a Mosque, Mike Tyson Has Reemerged as Boxing's
Enigmatic Main Event." *Sports Illustrated*, April 3, 1995.

Kram, Mark. "The Playboy Interview: Mike Tyson." *Playboy*, November, 1998.

McNeil, Liz. "Inside John F. Kennedy Jr. and Mike Tyson's Unusual Friendship." *People*, July 26, 2016.

McRea, Donald. 'Mike Tyson: All I Once Knew Was How to Hurt People. I've Surrendered Now." *The Guardian*, January 24, 2014.

"Mike Tyson Lennox Lewis Press Conference." (January 22, 2002.) Posted by "Haleem Iqbal." August 14, 2014.

Muscatine Alison. "Accuser Testifies in Tyson Trial." *Washington Post*, January 31, 1992.

Oprah Winfrey Show. Season 24, episode 21, "Mike Tyson and Robin Givens." Directed by Joseph C. Terry, aired October 10, 2009, on CBS.

Oprah Winfrey Show. Season 24, episode 25, "Mike Tyson and Evander Holyfield." Directed by Joseph C. Terry, aired October 16, 2009, on CBS.

Phillips, John. "Mike Tyson: To Zoloft or not to Zoloft, That is the Question." *Bert Sugar's Fight Game*, Number 16, November, 2000.

Randolph, Laura B. "Robin Givens, Life After Tyson." *Ebony*, March, 1990.

Samantha, Albert. "'Mike,' A New Show About Mike Tyson, Is An Indictment Of Rape Culture." *BuzzFeed News*, August 25, 2022.

Scott, A.O. "Movie Review: 'Tyson' Violence Embodied in a Boxer's Rise and Fall." *New York Times*, April 23, 2009.

Sports Illustrated. "Q & A with Tyson Director, James Toback." April 23, 2009.

Thompson, Anne. "Spike Lee Shoots Stage Show 'Mike Tyson: Undisputed Truth' for HBO." *IndieWire*, June 26, 2013.

Times Wire Service. "Mood Swings: In a TV Interview, Tyson's Wife Says Life Has Been 'Torture... Pure Hell'." *Los Angeles Times*, Sept 30, 1988.

Toback, James. "Commentary." *Tyson*. DVD. Directed by James Toback. Hollywood, CA: Sony Pictures Classics, 2009.

Turan, Kenneth. "'Tyson' is a Knockout In, Out of Ring." *Los Angeles Times*, April 24, 2009.

Tyson, Mike with Larry Sloman. *Iron Ambition: My Life with Cus D'Amato*. New York: Blue Rider Press. 2017.

Tyson, Mike with Larry Sloman. *Undisputed Truth* (New York: Blue Rider Press. 2013).

Tyson, Mike. Episode 91: "William Shatner." *Hotboxin with Mike Tyson*, December 17, 2019. Podcast.

20/20. "Barbara Walters: Mike Tyson and Robin Givens.". *20/20*. Directed by Barbara Walters, aired September 30, 1988 on ABC.

West, Evan. "The Decision: Mike Tyson's Rape Trial, 25 Years Later." *Indianapolis Monthly*, January 20, 2017.

Whipp, Glenn. "38 Women Have Come Forward to Accuse Director James Toback of Sexual Harassment." *Los Angeles Times*, Oct. 22, 2017.

Whipp, Glenn. "200 More Women Share Their James Toback Stories After 38 Accuse Director of Sexual Harassment." *Los Angeles Times*, Oct. 23, 2017.

Willis, George. *The Bite Fight: Tyson, Holyfield and the Night That Changed Boxing Forever*. Chicago: Triumph Books, 2013.

INDEX

INDEX

AUTHOR BIO

DAVID CURCIO is an artist and writer in Massachusetts. He has written articles and reviews for numerous film, book, and boxing sites, is a contributor to the anthology *Dangerous Visions and New Worlds: Radical Science Fiction, 1950-1985*, and has a regular column on boxing in cinema in *The Fight City*. *Smash Hit* is his first book.

Printed in the USA
CPSIA information can be obtained
at www.ICGtesting.com
LVHW040314031023
759964LV00002B/172